THAT'S GOT 'EM!

THAT'S GOT 'EM!

⤜ The Life and Music of ⤛

WILBUR C. SWEATMAN

MARK BERRESFORD

UNIVERSITY PRESS OF MISSISSIPPI
JACKSON

www.upress.state.ms.us

ℒ-2636805

The University Press of Mississippi is a member of the
Association of American University Presses.

Copyright © 2010 by University Press of Mississippi
All rights reserved
Manufactured in the United States of America

First printing 2010

∞

Library of Congress Cataloging-in-Publication Data

Berresford, Mark.
That's got 'em! : the life and music of Wilbur C. Sweatman / Mark Berresford.
p. cm. — (American made music series)
Includes list of known compositions by Sweatman.
Includes bibliographical references, discography, and index.
ISBN 978-1-60473-099-9 (cloth : alk. paper) 1. Sweatman, Wilbur C. S. 2. Clarinetists—
United States—Biography. 3. African American jazz musicians—Biography. 4. Jazz—History
and criticism. 5. Vaudeville—United States—History—20th century. I. Title.
ML419.S92B47 2010
781.65092—dc22
[B]   2009023904

British Library Cataloging-in-Publication Data available

CONTENTS

ACKNOWLEDGMENTS

I FIRST ENCOUNTERED WILBUR SWEATMAN in the early 1970s, when most of my school friends were listening to the likes of Led Zeppelin and the Rolling Stones. By the age of thirteen I had already discovered the Original Dixieland Jazz Band and was spending most Saturdays in a wonderfully ramshackle vintage record shop on Arkwright Street in Nottingham, run by lifelong classic jazz enthusiast and clarinetist Johnny Hobbs. Knowing of my love of the ODJB, John suggested I buy an American Columbia record of their contemporaries, the Louisiana Five. I rushed home to play it and promptly fell in love with Alcide Nunez's lyrical clarinet playing—a genuine survival of nineteenth-century New Orleans musical style. More intriguing was "Slide, Kelly, Slide" by Wilbur C. Sweatman's Original Jazz Band on the reverse. Yes, it may be the most atypical Sweatman recording, but I did not know that at the time.

I was intrigued. Who was this Wilbur C. Sweatman? Did he make any more recordings? Could I get hold of them? I soon found that the answer to the last question, as far as LP reissues were concerned, was an emphatic "No." However, I was starting to make useful contacts in the world of 78 rpm record collectors and soon, even in those pre-eBay days, more Sweatman recordings came my way. However, finding information on Sweatman proved to be a frustrating and fruitless enterprise. None of the standard jazz books had much to say about him, and those that did mention him did so in generally disparaging terms. I could not understand this—the records I had managed to obtain told a story of bold, happy, carefree music played with great proficiency and panache, far removed from the contemporary pap dished out by Joseph C. Smith, the Victor Military Band or Art Hickman's Orchestra. What was going on? Why was this man so disregarded and put down?

Gradually, over a number of years, the truth dawned on me. The first reason Sweatman was so disparaged and overlooked was because of the lack of understanding about him and his position as a non–New Orleans jazz pioneer. Second, he and others like him had had their stories ignored or dismissed as a mere sideshow to the received wisdom of the development of jazz. Sweatman is not the only jazz pioneer who has suffered such an undeserving fate at the hands of blinkered writers, particularly those active in the 1940s and 1950s.[1] Many of these writers, especially those active in the years leading up to the birth of the civil rights movement, naively allowed their left-leaning political views and anger and frustration at the treatment of blacks in the Southern states to color their musical opinions. Likewise, most of these writers saw the birth and dissemination of jazz in the simplest of terms (born in New Orleans, moved up the Mississippi to Chicago, and thence to New York and nationwide) and gave little consideration to the roles that vaudeville, circus sideshows, and black minstrelsy played in the development of jazz. Consequently many early performers, regardless of race, were not merely ignored, but disparaged as bandwagon jumpers and plagiarists. The pervading view that the cradle of jazz was solely based in and around New Orleans meant that many non–New Orleans musicians like Sweatman and others were accused of watering down "real" jazz music and of catering to, or even selling out to, white audiences.

For many jazz enthusiasts and writers, then and now, the ultimate expression of the New Orleans jazz tradition was the series of recordings made by King Oliver's Creole Jazz Band for the Gennett label in 1923. Many writers have been happy to dismiss any jazz recordings made prior to this as being "primitive," "contrived," "stiff," or "lacking in swing," even though New Orleans musicians, black and white, had been making records since 1917, including two exciting instrumental sides made in California by trombonist Kid Ory's band in 1922. Fortunately, more recent researchers and writers have shown that the birth of jazz cannot be couched in such simplistic, one-dimensional terms, and that a rich musical tapestry of syncopated music was being woven right across the USA that would come together as jazz as we understand it.

Producing this, the first publication to examine the career of one of the most important pioneers of ragtime, jazz, and African-American entertainment, has been an enormous task, spanning over fifteen years. As any researcher will confirm, I could have easily spent another fifteen years trying to unravel the minutiae of Sweatman's life, but a line has to be drawn somewhere. I feel that a balance has been struck between new information being made widely available and the possibility of carrying on ad infinitum with the final work possibly never seeing publication.

Much of my spare time has been spent journeying to archives, spending hours poring over microfilm viewers and computer monitors, and corresponding with the many people who have given freely of both their time and knowledge. Many more hours were spent listening to Sweatman's re-cords, both alone and with fellow enthusiasts, musicians and sound res-toration experts, putting the records into their correct keys and speeds and endeavoring to solve riddles of personnel, while cross-checking against records by other contemporary artists. I must extend particular thanks in this respect to musician and composer Ron Geesin, who patiently, and with the acute hearing of a professional musician, examined all of Wilbur Sweatman's recordings and put them into their correct pitches and speeds. Ron's knowledge of this music is virtually unsurpassed. As a young man he shared many musical experiences with Billy Jones, the English pianist who played with the Original Dixieland Jazz Band in London in 1919 and 1920. He also worked for some years in the early 1960s as the pianist with the Original Downtown Syncopators, an English jazz band devoted to rec-reating the flavor of the ODJB and other early jazz bands of the 1917–20 period. Ron has also contributed an essay on pitching the Sweatman discs, for which I owe him many thanks!

I am especially grateful for the immense help and assistance given by Doug Seroff and Lynn Abbott, who freely shared the fruits of their ongoing research into the black press of the pre-1920 period, much of which has been subsequently published in their two monumental studies of pre–Jazz Age African American entertainment—*Out of Sight* and *Ragged But Right* (both published by University Press of Mississippi). Without their generos-ity, support, and kindness this book would be but a pale version of what you see.

Special mention must be made of the enormous support and help given by the University Press of Mississippi's Editor-in-Chief, Craig Gill. It was Craig who first showed interest in this book and has been on hand at all stages in its move from manuscript to finished book. David Evans, General Editor for the University Press of Mississippi, read the final manuscript and made some useful suggestions and comments.

Writer, music critic, and good friend Malcolm Shaw, besides providing ongoing moral support, kindly volunteered to proofread the final draft, and his wisdom and good humor have been of enormous help in seeing this project through to fruition. Likewise, Frank Driggs, custodian of the finest archive of classic jazz photographs in the world, was unstinting in his gen-erosity, locating and providing unique (and some previously unpublished) photographs of Sweatman and his band.

It goes without saying that no work of this size can be completed by one person alone, and I would like to express at the outset my sincere gratitude to the following people and organizations for their generous assistance, kindness, and encouragement: Lynn Abbott, Dr. Elliott L. Adams, Scott Alexander, Tony Barker, Anthony Barnett, Bruce Bastin, Roger Beardsley, Edward A. Berlin, Mary Lou Brandt of the mayor's office in Brunswick, Missouri, Olivier Brard, Colin Bray, the British Newspaper Library, Tim Brooks, Samuel Charters, John Chilton, Bob Colton, Frederick Crane, the late John R. T. Davies, Ate van Delden, Nick Dellow, Frank Driggs, Sherwin Dunner, Max Easterman, Erin Foley, archivist of the Circus World Museum Library, Baraboo, Wisconsin, Ron Geesin, Vince Giordano, Lawrence Gushee, Reg Hall, the late Jeff Healey, Karl Gert zur Heide, Brendan Heneghan, Warren Hicks, Chris Hillman, John Hobbs, Warren Hodgdon, Franz Hoffmann, Richard Johnson, Reide Kaiser, the late Len Kunstadt, Steven Lasker, Joe Lauro, Dan Levinson, Rainer Lotz, Jim Lyons, Mike Meddings, Paul Merrill, Keith Miller, Mark Miller, the Minnesota Historical Society, Mike Mongillo, Joe Moore, Dan Morgenstern of the Institute of Jazz Studies at Rutgers University, National Archives–Central Plains Region, Kansas City, National Archives–South-East Region, East Point, Georgia, Bruce Nemerov of the Center for Popular Music Studies, the late Richard Newman, the New York Public Library, Robert Ray of the Miller Nichols Library, University of Missouri–Kansas City, John Reade, Paul Riseman, Brian Rust, Howard Rye, David Sager, Dr. Rainer Schneider, Charles Sengstock Jr., Doug Seroff, Malcolm Shaw, Bernard Shirley, Wayne Shirley of the Library of Congress, Music Division, Russ Shor, David Smith, Ken Steiner, Allan Sutton, Donald Thompson, Trevor Tolley, Bruce Vermazen, the late Edward S. Walker, Steven Walker, Chris Ware, Clifford Watkins, David Wondrich, Ralph Wondraschek, Laurie Wright, Art Zimmerman, and Theo Zwicky. I offer my sincere apologies for any names unintentionally omitted from this list.

INTRODUCTION

AS WE ENTER THE SECOND CENTURY OF JAZZ HISTORY, it is becoming increasingly difficult to evaluate the earliest years of its development. All of the musicians who were involved in the transition from ragtime and cakewalks to jazz in its earliest forms are now dead. Many of these important pioneers were largely ignored by historians when they were alive, unless they happened to fit into a populist view of mainstream jazz development: from New Orleans to Chicago and New York, thence worldwide. Ironically, it is this very period that is increasingly of interest to contemporary researchers and historians. Much valuable work, done by the likes of Rainer Lotz,[1] Larry Gushee,[2] Lynn Abbott, Doug Seroff,[3] Tim Brooks,[4] Reid Badger,[5] Howard Rye, and others, brings sharply into focus the musical activities of the quarter-century before the Original Dixieland Jazz Band (ODJB) made their first records in 1917. The pitifully small number of records by African-American artists before 1917 tells us enough to conclude that the traditionalist view of jazz originating solely in New Orleans is patently untrue.

It would be less partisan to say that musicians from the South brought to the North the blues element of jazz, but overwhelming evidence exists to demonstrate that early forms of jazz existed in the North long before the migrations of New Orleans and Southern musicians to the urban centers of the North in the mid-1910s. In researching and writing this book, it became apparent early on that the roles of black theater, tented touring shows, circus sideshows, and vaudeville played a much greater part in the early development of jazz than has generally been acknowledged. One could go so far as to state that, without an established, self-directed black theater and entertainment network already in place by the beginning of the twentieth century, the whole course of jazz history would have been altered massively. Its subsequent development would potentially have remained, for many more years, an underground, illicit music. Theaters and vaudeville, along with tent shows and black minstrel shows, gave syncopated music a vital platform by which it could reach a wide audience, thus shaking off its perceived "whorehouse music" origins and identity. Sweatman went one step further by extending this platform into the previously closed world of white vaudeville, whereby audiences unfamiliar with this new music could hear it without venturing onto the margins of society in order to do so.

Because of the injustice meted out to the early non–New Orleans pioneers by the first two generations of jazz scholars—in denigrating their careers, in not understanding the context of their careers in relation to the period of their activity, and in not documenting their life stories—it now falls to the present and future generations of historians to unravel this complex web by using whatever source materials survive.

For the purposes of researching an artist who made his career in the music industry, Sweatman's recordings are the most obvious and important primary source, but they only tell part of the story—and a somewhat jaundiced, skewed, and manipulated one at that. First, one has to take into consideration the fact that until 1925 all recording was done mechanically, without the benefit of electrical amplification and microphones. The resultant sound-image gives only a faint, acoustically distorted, and often artistically compromised idea of how a band or individual musician sounded. The acoustic recording process, whereby the artist sang or played into one or more metal horns connected to a diaphragm, used sound wave energy alone to vibrate the diaphragm, thus actuating a cutting stylus which engraved the sound waves onto a thick wax disc. If one tapes a piece of paper to the end of a cardboard tube and then shouts down the open end, then one has an idea (albeit simplified) of the process. The method had a recording range of approximately 150 to 4500 cycles or Hertz (Hz); by way of comparison, modern recording technology can record and reproduce from 20Hz to over 20 KHz, beyond the range of human hearing. The fundamental notes of a bass instrument simply could not be recorded, although the higher harmonics would be; the string bass, one of the most popular bass instruments in ragtime and early jazz bands, would barely be audible, and had to be either omitted or a substitute instrument with more "punch" used in its place. Usually a tuba, bass saxophone, or the nowadays very rare sarrusophone would be brought in to substitute for the string bass, completely changing the sound of the band in comparison to its "live" performances.

Second, the performers were nearly always made to work within the constraints laid down by the record company's Artists and Repertoire (A&R) or recording managers. These could include controlling the choice of repertoire to be recorded; the tempo, volume, and dynamics of a performance; even going so far as adding musicians to a band, if it was considered necessary to improve the balance for recording or to assist sales. The best-known example of such interference is the case of the Original Dixieland Jazz Band who, on returning from a hugely successful eighteen-month visit to Britain, were forced by Victor's Artist & Repertoire Manager, Eddie King, to add a saxophone for their subsequent record sessions. King's idea was to give a "smoother" sound, the resulting records often sounded like parodies of the much larger orchestra of Paul Whiteman, Victor's then-ascendant bandleader star.

Sweatman was also a victim of record company interference: his Columbia records, in part at least, are obvious attempts to emulate the style of the Original Dixieland Jazz Band, and one suspects the hand of company executives in this. A particularly egregious example of record company executives exerting control on Sweatman's recorded repertoire was Columbia's practice of interpolating additional tunes into Sweatman's (and, it has to be admitted, other contemporary bands') records. The main reason for this was that it was cheap—if the tune (and sometimes tunes) introduced into a performance emanated from the same publisher, then only one royalty payment was paid. This suggests that Sweatman and his musicians were unlikely to be aware of the material they were to be recording until the day of the session, which goes some way to explain what appears to be their apparent unfamiliarity with some of the more obscure tunes they were given to record.

Columbia, like their rivals Victor, wanted the early jazz bands they recorded to emphasize the noise, brashness, and cacophony of the weird new music; consequently, their recordings of Wilbur Sweatman, the Original Dixieland Jazz Band, and Earl Fuller's Famous Jazz Band have one volume setting—loud—and no attempt is made to introduce any dynamics or subtlety. We know from the recordings made by the ODJB for more enlightened record companies, such as Aeolian-Vocalion in the USA and the English branch of Columbia, that they regularly made use of dynamic volume control to introduce color and shade into their performances, and one sees no reason why Sweatman would not have done likewise, had he been given the opportunity.

For African American musicians even the act of getting onto record was a long and uphill struggle and, even when the trickle turned into a flood, the inherent racism in the industry ensured that they only played what the company wanted, and were unceremoniously tossed aside when considered of no further use to the company. Racism in the recording industry went as far as record companies assigning to themselves, or to satellite music publishing companies, the copyright of unpublished compositions that black bands and singers recorded for them. Strong-arm and bullying tactics were frequently used, threatening artists that they would never record again unless they sold the rights to their tune to the company or their publishing company, with minimal payment being made to the creator. Thus the record company got two paydays—one for the sales of the record and another for the royalty it paid itself as the publisher. This ploy was endemic throughout the industry, practiced both by minor companies such as Paramount and OKeh and by the industry leaders such as Victor, the dominant player in the business. Admittedly, the same practices were used against hillbilly musicians—usually where the performer was also the composer, especially one who was unlikely to have any knowledge of copyright law and the need to establish ownership of the material—but black performers usually got the poorest deals.

Another important prime documentary source is the theatrical press: trade papers such as *Variety*, the *New York Clipper*, and *Billboard* carried vast amounts of detailed information on performers' activities. Even more important, from a research perspective, are contemporary African American newspapers such as the *Indianapolis Freeman*, the *New York Age*, and the *Chicago Defender*, for their extensive coverage of musical news and events from a black perspective. These newspapers also acted as a poste restante service to touring performers, holding mail and providing a welcome lifeline of news, gossip and information about friends as well as about forthcoming work opportunities. As with the present-day press, however, the researcher must exercise discretion when trying to sort fact from fiction. Public relations, although in its infancy as a profession at the beginning of the twentieth century, was extremely effective. Therefore we need to exercise a considerable degree of caution and a not-inconsiderable amount of skepticism when reading of artists being booked for three years ahead, or having recording contracts offered them. This caveat aside, there is a wealth of invaluable material (most of which has still to be evaluated and reported by researchers) to be found in contemporary newspapers and periodicals—reviews of performances (sometimes detailing partial or entire band personnel), traveling routes, personal "human interest" details (gossip, to you and me), and much more.

Given all the above-mentioned pitfalls and hindrances, how do we give a critical evaluation of Wilbur Sweatman, an artist with a career that started in the last years of the nineteenth century and who was still active within the music industry until his death during Kennedy's presidency? An artist whom most enthusiasts of the Golden Age of jazz have heard of, but who, for most, is merely a footnote in the pages of jazz history, based mainly on a "circus turn" of playing three clarinets at once, and the fact that the young

Duke Ellington spent a brief and supposedly unhappy time with Sweatman in vaudeville in 1923?

In answering this question, one has to consider (a) the role Sweatman played in the transition from ragtime to jazz, (b) his part in the popularization of jazz on record, (c) his part in both the popularization and subsequent dissemination of ragtime and jazz by his many years of presenting his music in vaudeville to both black and white audiences, and (d) the influence he had on younger musicians, both stylistically and through the part he played in providing invaluable practical experience for and mentoring of aspiring young talent.

It is my intention to answer these questions by presenting as full a picture as possible of Sweatman's career, making use of resources available. The picture is far from complete—family source material is nonexistent, photographs are hard to locate (which is surprising, given both his popularity and the duration of his career in vaudeville), surviving record company ledgers give only the barest information about his records, and there is virtually nothing in their surviving files about the sidemen involved. Sweatman's own comprehensive files and papers disappeared after his death, and the only serious attempt to coax the reminiscences of nearly seventy years' involvement in music from this intensely private man remains unpublished. Sweatman's almost obsessive privacy was a major obstacle that interviewers and researchers in the 1950s had to overcome. He was cautious, particularly in dealing with white interviewers—partly out of distrust, partly because he did not want to be misrepresented, but also to guard his carefully built business interests from perceived threats. As *Record Research* editors Len Kunstadt and Bob Colton diplomatically noted: "It was true that Wilbur's very cautious manner to most everybody may have prevented him from recalling his past activities, but we were able to overcome his reticence and to gain his confidence."[2]

Faced with these difficulties, I have attempted to glean from whatever source any information that sheds light on Sweatman's life and career and present it in as objective a way as possible. In that respect, I had to confront a major obstacle fairly early on in the process of writing this book. With a career in vaudeville that lasted over twenty years, Wilbur Sweatman is mentioned in literally hundreds of vaudeville show reviews and in the theatrical trade press, with respect to where and when he was appearing. Usually this consists of a simple statement along the lines that Wilbur Sweatman & Company are appearing for a given week at a certain theater. While this information has value in showing the extent of Sweatman's travels and the geographical areas covered, it does not make for riveting reading. I therefore took the decision to exclude this information *unless* subsequent local or national reviews provide useful or pertinent information or criticism central to the overall picture of Sweatman's career or his private life.

Another aim is to redress the imbalance and give Wilbur Sweatman some of the credit he undoubtedly deserves as a pioneer of jazz, for he has suffered unjustifiable neglect and criticism at the hands of jazz writers, many of whom, to their lasting shame, were working at a time when Sweatman was still alive and working on an autobiography, the notes for which disappeared after his death. Credit must be given to the late Len Kunstadt and Bob Colton of *Record Research* magazine, who interviewed Sweatman on several occasions and who, through the pages of their magazine, helped give Sweatman some long overdue recognition.

It is also my intention to provide as authoritative as possible a discography of Wilbur Sweatman's recorded output. This has been a particularly onerous task because, as a rule, Sweatman used either musicians from a roster of men working through his booking agency, or those who happened to be available at a particular time. Thus we find the youthful trumpeter Arthur Briggs, later a figure of enormous importance and influence in the development of jazz in Europe, playing on a Sweatman session in early 1919—his first record date—and possibly on other Sweatman sessions, too. At that time, Briggs was working with Will Marion Cook's New York Syncopated Orchestra, immediately prior to their hugely significant visit to Britain and mainland Europe.

The main reason for the constantly shifting personnel in Sweatman's bands is that, from 1911 through to the mid-1930s, Sweatman's main field of activity was working in vaudeville, which entailed spending weeks and months on the road—a week in one town and then on to another. The great vaudeville conglomerations, such as the Keith-Albee and Orpheum circuits, Loew, Proctor, Pantages, Klaw and Erlanger, and others, owned chains of theaters nationwide and artists were booked from coast to coast. The rigors of this nomadic lifestyle were such that few New York–based musicians were willing or able to devote so much time away from home and family, preferring the relative stability of local nightclub or dance hall work.

Because of this instability in personnel and the fact that there were no publications at that time that took an active interest in jazz or jazz musicians, I have conducted my research using contemporary newspapers, theatrical and vaudeville publications, not to mention a degree of educated guesswork. However I believe that the information presented in the discography, both from a personnel and discographical perspective, is more accurate than anything previously published. That being said, no work of this type can be 100 percent accurate, given the passage of time and the rarity of some of the records listed, so I would appreciate and acknowledge any additions and amendments readers may choose to send to me.

THAT'S
GOT 'EM!

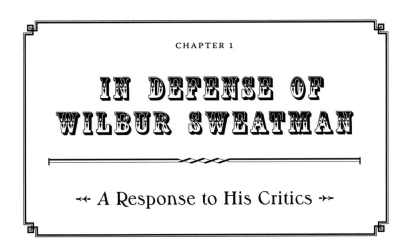

CHAPTER 1

IN DEFENSE OF WILBUR SWEATMAN

⤛ A Response to His Critics ⤜

HISTORY HAS NOT BEEN KIND TO WILBUR SWEATMAN. Key his name into a web search-engine and you will find numerous references—nearly all of them relating to a few weeks in early 1923 when a struggling pianist from Washington found himself in New York along with some friends, working in vaudeville with Sweatman. That vaudeville stint made a lasting impression on the young Duke Ellington, who learned much of the business of public presentation and stagecraft from the proud, middle-aged clarinetist. And so he should have. Sweatman, by that date, had been performing before the public since the mid-1890s, in locations that ranged from circus tent-shows and dime museums, to New York's prestigious Palace Theater, and vaudeville houses from coast to coast.

For years those jazz writers who even found sufficient space to mention Sweatman have looked on him with derision and scorn (one author even claimed that he was the Henry Mancini of his day!), mainly because of his minstrel/vaudeville roots and because he was best known for his trick of playing three clarinets simultaneously. That, however, is not the impression given by musicians and performers who knew Sweatman in his heyday:

"Sweatman was my idol. I just listened to him talk and looked at him like he was God."—GARVIN BUSHELL[1]

"[Sweatman] started recording for Emerson in 1915 . . . when the prejudice and discrimination were so thick you couldn't cut them with a
butcher's knife."—PERRY BRADFORD[2]

"He was a sensational, rapid, clever manipulator of the clarinet."
—DAVE PEYTON[3]

"When he introduced his style of playing in the leading vaudeville theaters, it was before some of the men now given credit for introducing
jazz were born."—TOM FLETCHER[4]

"Sweatman's band was 'Hotter than red pepper.'"—PERRY BRADFORD[5]

"I . . . learned a lot about show business from Sweatman. He was a good
musician."—DUKE ELLINGTON[6]

"He was big-time in all ways."—HARRISON SMITH[7]

Buster Bailey, Garvin Bushell, Cecil Scott, Gene Sedric, and many other
musicians fell under Sweatman's influence. His astounding top-to-bottom-
register break on the Columbia recording of "Think of Me Little Daddy"
was the talk among Harlem clarinetists in 1920; both Sedric and Bushell
independently recalled hearing it for the first time.[8] The roster of musicians
who worked with Sweatman over the years is not unimpressive for a man
whom jazz history has at best denigrated and at worst downright ignored:
Freddie Keppard, Sidney Bechet, Coleman Hawkins, Duke Ellington, Arthur
Briggs, Wellman Braud, Russell Smith, Cozy Cole, Sid Catlett, Sonny Greer,
Otto Hardwick, Herb Flemming, Ikey Robinson, Jimmie Lunceford, Claude
Hopkins, Teddy Bunn, and many others.

It is important to note that, as well as influencing and encouraging fellow
African American musicians, Sweatman was among the first black instrumentalists working in the idiom of syncopated music to perform regularly
with white musicians. In his vaudeville work Sweatman generally worked
with a pianist and drummer, usually fellow black musicians, but earlier in
his vaudeville career he worked as a "single," accompanied by the pit band of
the theater at which he was appearing. From 1911 onwards, when he started
to work on the white-owned United, Keith-Albee, and Orpheum vaudeville circuits, most if not all of these accompanying musicians would have
been white. Sweatman was also the first black instrumentalist to record in
the United States with a racially mixed group. Indeed, his 1916 Emerson

recordings are accompanied by white studio musicians. At other times in his career he worked with white instrumentalists on the bandstand, and recalled working with a white musician as a sideman in his own band on at least one recording session. White banjoist Michael Danzi, who spent much of his working life in Germany, recalled a recording session with Sweatman in 1924, and that the last gig he worked in the United States before leaving for Germany in 1924 was a wedding dance with Wilbur Sweatman's band. In this sense Sweatman can be seen to be many years ahead of his contemporaries, both black and white, and one has to look to the more racially tolerant Europe to find comparable contemporary parallels.

Even discounting the well-known names who played with Sweatman and the influence he had on many other musicians, Sweatman's name should still be writ large in the history of African American music; for he was without doubt one of the first black musicians to become nationally known, from both his years of touring in vaudeville, playing to both black and white audiences, and through his pioneering record career. It is apparent from reading newspaper reviews of Sweatman's early vaudeville appearances (ca. 1911–12), that there were very few other black instrumentalists working in the syncopated music medium on the American vaudeville stage and, in this particular field, Sweatman was pre-eminent.

Sweatman is also important for being one of the first African American artists, if not *the* first, to appear on the vaudeville stage in ordinary dress clothes and without the use of demeaning burnt-cork blackface makeup. No less an authority than fellow African American musician, composer, and vaudevillian Eubie Blake credited Sweatman as being the first to break the blackface barrier in his vaudeville performances.[9]

More than anyone else, Sweatman opened the door to recording work for black musicians. True, James Reese Europe's Society Orchestra had recorded as early as 1913, but one has to bear in mind that (a) this was through the patronage and influence of Vernon and Irene Castle, the white popularizers of ballroom dancing, who were then at the height of their success, and for whom Europe was musical director; and (b) Europe was a well-known and respected figure in black and white social and musical circles alike. Sweatman, with no white benefactors to influence recording company executives, managed by sheer determination and talent to break down the racial barriers then prevalent within the recording industry.

Some jazz writers suggest that it is a complete misconception that black artists in the United States were prevented from recording in large numbers, and cite the example of the Creole Band, who were approached by the Victor Talking Machine Company but turned down the offer to record.

They have made the point that record companies, being first and foremost interested in making money, would record anybody if there was an opportunity to make a profit. The facts, however, speak for themselves. With the notable exceptions of Bert Williams, George Walker, James Reese Europe, the Fisk University Jubilee Singers, and a handful of others, very few black artists did record (in the U.S., at least) before 1917. Therefore one has to conclude that this was either because of racist attitudes within the companies themselves, a lack of contact with black artists and their managers or agents by company talent scouts (undoubtedly a major factor), the mistaken belief that most blacks were too poor to buy records, or the fear of their products being boycotted in Jim Crow states in the South. On the latter point, one can cite the case of the Thomas A. Edison Company, the majority of whose customers were based in rural farming communities. Despite the enormous popularity of records by black female blues singers from 1920 onwards, it was not until 1923 that Edison issued records by a black female blues performer (Helen Baxter) and a black band (Charles A. Matson's Creole Serenaders). While it is certainly true that the Edison company was not the quickest record company off the mark to spot market and cultural trends and gain a lead on their competitors (time and again this can be seen in the company's operations—Edison himself rejected an audition test by an up-and-coming singer by the name of Al Jolson, and personally passed judgment on new talent despite both his profound deafness and his well-documented musical conservatism that bordered on the simplistic), there has to be considered the fear of a backlash from their southern, racially sensitive customers.

As early as 1916 Sweatman was recording for Emerson, and from 1918 to 1920 he was the main supplier of jazz for Columbia, with 24 issued sides to his name in that period. This is all the more a remarkable achievement when one considers that the Original Dixieland Jazz Band, at that time the best known jazz band in the world, and made up of white musicians to boot, had only 23 sides issued by Victor in the four years from 1917 to 1921. Sweatman was also instrumental in helping composer, publisher, and promoter Perry Bradford to get Mamie Smith, the first female blues singer to record, into a recording studio, a fact Bradford generously acknowledges in his autobiography *Born with the Blues*.[10]

Critics have also leapt on Sweatman's 1918–20 Columbia recordings as being but pale imitations of the Original Dixieland Jazz Band, "made to order" by Columbia to compete with the ODJB's highly successful series of Victor recordings. To an extent, this is based in fact; the Columbia bosses were desperate to compete on equal terms with their longtime rivals Victor in the "jass" craze—both companies were milking the national obsession with social dancing for all it was worth. It was inevitable that Columbia's answer to the ODJB would, to some extent, be based on the hit-making Victor band in much the same way as when, in the 1960s, the Monkees were shamelessly touted as America's answer to the Beatles.

However, there the similarity ends. Sweatman's career was in full swing before the ODJB's youngest member, drummer Tony Sbarbaro, was even born (1897) and much of the music on Sweatman's Columbias can be interpreted as a stylistic fingerprint reaching back into the late nineteenth century. This is even more apparent on the sides made in 1919 (when the ODJB were safely off the scene, frightening listeners and dancers in an England awash with postwar euphoria), when Sweatman apparently filled his band with members of the Clef Club Orchestra and Will Marion Cook's New York Syncopated Orchestra. The massed banjos and mandolin-banjos on "I'll Say She Does" and the big band sound of "That's Got 'Em" accurately reflect both what has been and what will be in African American music and, as such, should be applauded rather than disparaged.

The main criticism leveled at Sweatman by jazz writers has been that he was a "gaspipe" clarinetist and, as such, he has been shoehorned into the same category as Ted Lewis, Boyd Senter, and Wilton Crawley. This is a great injustice. It is true he lacked the lyrical tone, fluidity, and invention of the best New Orleans clarinetists, and did not possess the technique of a player like Buster Bailey; but one has to bear in mind that when we listen to his playing, we are hearing a man whose style was rooted in the late nineteenth century, when most of the subsequent jazz greats were either in short trousers or not even born! As such his playing is as unique and true a representation of his time and its influences as that of Johnny Dodds or Benny Goodman was in theirs. Sweatman, like most African American musicians of his generation, considered himself an entertainer, and if part of that process of entertainment involved "novelty" effects and the like, and the public paid good money to hear it, then it was incorporated into one's performance, as and when required.

Putting aside Sweatman's Columbia recordings—his best-known—one only has to listen to his 1917 Pathé records to realize that something different is happening. There are no novelty effects, no gaspiping or whoops and cackles. This is very hot but disciplined dance music, revealing another side to Sweatman's musical personality, one that has less to do with vaudeville stage gimmickry or record company interference. This no-nonsense approach can also be heard on his post-Columbia period records, particularly the 1926 Grey Gulls and the superbly swinging 1935 Vocalions.

Those writers who have seen fit to mention Sweatman usually do so in relation to the very short stint that Duke Ellington spent with the band in 1923, and with little thought to either accuracy or objectivity. Ellington, ever the supreme self-publicist, consistently downplayed any references to his early career if he was not the star of the show (for this reason Elmer Snowden's reputation also suffered at the hands of both the Duke and his acolytes) and always claimed he only spent a short time with Sweatman, a period of apparent misery and frustration. This is not so—apparently Ellington also worked with Sweatman in 1924 and may well have recorded with him, and there is some evidence (albeit very tenuous) to suggest that he may have been associated with Sweatman as early as 1919. Writers and journalists whom Ellington told of his time with Sweatman were apparently happy to take his version without corroboration. One writer in the 1930s, when Ellington was the darling of the intellectual elite, spoke of Sweatman as "a mammoth of a man" and in terms that made it appear as though Sweatman was some prehistoric musical dinosaur who had long disappeared from the face of the earth. In fact, at that time Sweatman was, quite slim, below average height, and still musically active!

CHAPTER 2

MISSOURI CHILDHOOD

THE SMALL MISSOURI TOWN OF BRUNSWICK ("Home of the Pecan") is located in Chariton County and stands at the confluence of the Grand and Missouri rivers, between St. Louis and St. Joseph, some ninety-odd miles from Kansas City. On Wednesday June 13, 1804, Lewis and Clark encamped there, their hunters killing a bear and a deer. William Clark noted that it was "a butifull place the Prarie rich & extensive."[1] However, it was not until 1836 that the town was founded, by James Keyte, an enterprising businessman and Methodist preacher. He had arrived in Missouri from England in 1818 and allegedly named the town after his old home on Brunswick Terrace, in the northern England mill town of Accrington, Lancashire (the street is still there, near the railway station). Keyte was a natural entrepreneur, and he served the small community in many capacities besides preaching: he ran the post office and general store, a saw mill, a building business, and also a packet boat business—all vital roles in a developing small town.

Brunswick was the most northerly port on the Missouri River before St. Joseph and, as such, was guaranteed a considerable amount of trade from the outlying farms and communities. Tobacco was the staple crop of the area, along with wheat, potatoes, onions, and watermelons, and a brisk trade was soon established both in and out of the town's warehouses and wharves. Several tobacco and hemp factories and pork packers were established in the town and these, along with the founding of a number of other towns in north Missouri that relied upon Brunswick as an entrepot, guaranteed the town a prosperous outlook.

An indication of the volume of business passing through the town can be gauged from the fact that in 1849 there were 534 steamboat arrivals at the town docks. Allowing for the fact that the Missouri river froze in winter, preventing any water traffic, this would indicate something of the order of three boats per working day, arriving in town. In the winter months the tobacco crop would be hauled into town from outlying plantations by teams of oxen, fifty to a hundred strong, which would leave with dry goods and provisions.

The first blow to Brunswick's fortunes came in 1856, when the Hannibal and St. Joseph Railroad surveyed a line across northern Missouri and bypassed Brunswick in favor of nearby Laclede. Railroads, as a shipping medium, were faster, cheaper, and more reliable than riverboats, and the town slipped into decay. In 1868 Brunswick was finally connected to the Hannibal and St. Joseph Railroad; the resulting trading opportunities saw the town's fortunes improve once more and its population increase.

The Civil War found Brunswick, like the whole state of Missouri, internally torn between the Union and the Confederacy. After a strife-ridden first year of attempted non-involvement, which led to "civil war within the Civil War," Missouri was held with some difficulty by the Union from 1862 forward. But since everyone in Missouri came from somewhere else, each inhabitant had a strong opinion, especially on the slavery question. The South's abandonment of Missouri and Arkansas, after Pea Ridge in 1862, led to the rise of guerrilla groups (originating the term "bushwhackers") like Bloody Bill Anderson's gang, Quantrill's Raiders, and the Jesse James Gang, who kept going even long after Appomattox.

Brunswick's mayor, Allen Kennedy, and civic officials declared support for the Union cause but, as several families had moved to Brunswick from the southern states, this stand was not favored by all of the town's inhabitants. Brother fought brother; families and friendships were torn apart by the war. As a result of this ill feeling the law was often powerless to prevent violence and vandalism, and several properties and businesses were burnt by rival groups, including Mayor Kennedy's warehouse.

As if manmade troubles were not enough, nature also played a hand in Brunswick's misfortunes. The town was situated on a bend in the river that gradually shifted, eating away at the terrain on which it was built, frequently inundating houses and businesses, which as a result moved further away from the river to the safety of higher ground. Today, the Missouri River is some two miles from the town.

It was in Brunswick that Matilda Sweatman gave birth to a son, Wilbur Coleman Sweatman, on February 7, 1882. Both his father, Coleman, and his mother were born in Missouri, but three of their parents were from Virginia.[2] Matilda was born in September 1857 in Missouri, but her mother was born in Tennessee, having moved north before the Civil War. Coleman and Matilda were apparently of mixed racial origin; from their parents Wilbur and his older sisters, Eva and Lula, inherited their light skin color. Wilbur, his mother, and his sisters were sometimes noted in census returns as "mulatto." What constituted their racial mix is uncertain. Eubie Blake knew Wilbur Sweatman both professionally and socially, and in an interview referred to him as "an Indian," a Native American.[3]

Coleman Sweatman, born in 1853 or July 1859 (depending on which census return is referred to), ran his own barbershop, one of three in Brunswick that were listed in the *Missouri State Gazetteer and Business Directory* of 1881. Black barbershops in the post–Civil War period held a unique status among the black populace: it was one of the few places outside of the church where black men could safely congregate—a sanctuary to discuss common interests regardless of education or occupation. It was also one of the few entrepreneurial opportunities open to blacks at that time, and as such was a gateway to financial independence. The black barber was a respected member of the community, and it was not at all unusual for them to cater to white customers as well—particularly in a small, racially mixed town like Brunswick.

Sweatman's very name has caused researchers enormous problems over the years and continues to do so. His forename has generally been spelt *Wilbur*, which is the usual spelling of this name. However, his World War I draft registration card gives his forename as *Wilber*, and his signature, affirming the veracity of the details on the card, clearly uses an *e*. But this does not provide a cut-and-dried solution to the problem. His 1910 marriage certificate manages to employ both spellings in the same document. And to add further complication, the labels of his Columbia records show both *Wilber* and *Wilbur* with apparent randomness—some have been reported where both spellings appear on opposite sides of a record! If that is not sufficiently complicated, there appears to be little consistency on Sweatman's own part as to how he spelled his forename. Up to early middle age Wilber seems to have been his personal choice (but not consistently), but by the 1920s he seems to settle on Wilbur. His own publishing company founded in 1924 was titled Wilbur Sweatman Music Publishing Co., and copyright entries at the Library of Congress from this period onward use this spelling. His 1942 draft registration card clearly shows *Wilbur*, as does his signature on the card. A decision has had to be taken in writing this book whether to use *Wilbur*, *Wilber*, or both and, in the interest of maintaining some degree of consistency, I made the decision to use *Wilbur* throughout, unless *Wilber* was used in a contemporary account, report, advertisement, or document.

His middle name, Coleman, taken from his father, was only revealed to me on seeing his WWI draft card. I had labored in vain for many years, checking Federal census returns, marriage certificates and other official documents trying to find what the *C* stood for, only to find either no middle name shown or merely the initial. Again, there is inconsistency—on his 1918 draft card it is spelled *Coleman* but the *e* has apparently been obliterated. His 1942 draft card clearly shows *Colman*, but trade directory entries for his father's barbershop business show the spelling as *Coleman*.

The surname *Sweatman* is not common either in the USA or in England, where it originated. Its English origin comes as a derivation of *Sweet* or, in medieval English, *Swete*, a nickname for a popular or well-liked person. Other names derived from this origin include *Sweetman*, *Swetman*, *Swatman*, and, in German, *Sussman*. Sweatmans are known to have emigrated to America from most counties of England, in particular Kent, Sussex, Cheshire, Wiltshire, Lincolnshire, Yorkshire, and Gloucestershire. Rather than a slave name, given by a farm or plantation owner of that name to his slaves, it seems likely that Wilbur Sweatman had some English blood pulsing in his veins. Sadly, all attempts at tracing direct ancestors have so far proved fruitless. According to the 1920 federal census the distribution of Sweatmans across the USA was somewhat uneven; by far the most numerous were in Georgia, South Carolina, and Texas, with Illinois following. A large swath of midwestern states—from Michigan and Kentucky across to Wyoming and down to New Mexico—was virtually devoid of a single Sweatman family.

Wilbur was the third child born to Coleman and Matilda Sweatman; Eva Leontyne, the eldest, was born in March 1878 and went on to become a schoolteacher, specializing in music. Lula (affectionately known as Sissie) followed in November 1879 and, like her father and mother, worked in the family barbershop before eventually following her older sister into teaching. The Sweatman household was in a racially mixed working-class area of Brunswick, with several of their neighbors being immigrants from Germany and Switzerland. To help make ends meet Matilda, or Mattie as she was known to her friends and family, in common with many other housewives of the time, took in lodgers. When the 1880 census was taken, two years before Wilbur's birth, the Sweatman household comprised the two parents and their two daughters plus Emma Sweatman aged 16, sister of Coleman Sweatman, and two lodgers, Oliver Black aged 25 ("mulatto"), a preacher, and Spencer Morgan aged 27 (also described as "mulatto"), a barber and presumably an assistant to Coleman in his barbershop.

Wilbur's first musical instrument was piano, which he was taught by his elder sister, Eva. He later taught himself to play the violin before subsequently learning to play clarinet, on which he was also self-taught. Still later, he became proficient on bass clarinet, trombone, and organ, but his first love was the clarinet. Unusually, Sweatman appears never to have learned to play saxophone; he never played it on his records, nor was he ever photographed with one among his array of clarinets. Several contemporary newspaper reports mention him playing the saxophone, but this is presumably a case of slipshod reporters mistaking Sweatman's bass clarinet, with its curved bell, for a saxophone.

Sweatman was not the only entertainer of note to hail from Brunswick; the celebrated nineteenth-century white theatrical comedian Sol Smith Russell was born in Brunswick in 1848.[4] Of more interest to jazz enthusiasts—albeit those of the most esoteric inclinations—is the black clarinet and tenor saxophonist Vernon Roulette, who played with Jimmy Wade's Moulin Rouge Orchestra in the early 1920s and recorded with them for Paramount in 1923.

A devastating blow for the infant Wilbur and his sisters occurred in the mid-1880s, when their father Coleman Sweatman walked out of the family home. He moved to St. Joseph, Missouri, over 120 miles from Brunswick, where he continued to work as a barber. By 1889 he was listed in Hoye's City Directory of St. Joseph as working at Edward Brown's barbershop at 312 South 3rd Street, but by 1894 was running his own barbershop, The Mirror, with a small staff of assistants at 220 Felix Street. On January 1, 1894, he married Willeta Phelps, a mother of two (including his own son, Gus, born in 1885), at the New Hope Baptist Church and was living at 610 North 18th Street. By 1898 they had moved to 1217 Edmond Street, one block south of his Felix Street barbershop.

Mattie Sweatman was left not only to bring up a family of three young children, but to work to support them, too. She took on the job of continuing the barbershop business but, to help make ends meet, continued to take in lodgers. Wilbur would grow familiar with transient visitors filling the family home, and in some way this may have contributed to his own periods of rootlessness and desire to keep on moving, exemplified by his years of seemingly endless touring in vaudeville.

In the absence of a father figure and a with mother working long hours to provide for her family, Wilbur was cared for by his older sisters, Eva and Lula; his relationship with them was to remain close their entire lives. In particular, Eva's musical aptitude rubbed off on young Wilbur, and he would benefit greatly from her knowledge and abilities, both as a musician and a teacher.

Missouri schools were segregated until the 1950s. Sweatman would have attended the Elliott School, named after the family who gave the land on which it was built. On leaving school Wilbur, not surprisingly, started work at his mother's barbershop business, but his interests lay far away from cutting, dyeing, and straightening hair and shaving faces—he had already been bit by the music bug. He recalled to *Record Research* editor Len Kunstadt that, as a youngster in 1893, he saw a group of African singers and dancers in Excelsior Park, Kansas City.[5] It now appears, however, that what he saw was the Dahomean Village in Troost Park, Kansas City, in September 1894.

One of the best-known and certainly one of the most written-about features of the Midway during the great World's Columbian Exposition, held in Chicago between May and October 1893, was the Dahomean Village, populated by Fon people from the west African country of Dahomey (now the Republic of Benin). Dahomey, like many coastal west African nations, was a major slave-trading center in the eighteenth century, with the king and other traders supplying slaves for shipment to America and the Caribbean.

Unlike the majority of the Midway's attractions, the organization of the Dahomean Village had less to do with the extraction of money from guileless punters than with an ethnographic experiment, complete with bare-breasted women, warriors, musicians, and dancers. Much has been written about the 1893 World's Fair, especially about its alleged role in the birth of ragtime; and key to this development appear to have been the various entertainments available on the Midway Plaisance. The best-known of these were the "hoochie-coochie" dancers—"Little Egypt" being the most notorious—and the Dahomean Village. The Midway, the site of which is still called Midway Plaisance Park, situated between East 59th and East 60th Streets, was over a mile long and packed with virtually every form of novelty and entertainment known to man. The original Ferris wheel was sited there; a short distance away, on the north side of East 60th Street between Wharton and Ellis Avenues, was the Dahomean Village. Although there is no evidence to either prove or disprove that ragtime was performed on the Midway, it is said that many black pianists found work, both in the sideshows of the Midway and in the "sporting houses" of the nearby Levee District. Among the pianists known to be in Chicago at that time was Scott Joplin, but, again, there is no evidence that he performed on the Midway.

Rudi Blesh and Harriet Janis in their groundbreaking study of ragtime and its development, *They All Played Ragtime*, contextualized the role of the Midway and the Dahomean Village in the chronology of the development of ragtime as a distinct musical form:

> The World's Columbian Exposition had, in fact, prepared the way for rag-time, even though a few years elapsed before its publication started. While the sensational dancing of Little Egypt is likely to be remembered by old-timers [they were writing in the 1950s], the Dahomean Village was an equally sensational attraction. Between the two of them a spate of exotic dances became the talk, from the hootchie-cootchie to the bombashay.
>
> The village was uniquely authentic amid the spurious curiosities of the Midway. Its native occupants entertained all day with drumming and chants. They came from the African West Coast, where America's slaves had once been captured, and the rhythms of the drum batteries and the haunting chord-chains of their chorales held in their essence the trans-forming contribution that the Negro has made to American music.[6]

No less an authority than Henry E. Krehbiel, pre-eminent among American music critics at the time, wrote admiringly of their rhythmic drumming and singing in a laudatory review in the New York Tribune: "The players have the most remarkable rhythmic sense and skill . . . but it is impossible to convey an idea of the wealth of detail achieved by devices of syncopation, dynamics, etc., except by scoring the part of each instrument." He goes on to describe the village's harpist: "With his right hand he plays, over and over again, a descending passage (dotted quarters and eighths) of thirds; with his left hand he syncopates ingeniously on the highest two strings."[7]

After the Chicago World's Fair closed in October 1893, the European managers of the Dahomean Village embarked on a tour of state fairs and amusement parks across the country, and on September 1, 1894, set up the village at Troost Park in Kansas City for a two-week engagement. This is almost certainly the troupe of African singers and dancers that Sweatman recalled seeing.[8]

As a teenager in Brunswick in the mid-1890s, Sweatman was ideally placed to be influenced by the evolution of ragtime—Sedalia, the musical home of Scott Joplin, Arthur Marshall, Scott Hayden, Brun Campbell, and publisher John Stark (although only Hayden had been born there), was a mere sixty miles away. These and other itinerant pianists, along with trav-elling tent shows and their bands, would have passed through Brunswick, bringing the new music with them. The sounds of ragtime would also be found on the numerous showboats that plied the Missouri River, carrying with them a retinue of traveling musicians and entertainers. The show-boats would usually arrive on a Monday, flags and banners flying and steam calliope cheerfully heralding their arrival. After disembarking, the show's artistes, headed by a band, would parade through the streets of the town, drumming up business and filling the town with a vibrant mix of color and music. Saturday evening would see their final show, and the boat left town on Sunday morning for their next port of call. Without doubt, Sweatman would have heard some of the great pianists and bands of the time passing through town, further fueling his musical aspirations. The influence of the early ragtime performers on Sweatman was profound. His style of play-ing was strongly influenced by the orchestral ragtime bands he heard and played in as a teenager, and was to remain virtually fixed for the rest of his career—even his 1935 Vocalion recordings show him to be still performing in a strongly ragtime-influenced style.

CHAPTER 3

"PICKANINNIES," ERNEST HOGAN, AND A WORLD TOUR

OPPORTUNITIES FOR PROFESSIONAL BLACK MUSICIANS IN THE MID-1890S were severely limited—for a pianist it was often the bar or whorehouse; for other instrumentalists it was either working with a musical act in a travelling tent show, or playing with a circus sideshow or minstrel band that provided regular work. The importance of vaudeville and touring tented shows in the development of jazz has largely been ignored; only recently has the pivotal role of touring minstrel shows and circus sideshow bands in the formative period of jazz and blues evolution been researched in any depth. A small but dedicated group of jazz historians, most notably authors Seroff and Abbott in the USA and Rainer Lotz in Germany, have started to reveal the fascinating story of these African American entertainers and early jazz musicians who worked in traveling shows in the pre-1920 period, both at home and in Europe.

One of the main areas of employment for young black performers in the entertainment business was the so-called "pick act." Usually working as part of a white vaudeville act, the "picks" or "pickaninnies" would consist of talented young black dancers, singers, and occasionally instrumentalists brought in to bolster and add variety to an act. For a young black performer it was the quickest way of entering show business and working with an established (and usually white) star. Among the predominantly female performers who used picks as part of their stage act were the likes of Sophie Tucker, Nora Bayes, Grace La Rue, and May Irwin. Amazingly, a recording of an American pick act dating from 1902 survives, providing a unique opportunity to hear how one such act sounded. Belle Davis was a beautiful, statuesque, light-skinned black singer from New Orleans who, after several years as a star of black touring companies such as Sam T. Jack's Creole Burlesque Company and John W. Isham's Octoroons, toured Europe extensively, billed as Belle Davis and Her Piccaninnies. In the spring and early summer of 1902 this act recorded four incredibly rare titles for the Gramophone & Typewriter Company in London for issue on their Gramophone Concert Record, Berliner, and Zonophone labels.² "The Honeysuckle and The Bee" shows Davis to be a formally trained mezzo-soprano, but the "pick" vocal backing of Irving "Sneeze" Williams, Fernandes "Sonny" Jones, and probably Harry Fleming (all of whom went on to notable careers in European theater) weave wonderful harmonies around the chorus.³

Working as part of a pick act had its downside. To quote Marshall Stearns: "No doubt the practice provided a fine schooling and developed a youngster's ability, as well as teaching him show business. But the profits were one way. The employer was white and adult, while the pick was Negro and a child—so picks never got rich. It was child labor, theatrical style. Many dancers started as picks only because it was one of the ways for a Negro to get into show business."⁴

From this nursery for black performers came the likes of Bill Robinson, Luckey Roberts, Coot Grant, Irene Gibbons (Eva Taylor), Jimmy Yancey, and Wilbur Sweatman. Sweatman's entry into a professional musical career came in the mid-1890s when he joined the "Pickaninny Band," led by the respected and highly influential Nathaniel Clark Smith.⁵

Although now virtually forgotten by all but the keenest students of black American musical history, Nathaniel Clark Smith was an important African American composer, bandmaster, and the foremost black musical educator of his age, often described as "America's greatest colored bandmaster." He exerted his greatest influence in the role of music educator of many young musicians who subsequently worked in the jazz and dance music fields. His many years in music education saw him teaching a galaxy of soon-to-be jazz greats, including Earl Hines, Bennie Moten, Julia Lee, Hayes Alvis, Walter Page, Harlan Leonard, Lamar Wright, Ray Nance, Thamon Hayes, Leroy Maxey, Lionel Hampton, Eddie Cole, Milt Hinton, Herman Walder, and Cab Calloway. Facts about Smith's early life and career have been seriously garbled and distorted over the years and sorting fact from fiction and forming some sort of chronology is difficult. ⁶

Born in Fort Leavenworth, Kansas, in 1866 (though many sources claim he was born in 1877, despite the fact that he was listed as a fourteen-year-old printer in the 1880 census), Smith's youth was a varied mix of careers. These included journalism, military service, printing, and working for the Carl Hoffman music publishing company. He married and settled down in Wichita, Kansas, where he lived for three years, during which time he formed his Pickaninny Band. He studied at the Guildhall School of Music in London in 1899, prior to a nine-month Pacific tour with his Pickaninny Band with the M. B. Curtis All-Star Minstrels. On his return he found work with the Lyon & Healy music publishing company in Chicago and, through the generous financial assistance of Patrick Healy, attended Chicago Musical College, where he studied composition and orchestration under Felix Borowiski and voice under Prof. J. R. Miller. He received his Bachelor of Music degree in 1905, and shortly thereafter formed Chicago's first black symphony orchestra, which may have been the first in the USA.

In June 1904 Smith volunteered for a three-year enlistment in the Eighth Regiment Infantry, Illinois National Guard, and was appointed bandmaster. It has often been reported he was with the regiment in Cuba during the Spanish-American War of 1898, but this is incorrect. From 1906 to 1913 he was music director at the Tuskegee Institute in Tuskegee, Alabama, but his overbearing personality and strong opinions frequently led him into clashes with Tuskegee's head, Booker T. Washington, and he resigned in the fall of 1913. In 1914 he moved to Kansas City to teach music at Western University (1914–16) and Lincoln High (1916–22). Many of the best-known Kansas City jazzmen—Walter Page, Harlan Leonard, Leroy Maxey, Julia Lee, and Thamon Hayes—studied under Smith during his tenure at Lincoln High School. Saxophonist Harlan Leonard, an important figure in Kansas City jazz from the 1920s to 1950s, paints a vivid mental picture of Smith:

> Major Smith had a vivid and commanding personality. He was short, chubby, gruff, military in bearing, wore glasses and was never seen without his full uniform and decorations. His language was rather rough and occasionally shocking to the few ladies who were taking music classes, though never offensive. Major Smith simply ran a tight ship. . . . He *was* the music tradition at Lincoln High School. He discouraged dilettantes and time wasters and encouraged talent. Major Smith was not an outstanding player himself but he knew all of the instruments and he could teach. He drilled the Lincoln marching bands until they were the best in the area, some said the best of their kind in the Middle West. He made music seem exciting and important and over the years . . . won a reputation for turning out a steady stream of well-prepared musicians who succeeded in the profession.[7]

Another well-known musician to feel the wrath of N. Clark Smith was Herman Walder, a top Kansas City saxophonist and arranger and a musician widely regarded as an important early influence on Charlie Parker: "Oh, that cat was a masterpiece. Man, I remember, he come by me and I made the wrong note. Man, he took that baton and he hit me right on top of the head . . . till I got it right. . . . He was a masterpiece, but after he left, we had a helluva band."[8]

In 1922 Smith accepted a teaching position at Wendell Phillips High School in Chicago, where he taught many more future jazz musicians, including Lionel Hampton, trumpeter Leon Scott and bassist Hayes Alvis. New Orleans trombonist Preston Jackson recalled Smith and his fearsome reputation as a disciplinarian: "He was . . . a man who didn't tolerate lack of discipline and it is fellows like him who turn out the best musicians . . . there were so many fine musicians—I'd say that N. Clark Smith really produced the goods."[9]

Smith moved to St. Louis in 1931 to teach music at Sumner High School but returned to Kansas City in 1935, to concentrate on music publishing. He suffered a stroke while directing the Musicians' Union Local 627 orchestra at their headquarters and died on October 8, 1935.

In the light of N. Clark Smith's activities in 1898 and 1899 described above, it seems likely that Sweatman's tenure with the Smith Band was during the years 1895–98 and possibly a period from the summer of 1899 to the late spring of 1900; unfortunately no newspaper reports of the band's activities mention Sweatman by name as being a member. However, the Pickaninny Band was sufficiently well-known in the Midwest to merit frequent mention in African American newspapers of the period:

> Probably the most attractive feature of the Apple Carnival parade was Prof. N. Clark Smith's Pickaninny Band of Wichita. Sousa, so it is said, calls this band the best kid band in the world. Sousa heard the band play in Wichita last summer, and he ought to know what he is talking about. After Sousa wrote his famous march, 'King Cotton,' Prof. Smith was the first one of his friends to receive a copy. This certainly was a great compliment, and also a recognition of true genius. The band was not here in its entirety, several of the members having gone home to Wichita from Kansas City Sunday night. The band came to Leavenworth at the request of Elliot Marshall of the Burlington Railroad company, having heard it play in Kansas City last week. Thinking it would be a great hit for the Apple Carnival parade, he sent Prof. Smith a telegram. The band numbers 22 members and is led by Master Willie Smith, who is only 9 years

old. It easily surpasses Topeka's Dispatch band, which was here last summer. The band has made such a great success that Prof. George Jackson
of the Dispatch band, is also organizing a Pickaninny Band.[10]

Another report later in November indicates the popularity of 'Pick'
bands and gives a possible clue to when Sweatman joined the band, given
the proximity of Brunswick to Kansas City:

> Prof. Smith and his Pickaninny Band have located permanently in Kansas
> City, MO., where both the band and the bandmaster are progressing
> nicely. We are informed that the band will have forty members next year,
> and that a tour will be made of Kansas and Missouri and other states.
> "Down In Dixie," a show which has been playing in Kansas City, MO.,
> this week, has a Pickaninny Band, so we are informed by Prof. Smith.
> "The Crackerjack," which is playing in Iowa also has one. In fact pickan-
> innies seem to be all the rage, even a pickaninny preacher having made
> her appearance in New York. Every pickaninny born nowadays seems to
> have a bright future. His future is centred in the fact that some day he
> will be a member of a Pickaninny Band.[11]

Smith even immortalized his Pickaninny Band in music, composing "The
Pickaninny Band March" in 1895, at which time Sweatman would have been
twelve or thirteen years old.[12]

In the summer of 1899 Smith and his Pickaninny Band were contracted
to join comedian and composer Ernest Hogan's troupe for a tour of Australia
and the Far East, under the auspices of impresario M. B. Curtis. Maurice
B. Curtis was a white actor-manager and property developer with a notorious reputation—he had been tried and acquitted for the murder of a police-
man in San Francisco in September 1891 and was considered a dangerous
man to know and deal with. Born Mauritz Strelinger in Bohemia (now the
Czech Republic) around 1850 (other sources give 1852), he adopted the name
Curtis when he became an actor in the 1870s. He made his fame when, in
1881, he bought the rights to a comic play by Irish-born playwright George
H. Jessop entitled "Sam'l of Posen, the Commercial Drummer" ("commercial drummer" was a nineteenth-century slang term for a travelling sales-
man). He toured with the play for years with great success, earning enough
money to invest in land, buying vineyards and a substantial slice of Berkeley
in California, developing it with houses and hotels. Curtis's luck changed
after the murder of police officer Alexander Grant and Curtis's subsequent
trials for Grant's murder. In 1893, after four trials, two hung juries, and one

procedural dismissal, Curtis was found not guilty, but his reputation was in tatters and his investments sold. The outcome of this was that Curtis moved his operations to Australia, booking many well-known vaudeville and theater stars to appear there as well as producing his own shows.[13]

Curtis could hardly fail to notice that a black theatrical company managed by a former member of the Fisk Jubilee Singers, Orpheus M. McAdoo, had scored a great success in South Africa and was continuing to do so in Australia. Seeing the possibilities of emulating the success of McAdoo's Minstrels, he returned to the States to organize an even larger, more star-studded company of black singers, dancers, comedians, and musicians, led by comedian and singer Ernest Hogan. Hogan, billed as "The Unbleached American," was the leading African American comedian of his day and is best remembered nowadays as the writer of the song that was to prove his damnation for all the wrong reasons—"All Coons Look Alike to Me." Born Reuben Crowders in Bowling Green, Kentucky, on April 17, 1865, Hogan's first job, while still a boy, was as a bootblack. He made his first professional stage appearance in 1878 with Callendar's Georgia Minstrels, an early theatrical enterprise of famed Broadway producers Charles and Daniel Frohman. By the 1890s he was running and starring in his own productions as well as actively composing early ragtime-influenced tunes. In 1905 he was instrumental in bringing a troupe of talented young black singers and musicians billed as "The Memphis Students" to Broadway—a production of seminal importance in New York black theater history, and one that helped start the careers of a number of notable figures in the black musical world, including composer and bandleader James Reese Europe. Overwork and ill health—possibly tuberculosis or syphilis—took their toll on Hogan, and he died in May 1909 at just forty-four years old.

The M. B. Curtis Afro-American Minstrel Company (sometimes billed as the M. B. Curtis Afro-American All Star Carnival) sailed for Australia from Vancouver, British Columbia, on June 1, 1899, on the first leg of a tour that was planned to take them to China, Japan, the Philippines, and Europe. Besides Ernest Hogan, the troupe featured several celebrated black performers of the time, including singer and actress Muriel Ringgold, comedian Billy McClain, Katie Carter, and Tom Brown. The troupe opened at the Criterion Theater in Sydney on July 2, 1899, and immediately became embroiled in fierce rivalry with the McAdoo company, who were also playing in Sydney. Matinee days were switched to coincide with the McAdoo company's matinees, and Curtis made no secret of his desire to run McAdoo out of Australia. By mid-July McAdoo's Georgia Minstrels and Alabama Cakewalkers had left Sydney on tour—a tactical victory for

Curtis, but a short-lived one. A downturn in business and clashes between Curtis and several key performers over salaries and billing saw Curtis leave the country suddenly in early August, leaving the company stranded and unpaid. McAdoo's troupe, anxious to help their stranded fellow performers, donated $225 to the Curtis company and, in mid-August, the U.S. Consul arranged for them to travel to Auckland, New Zealand. A rather tardy (and, considering the reality of the situation, inaccurate) report of their progress in Australia appeared in August in the *Kansas City Star*, under the heading "Pickaninnies In Clover":

> The pickaninny band of this city is in clover in Australia. That is the report the members send to their friends here about their tour of that country with "M. B. Curtis' Afro-American Minstrel Carnival," of which Ernest Hogan is the star. There are fifteen players in the band under N. Clark Smith's leadership. They left here in May for a summer in Australia, with a tour of the United States and a trip to the Paris exposition to follow.
>
> . . . In two months Hogan and the band and minstrels will be in Kansas City playing their way East from the coast. New minstrel talent and costumes will be secured and the band will sail in time to be in at the opening of the Paris exposition, as its contract demands.[14]

In New Zealand the troupe formed a cooperative, under Hogan's management and direction, and started to attract favorable attention from both theatergoers and critics alike, not least for a new dance that they introduced to the southern hemisphere—the cake walk. A program for their appearance at the Wellington Opera House in 1899 shows that the show began with a "Grand First Part, depicting the Interior of the Palace of the Emperors of Minstrelsy and gathering of the Mastodon Senate. Grand Opening Overture by N. Clark Smith's Pickaninny Band."[15]

After eight months of touring, financial uncertainty, and endless arguments and fights over money and billing, many of the Hogan troupe were more than a little tired of Australia and New Zealand and feeling decidedly homesick. In March 1900, the troupe sailed for Honolulu for an engagement at the Orpheum Theater, arriving there on the 14th. The troupe was subsequently denied passage back to Vancouver by the Canadian-American Royal Mail Steamship Line, and it took legal action on the part of Hogan and other members of the troupe before they were allowed to sail home.[16] In the interim Hogan raised money for the troupe by writing and staging three new productions, each staged for two weeks for bemused Honolulu theatergoers. The Honolulu fiasco meant that the planned appearance of the Pickaninny Band at the 1900 Paris Exposition Universelle never materialized; instead it was left to John Philip Sousa and his band to introduce ragtime, or "le temps du chiffon," to an incredulous French public.

Whether Sweatman was a member of the N. Clark Smith Pickaninny Band that ventured with the M. B. Curtis/Ernest Hogan troupe to Australia in 1899 is impossible to ascertain with any degree of certainty. Tantalizingly, an almost complete roster of the Hogan/Curtis troupe survives, listing singers, actors, dancers and others connected with the show, on-and off-stage, but, sadly, the personnel for Clark Smith's Pickaninny Band is not individually listed.[17] Surviving documents relating to the tour are inconclusive, and an extensive search of passport applications for the period has failed to reveal an application made in Sweatman's name. However, although the Department of State has issued passports since 1789, except for brief periods during the Civil War and World War I and its immediate aftermath, there was no statutory obligation for American citizens to hold a passport when travelling abroad until the 1920s. It seems unlikely that documentary evidence will now surface, but the gap in Sweatman's career from ca. 1898 to 1901 points to the likelihood of his having made the trip. The late Len Kunstadt's all too brief published notes of his interviews with Sweatman which appeared in *Record Research* magazine shed no light whatsoever on this period of his career.

While with the Smith Band, Sweatman was befriended by a fellow member his own age who later became a leading figure in the development of early jazz, not only in the United States but also throughout Europe, South America, India, and Southeast Asia. This was cornetist William Crickett Smith, the same "Master Willie Smith" mentioned in the newspaper report of November 2, 1895. Smith ("Crickett" was his given name, not a nickname as has often been stated) was born in Emporia, Kansas, on February 8, 1881.[18] After working with N. Clark Smith's Pickaninny Band, Smith's activities over the following ten years are difficult to trace, but he is thought to have worked with Sweatman at the Pekin Theater in Chicago in about 1908. In 1911 he joined the Musical Spillers, a highly popular and influential group of black multi-instrumentalists led by William Newmeyer Spiller, with whom he toured throughout the USA and Canada, and even appeared in England from late 1912 until February 1913.[19]

By 1913 Crickett Smith had joined James Reese Europe's Society Orchestra, with whom he recorded in December of that year; the following year he worked with Sweatman, when the latter briefly led the pit band at Harlem's Lafayette Theater. From 1915 to early 1919 he was featured with Ford Dabney's Band during its long engagement with Ziegfeld's Midnight

Frolic atop the New Amsterdam Theater and recorded with both Dabney (1917–19) and Sweatman (1918). He returned to Europe in the summer of 1919 with Louis Mitchell's Jazz Kings, where he influenced many first-generation European jazz musicians, through live performances at Le Perroquet nightclub and records he made with the Mitchell band for Pathé in Paris in 1922–23. When Louis Mitchell quit Le Perroquet to open his own nightclub, Mitchell's, in November 1923, Smith assumed leadership of the Mitchell band. Replacing Mitchell with drummer/vocalist Creighton Thompson, Smith changed the band's name to the Real Jazz Kings and continued to work at Le Perroquet in the Rue de Clichy, close to the Gare Saint-Lazare. In the late 1920s he worked with pianist Glover Compton's house band at Joe Zelli's Royal Box on the Rue Fontaine, a favorite Montmartre hangout for expatriate and visiting Americans.

In the 1930s Smith worked in South America, Java (now part of Indonesia), Ceylon (now Sri Lanka), and India in a variety of bands, both black and white, most notably those of Herb Flemming, Leon Abbey, and Teddy Weatherford. Around 1941 he returned to the States and, when he registered for the draft on December 28, 1943, declared that he was "unemployed at present" and living at 34 St. Nicholas Place in New York. He is thought to have died in New York around 1947, although some sources have incorrectly claimed that he died in India in 1943 and that his embalmed body was shipped home.[20]

Regardless of the degree of success of the M. B. Curtis–Ernest Hogan Pacific tour, and whether Sweatman was a part of it or not, one thing is certain: by the summer of 1900 he was in Brunswick, Missouri. The precise date for the Hogan troupe sailing from Honolulu has not been established, but it is estimated to have been in early to mid-May. By the beginning of June Sweatman was back in his home town of Brunswick. The 1900 Federal census, taken in Brunswick on June 8th, reveals Mattie Sweatman as the head of the household ("Divorced"), with Eva ("School teacher"), Lula ("Music teacher"), and "Wilber" all resident and with no lodgers. Both Mattie and "Wilber" are shown to be employed as barbers.

A note in the "Brunswick Pick-Ups" column of the *Indianapolis Freeman* of July 27, 1901, notes that "Mrs. Hattie [sic] Sweatman, tonsorial artist, runs two chairs also bath rooms."[21] Curiously, the same column mentions a Sweatman and Smith Restaurant in Brunswick, and one presumes that this was in some way associated with the barbershop business, being run by Mattie and, in all probability, Wilbur. The same article also notes that "Miss Eva Sweatman, who has been teaching school in Kansas City, has returned home to spend Vacation." Eva must have commuted on a regular basis between Kansas City and Brunswick, as she was doubly enumerated in the 1900 Census. As well as being recorded in Brunswick on June 8, she was enumerated on June 2 as residing at 1825 McGee Street in Kansas City, boarding with her aunt Willa Bigby and her husband Luther. The *Freeman* article goes on to state that there was a black band based in Brunswick, and one is tempted to think that Wilbur may have joined it on his return to his hometown.

In mid- to late 1901 Mattie Sweatman moved her family from Brunswick to Independence, Missouri, a suburb to the east of Kansas City. This threw eighteen-year-old Wilbur, already a seasoned performer, into a vibrant African American musical community where opportunities to further his chosen career would be a key to the future. In a 1959 interview with Marshall and Jean Stearns for their pioneering book on African American dance, *Jazz Dance*, Sweatman recalled the Baptist church in Independence: "When I was a kid in Kansas City, in Independence, Missouri, there was a Baptist Church where people were very religious and they'd get happy and do the Eagle Rock [the name of the church was the Eagle Rock Baptist Church]. This happened before I was born even. All those steps have been interpreted as long as there was any rhythm."[22]

By late 1901 Sweatman had moved again, this time to St. Louis, and was earning a living as a professional musician in a city already bursting with musical talent—Scott Joplin had recently arrived from Sedalia and ragtime composers and musicians of the caliber of Tom Turpin, Scott Hayden, Joe Jordan, Louis Chauvin, and Arthur Marshall were making their presence felt. In 1959 Sweatman recounted to Marshall and Jean Stearns his reminiscences of playing there at a black "dancing school": "They used to do quadrilles, lancers, polkas. They didn't have to call the steps—everybody knew them by heart. But when in New Orleans on a circuit, I'd go where the music was being played and where they were dancing. They always called the dances there."[23]

It may seem odd that a professional musician would take an engagement at a dancing school. However, black entrepreneurs at the time faced enormous obstacles in obtaining licenses to run entertainment premises, especially if their local competitors happened to be white, and dance halls and cabarets were no exception. It was easier to obtain the necessary license to open a dancing school, which, although posing as an educational establishment, was actually a dance hall. James P. Johnson recalled playing in a similarly styled "dancing school" on West 62nd Street in New York around 1912–13 that, although officially named Drake's Dancing School, was known to all and sundry as the Jungles Casino.

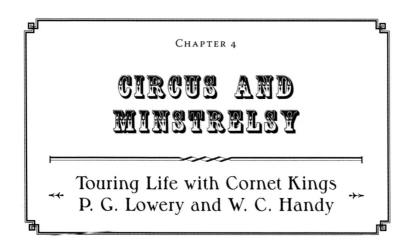

CHAPTER 4

CIRCUS AND MINSTRELSY

Touring Life with Cornet Kings P. G. Lowery and W. C. Handy

IN APRIL 1902 Sweatman joined the legendary P. G. Lowery's Concert Band as orchestra leader and violinist, as well as playing clarinet in the larger concert band. According to a report in the *Indianapolis Freeman* some eight years later, he was the youngest orchestra leader on the road.[1] This was a remarkable achievement for a twenty-year-old, and is not only indication of the esteem that Sweatman was held in by his contemporaries but also evidence of his ambition to succeed in a fiercely competitive field.

It is worth explaining how Sweatman could be leader and violinist of Lowery's "orchestra" and also play clarinet in Lowery's Concert Band. Lowery's Concert Band was for many years a feature attached to travelling circuses, working separately from the main circus arena, both as a marching band ballyhooing the circus' arrival in town and then playing to attract audiences into the big top and the sideshows. Once in the circus complex, audiences were given the choice of either seeing the main big top show or waiting for a later performance and passing the time by visiting the numerous sideshows. Lowery organized a minstrel sideshow, and the music was provided by the orchestra—a small group from the main band who accompanied the singers and performers. Sweatman thus had two roles—to play clarinet with the main concert band and also to lead the sideshow band.

From the early years of the century into the 1930s, circus sideshow bands were a regular source of work for black musicians. This area of jazz history, along with travelling minstrel and vaudeville shows, has been largely overlooked by jazz historians. Despite their fame and prestige, black bands such as Lowery's were not permitted to play in the main big top—this apartheid within the circus world was to last until the late 1970s. Black bands were an enormously popular part of the whole circus experience, the parade through town undoubtedly being the most popular. Headed by the white circus band, the troupe would usually start at noon and would include caged wagons containing the animals, plus the clowns and the black sideshow band either marching or riding atop its own richly decorated wagon.

At the circus pitch they played in a segregated sideshow tent, usually comprising a minstrel show accompanied by a small orchestra, generally of no more than ten musicians made up of men from the main marching band. The minstrel show featured comedians, singers, dancers, and "specialty acts" such as hoop rollers or jugglers, and the bandsmen would be expected to read musical scores to accompany them. Very occasionally they would be invited to perform in the big top at the end of the main show, in an extra "after show" entertainment that the public paid extra to watch. Musicians with the ability to "double" on brass, reed, or stringed instruments, or who could turn their hands to comedy, dancing, singing, or could perform a novelty act, were highly prized. Musicians of the caliber of W. C. Handy, Willie "Bunk" Johnson, Willie Hightower, Alvin "Zoo" Robertson, Lorenzo Tio Sr., Charles Creath, Jasper Taylor, and Buddy Petit joined minstrel, circus, and sideshow bands—often for the summer touring season during which, in the days before air conditioning, theaters, dance halls, and cabarets frequently closed until the fall.

The work was grueling, both physically and mentally; musicians were expected not only to double on other instruments but also to have some ability in other areas of entertainment, be it singing, dancing, or performing comedy routines. Added to this was the physical work of erecting and dismantling the circus tents and seating, and packing it away and carting it to the nearest railway station. Although bandmasters such as Lowery insisted that his musicians not get involved in the physical work of erecting and taking down the circus tents, many circus owners expected it of the bandsmen.

The most prized ability, and one that was expected as a matter of course by circus bandleaders, was the ability to read music well. This flies in the face of the romantic notion of early jazzmen being gifted musical illiterates, pouring forth a stream of endless improvised melody, oblivious to the rules and conventions of "proper" music. In reality, musicians groomed in the world of the tent show and the circus were those most in demand in other areas of musical activity. Orchestra leaders, especially those working in theaters and cabarets, valued highly the circus musicians' sight-reading and improvisational abilities, coupled with their ability to "follow" a stage performer in their routine. Then as now, a mistimed cymbal crash or a badly judged cue could kill a performance stone dead. This did not stop ambitious fakers with aspirations of a career with a tent show band trying to pull the wool over a leader's eyes. Veteran black comedian Tom Fletcher, who worked in minstrel and tent shows as a young man, recalled how they were dealt with:

> When you joined a show as a musician there never was any band re-hearsal. The band leader, when parade time came, would pass out the books that had all of the tunes, but with the names of the tunes cut off. The idea was to see whether you had told the truth about being a bands-man. When everyone had his book the leader would give the signal to start playing the march. [He] would get a chance to see who was cheating or wasn't a good music reader. If they were good singers or dancers the leader would let them keep their books but they would have to go off by themselves where they wouldn't disturb anyone and learn the tunes.[2]

Of the many black circus and concert bands working in the early years of the century, that of cornet virtuoso Perry George Lowery (1870–1942) was the best known and most highly regarded.[3] The Lowery band's reper-toire, in common with other circus sideshow bands, ran the whole gamut of orchestral music, circus overtures, operatic arias, marches, concert ar-rangements of popular tunes of the day, and orchestral ragtime. Lowery, who was the first African American graduate of the Boston Conservatory of Music, was a friend of Scott Joplin, and from relatively early on in Joplin's career championed his compositions. Advertisements for the Lowery Band in the black press at the turn of the century noted his performing Joplin compositions, and indeed Joplin's 1902 "A Breeze From Alabama" is dedi-cated to Lowery.[4] P. G. Lowery's reputation as a music teacher was as great as N. Clark Smith's, and the contemporary press frequently commented on the quality of Lowery's musicians, or made mention of the fact that that they were members of "The Lowery School." As authors Lynn Abbott and Doug Seroff noted in the book *Ragged But Right:* "P. G. Lowery was idolized by his contemporary musicians, and there is ample evidence that the 'Lowery School' was a primary factor in the development of modern African American popular music and jazz."[5]

Lowery regularly employed musicians, besides Sweatman, who would go on to make names for themselves as jazz musicians. These included cornetists Roger Quincey Dickerson, Charles Creath, and possibly Willie "Bunk" Johnson, trombonists Earl Granstaff, Alvin "Zoo" Robertson, and Harvey Lankford, and clarinetists Horace Eubanks and William Thornton Blue—all familiar names to enthusiasts and students of 1920s classic jazz. The best known, as far as their subsequent careers as jazzmen is concerned, were two legendary cornetists—Charles Creath and Willie "Bunk" Johnson. Charles Creath (1895–1951), played with Lowery's sideshow band with the Hagenbeck-Wallace Circus for the 1916 and 1917 seasons until illness, probably tuberculosis, forced him to quit. In the 1920s Creath led one of the best-known black bands in St. Louis and his records on the OKeh label between 1924 and 1927 demonstrate a masterly use of mutes and a soulful tone.

More controversially, and less substantiated, the New Orleans trumpeter, and leading figure of the 1940s jazz revival movement, Willie "Bunk" Johnson regularly claimed to have been with Lowery's band and even to have toured with them to Europe. Lowery spent much of 1918 directing a band at the government explosives factory in Nitro, West Virginia, and the *Indianapolis Freeman* of September 7, 1918, lists one W. Johnson as a member. However, Johnson's World War I draft registration card shows that on the day Uncle Sam caught up with him, just one week later, on September 12, 1918, he was residing at 140 Bank Street, Lake Charles, Louisiana, where he was working with drummer Paul Jones's orchestra.[6] Until substantive documentary evidence is forthcoming, Bunk's tenure with Lowery must be treated with a considerable degree of skepticism (he was not called "Bunk" for nothing). Taken at its least credible level, the assertion demonstrates that such was Lowery's reputation that musicians were prepared to lie about having played in his band.

The minstrel show required performers as well as musicians, and Lowery chose well in this area. Dancer and comedian Ulysses S. "Slow Kid" Thompson, later to be associated with and married to the celebrated black Broadway and international theater star Florence Mills, and blues singer Callie Vassar, who recorded four blues songs for the Starr Piano Company's Gennett record label in 1923, were both featured in Lowery's sideshow minstrels.

The *Indianapolis Freeman* of May 10, 1902, notes that the Lowery Band was working with the Forepaugh and Sells Brothers Circus for the fourth season and that their tour commenced in Philadelphia on Monday, April 21, 1902. It continues: "We regret that C.D. Jackson our orchestra leader is not with us but his place is ably filled by W.C. Sweatman, violin and clarionetist [*sic*]." Of C. D. Jackson little information is known, but Jackson's immediate predecessor as leader of the Lowery band was New Orleans–born violinist Antoine Charles Elgar (1879–1973) who, like Sweatman, was to play a pivotal role in the development of jazz in Chicago in the early years of the twentieth century. Elgar spent two seasons with the Lowery band before moving to Chicago in 1902, where he worked initially as a jobbing musician and music teacher, specializing in the violin (his pupils included future jazz stars Darnell Howard and Eddie South). When musical work was insufficient to pay his bills, he also worked in a cigar factory.

Fortunately for posterity, Perry Lowery was a regular contributor to the *Indianapolis Freeman*'s stage and music pages, providing on-the-spot reports of the troupe's activities, news and not a little self-promotion. These reports provide masses of information and names, down to details about the waiters and porters on their railroad car. A flavor of Lowery's reports and the entertainment offered by his troupe is given in this report to the *Freeman* in May 1902:

Another strong feature in the vaudeville department is the Four in Hand Quartette under the personal direction of Ambrose Davis ably supported by Wm. Johnson, Arthur Wilmore and Jack Watkins. Their single specialities are all first class. Too much cannot be said of the ladies, they are good-looking, good dressers, well behaved and are clever performers. Everybody knows Miss Sallie Lee formerly of the Octoroon company. Miss Essie Williams is with me this season and adds greatly to both the appearance and value of the company. Miss Gracie Hoyt from N.Y. has made many friends in her earnest work. In fact everybody is stuck on our girls.

Our business staff is filled as follows: P.G. Lowery, manager and director of the band; J.J. Smith, assistant band master; W.C. Sweatman, leader of Orchestra; Ambrose Davis, stage manager; C.B. Foster, assistant; Jas S. Morton, librarian; Sallie Lee, authorized agent for The Freeman.[7]

The Adam Forepaugh and Sells Brothers Circus (often referred to in contemporary press reports as "4-Paws") with whom the Lowery band toured, was one of the best-known in the country. Adam Forepaugh (1831–1890), a Philadelphia horse dealer and butcher, had made one fortune at the onset of the Civil War, selling horses to the Union army. He got into the circus business in 1864, when he sold forty-four horses for $9,000 to John V. "Pogey" O'Brien, a notoriously unscrupulous circus owner. O'Brien was unable to pay the debt in full, so Forepaugh took a share in his circus in lieu of payment. By astute acquisition of other circus troupes and their acts he was able to develop a top-quality circus that rivaled the great Ringling Brothers and Barnum and Bailey circuses, and personally ran it from 1866 until shortly before his death in 1890. It was acquired by James A. Bailey (of Barnum and Bailey fame) and James E. Cooper in 1889; when they combined it with the Sells Brothers Circus, which they also owned. It was, along with the Barnum and Bailey and Ringling Brothers ircuses, among the very best in the United States. In 1896 Bailey took the Barnum and Bailey Circus for a six-year tour of Europe, and the Forepaugh and Sells Brothers operation took over the best circus bookings in the Eastern states.

Sweatman joined the Lowery Band in New York, where their first appearance was at the Douglass Club, a well-known professional club for black performers located on West 31st Street. Besides its core of black theatrical performers, the Douglass Club was a favourite venue for both black and white members of the "Sporting Set," who could freely mingle and enjoy the free entertainment put on by members, many of whom would have sung or played the same songs to a paying public just hours or even minutes before. With such men as "Diamond Jim" Brady, Harry K. Thaw, and Alfred Vanderbilt as regular visitors, the tips for these "free" entertainments could be considerable, and one reason there was never a shortage of volunteer performers. A few days later, on April 2, 1902, the Lowery Band appeared at the season's opening performance of the Forepaugh–Sells Brothers Circus at Madison Square Garden, where they stayed for seventeen days. A report in the *Indianapolis Freeman* of April 26, 1902, notes the band being in New York and gives the following roster of bandsmen:

> Jeff J. Smith [cornet], Thos. May [cornet], Geo. P. Hambright, Mr. Sweetnam [*sic*] [clarinet and violin], Henry Rawles [baritone horn], John P. Jones [poss. baritone horn], James B. Hall [baritone euphonium], James Morton (shown in other rosters as Martin), Fred W. Simpson [trombone, a legendary Indianapolis-born trombonist who may have recorded along with New Orleans clarinetist Lorenzo Tio Sr. as early as 1898 when both were members of the Oliver Scott Colored Minstrels orchestra],[8] Wm. May [tuba], Saml. Elliott [drums and stage manager], Chas. Foster.

The Wichita-born May brothers, Thomas and William, were lifelong circus musicians of renowned ability and musicianship—William May in particular was often cited in the black press as being the benchmark by which all other bass players were measured. The May brothers' circus career predates even Lowery's: they were with the Sells Brothers Circus under the baton of celebrated leader Solomon P. White as early as 1891, and in fact William May was still with Lowery on the latter's final tour with Cole Brothers Circus in 1942![9]

A faded photograph (reproduced for the first time in this book) survives of the Lowery band and troupe taken during the 1902–03 season, signed on the reverse by Sallie N. Lee and Thomas May. It shows a youthful clarinetist, almost certainly Sweatman, standing alongside a proud-looking Lowery. To Lowery's left stands an equally proud and dignified Thomas May. They and the other bandsmen are resplendent in their caps and band uniforms, trimmed with braid decoration and epaulets. Above them, on a makeshift draped stage, sits Sallie Lee in a dress with leg-of-mutton sleeves and ruffles, flanked by two other female entertainers, presumably Essie Williams and Gracie Hoyt. Standing behind them, wearing street clothes, are four men, presumably the "Four in Hand Quartette"—Ambrose Davis, William Johnson, Arthur Wilmore, and Jack Watkins.

Veteran black showman Tom Fletcher recalled his first encounter with Sweatman:

> I met Wilbur Sweatman when he came to New York in the early 1900s to join the Forepaugh and Sells Brothers Circus as a member of Professor P. G. Lowery's Band. In those days, when the circuses played at old Madison Square Garden there would be a street parade the night before the opening, with bands, animals, actors, clowns, everything except the freaks. The colored band made the parade in New York and the season Sweatman was with the band the crowds that lined the side walks started following the band just to hear Sweatman playing his clarinet. Everybody was saying they had never heard anybody play the instrument like that before. Sweatman was the sensation of the parade.[10]

After Madison Square Garden, the circus moved to Philadelphia on April 21 for six days, then to Baltimore (where over nine thousand people paid to see them) and to Washington, D.C. Reports in the *Indianapolis Freeman* show that the troupe had a tremendously successful season that included performing for social events as well as regular circus work. One such event was a concert in Washington organized to celebrate the work of pioneering journalist Edward Elder Cooper, founder of the *Indianapolis Freeman* and the Washington *Colored American*.[11] The tour continued through Maryland and West Virginia in early May before doubling back to Pennsylvania, ending the month in New Jersey and Brooklyn. June started in New York State before heading up into New England, where they spent seventeen days touring.

They then crossed into Canada, where they toured major towns of Quebec and Ontario for the better part of three weeks, before crossing the border again and opening in Buffalo on July 21, 1902. A further week of one-night stands in upstate New York followed, then a few more days in northeast Pennsylvania before heading west into Ohio via a one-night stand in Wheeling, West Virginia. From early August until late September the Forepaugh and Sells Brothers Circus blazed a trail of one-day and one-night shows through Ohio, Indiana, Illinois, Iowa, and Wisconsin, journeying from town to town via train, Lowery's bandsmen travelling with him in his own private railroad car.

At the end of September the troupe headed south, and Lowery's private car became a necessity, as it offered both shelter and security in the racially charged atmosphere below the Mason-Dixon Line. Starting in Chattanooga, Tennessee, on September 29, 1902, they worked their way through Tennessee to Memphis on October 4th. The rest of October saw them pitching their tents throughout Alabama, Georgia, and the Carolinas, making a quick incursion into Florida for one day in Jacksonville. On October 25 the *Indianapolis Freeman* noted that Sweatman was with Lowery's Band in Savannah, Georgia, and that he ". . . would like to hear from H. St. Clair and sends regards to K.C. folks."[12] From Jacksonville, they headed back into Georgia for a week before playing Montgomery and Selma, Alabama, then crossing into Mississippi for a week. The final destination of the 1902 season was New Orleans, where they pitched tents for four days. Veteran New Orleans trumpeter Lee Collins, although too young to have seen the 1902 appearance of the Lowery band, recalled the thrill of seeing a later visit by Lowery to the Crescent City in 1928, when Collins was leading the band at the Astoria Gardens:

> One thrill I remember was the night that P. G. Lowery came to the Astoria. Lowery . . . was with the Barnum and Bailey shows and was known as the greatest cornet soloist. He could make high C over high C like it was nothing at all; he was the greatest of all time. The way he blew made goose pimples come over me; I had never heard a cornet player like him in my life before. Lowery was a fine-looking man and had come out of the Tuskegee Institute—where I always wanted to go and would have if my grandfather had lived longer. Bunk Johnson told me once that he worked under P. G. Lowery and that he went with the circus on a tour of Europe. I don't know if that was true or not, as Bunk did a

little stretching of the truth from time to time, but I do know that it was a great thing for all the musicians to listen to Lowery when he came to New Orleans with the circus.[13]

Throughout the 1902 touring season, Lowery suffered from an unspecified illness, which meant that he missed many dates. As early as May the *Indianapolis Freeman* was reporting that Lowery was missing performances, which would have increased the load of orchestra leader already on Sweatman's shoulders. Lowery's illness prevented him touring with his Nashville Students company in the winter season, which traditionally commenced on the closure of the Forepaugh-Sells Brothers Circus tour. He spent the whole of the winter season at his home in Reece, Kansas, where he directed the town's band and gave private music lessons.[14]

Even by this early date, Sweatman must have been sufficiently well regarded to have risen to the position of orchestra leader of one of the best-known black concert bands in the country at such a young age. Lowery's illness would have undoubtedly also meant that greater responsibility was thrust on his youthful shoulders: organizing advance publicity for their appearances, band rehearsals, discipline of the musicians, and being the public face of the band at their performances—skills that were to be of enormous value and importance in his later career. Sweatman's stagecraft and meticulous attention to detail, honed while working with the likes of Lowery, N. Clark Smith, and W. C. Handy, are often mentioned in contemporary accounts of his stage act. Years later, even Duke Ellington was to credit Sweatman with teaching him much about stagecraft, presentation and the business of show business.

Ragtime was, by 1902, a prominent part of the circus sideshow band repertoire. As previously noted, Lowery was an early champion of the work of Scott Joplin. Lowery biographer Clifford Edward Watkins notes: ". . . Lowery was impressed by Joplin's music and increasingly performed his compositions, and the two men developed great respect for each other. . . . During his 1901 tour with the Forepaugh and Sells Brothers circus, Lowery featured himself performing Joplin's 'Sunflower Slow Drag' in addition to the usual band songs and classical transcriptions."[15]

At the end of the 1902 season, Sweatman, along with cornetist and assistant bandmaster Jeff Smith, handed in his notice and left the Lowery band to join the legendary Mahara's Minstrels troupe. He joined as assistant orchestra leader, playing violin in the orchestra and doubling on clarinet in the full band, which was led by another great black cornet soloist of the day, William Christopher Handy. Mahara's Minstrels were, along with the

Georgia Minstrels, the most famous black minstrel troupe in the United States. In common with most other black minstrel troupes, Mahara's Minstrels were managed by white owners, in this instance by Irish brothers W. A., Frank L., and Jack Mahara—in Handy's own words, ". . . the fightingest triumvirate of Irishmen that ever hoodwinked the railway company."[16] While making money for themselves was always more important to the Mahara brothers than benevolence to black musicians and entertainers, they had an obvious eye for talent, and their troupe was considered one of the top finishing schools for black professional entertainers and musicians. Frank Mahara, in particular, was well-liked by those who worked for him. Handy noted:

> He had a passion for detail. He required that everything be just right. For him the minstrel show was not just a fabulous mine of profits but a company of human beings each of whom required personal consideration. The music, the uniforms, the program and the talent, even the food he bought and the Pullman car in which we travelled, had to be the best obtainable. He also saw to it that our Pullman had a hidden compartment . . . which we came to call the "bear wallow" or the "get-away." In this secret hold we carried reserves of food, not to mention a small arsenal.[17]

In common with most touring shows, the Mahara brothers ran two Mahara's Minstrels companies, each taking separate routes, with Frank Mahara taking responsibility for the running of the Number Two show with which Handy toured in the 1902-03 season. Under Handy's tutelage many pioneering jazz musicians gained invaluable experience. Handy's autobiography, *Father of the Blues*, gives a vivid account of his time with Mahara's Minstrels, and is essential reading for anyone interested in the history of black entertainment and early jazz and blues. As with the Lowery troupe, Sweatman doubled in both the band, which marched through the streets ballyhooing their appearance in town, and in the smaller orchestra, which was used to accompany the singers, dancers and other acts in the sideshow. In this latter role Sweatman played violin.

A note in the *Indianapolis Freeman* of December 6, 1902, provides details of the roster of musicians with Mahara's Minstrels: "Joe Pleasant [tuba], F. [Fountain] B. Wood [trombone], Pearl Moppin [trombone], W.B. Taylor, Albert Fredericks [trombone, violin], H.M. Prince [alto saxophone], H.D. Coleman ["alto," cornet], Geo. Wright [cornet], Wm. Johnson ("battery"), H.J. St. Clair [cornet], J.J. Smith [cornet], W.C. Sweatman (clarinet), Fred Richardson (clarinet), Geo. Reeves (drums), and W.C. Handy."

It is interesting to note the presence of cornetist H. J. St. Clair in the band—presumably the same man from whom Sweatman wanted to hear at the end of October, according to the report in the *Indianapolis Freeman*, and possibly the instigator of Sweatman's leaving Lowery and joining Handy's band. Two other names in this roster deserve special attention: alto saxophonist H. M. Prince is the same Henry Morgan Prince (1885–1969) who was the singer, dancer, and comedian with Bill Johnson's Creole Band in the period from 1914 to 1917; and drummer George "Pippin" Reeves was to be a regular member of Sweatman's groups up to the late teens, and thereafter the drummer with the pit band for Sissle and Blake's ground-breaking all-black musical comedy *Shuffle Along* in 1921–22.[18]

Handy and Lowery were both accomplished cornetists of the highest order, with a mutual respect for one another's abilities. Their paths had first crossed in the mid-1890s, and at the Trans-Mississippi Exposition, held in Omaha, Nebraska, in the summer of 1898, they met head to head in a memorable "cutting contest." Lowery, who was working as a featured cornet soloist, was invited by Handy's musicians to the Mahara's Minstrels show site. Before too long, the two cornetists were sizing up one another's musical abilities. Handy recalled the evening: "We got together and took each other's measure like a pair of gamecocks in a crowing match. I called for a number, and he gave it back to me with plenty of gravy and dressing. He named his terms, and I came back with my Sunday best. From that day my great ambition was to outplay P.G."[19]

For his part, Lowery had the utmost respect for Handy's abilities and, in 1900, set down his thoughts on the subject in an article in the *Indianapolis Freeman* on leading black cornetists. Describing him as "my friend, Wm. Handy," he wrote: "I feel safe in saying he deserves more credit than is dealt to him. His street work is very brilliant (but not blasty); his orchestra work is smooth and tasty and he certainly plays a song to suit me . . ."[20]

It was during his tenure with Handy and Mahara's Minstrels that Sweatman perfected the art of playing first two and, in 1917, three clarinets simultaneously in harmony.[21] This feat would, over the years, carry him to national vaudeville fame. Subsequently, "purist" jazz writers would decry this as the lowest gimmick to which the "copyists" would descend in the quest for novelty effect and, as such, deserved nothing less than eternal damnation. These writers failed to understand that, for a black musician to gain public recognition when the normal avenues of a musical career were at best restricted and at worst barred, it was necessary to possess a trick or novelty that would appeal to the customers in the few areas open to black performers. As academic and author Lawrence Gushee noted:

Musical acts . . . were pretty much obliged to have gimmicks, such as elaborate, often exotic, costumes or peculiar instruments, or to present their acts in a kind of choreography. The lesson that had to be learned was that vaudeville audiences were not there to be edified, as at a concert, but to be entertained. And music without words is not that entertaining by itself. This aspect of vaudeville was alive and well when dance bands began to appear on the vaudeville stage and found themselves obliged to impersonate Arabs, Eskimos, soldiers, sailors, and what have you.[22]

What is not mentioned in jazz books is that Sweatman reserved his three-clarinet trick solely for his minstrel show and, later, vaudeville performances—purely as an attention-grabbing novelty. In fact, the only tune that contemporary reports mention receiving this treatment was Ethelbert Nevin's "The Rosary," in much the same way that he featured Arthur Lamb and Henry Petrie's "Asleep in the Deep" as a bass clarinet solo.

Before the close of the touring season, probably at the end of May 1903, Sweatman, along with two key members of the band, quit the Mahara's Minstrels. The *Indianapolis Freeman* reported that: "J. Jeff Smith, W.C. Sweatman and George Reeves, have just closed with Mahara's No. 2 show, and are now in Minneapolis, Minn., at 112 Second Street. They send regards to Tom Logan, Kid Alston and all friends."[23] Tom Logan was a Kansas City–based minstrel entertainer and manager, renowned for his character parts, and a close friend and confidante of Ernest Hogan. Back in 1899 Logan had been stage manager for the M. B. Curtis Afro-American Minstrel Company on their Australasian tour and was later associated with Hogan in his show *Rufus Rastus*.[24] That Sweatman was a friend of such a well-established figure in black entertainment circles as Tom Logan is indicative of the esteem that Sweatman received in professional circles, and an example of how far his career had progressed in a relatively short time—he had barely turned twenty-one. Clarence "Kid" Alston was a distinguished minstrel show band leader, long associated with the Al G. Fields Real Negro Minstrels.[25]

On his departure from Mahara's Minstrels, Sweatman was replaced by Horace George who, due to the demands of his employers and audiences alike, also took up the trick of playing two and, eventually, three clarinets at once. This led to a long and bitter feud between Sweatman and George over who was the originator of the three-clarinet trick and which, over the years, sporadically erupted into a vitriolic exchange of letters published in show business papers. One such outburst occurred in August 1919, when Sweatman lodged a complaint with the National Vaudeville Association (the vaudeville artists' trade union) requesting that George (then working in vaudeville with pianist, composer, and singer Shelton Brooks) refrain from claiming to be the originator of playing two and three B♭ clarinets simultaneously. The trade paper *Variety* subsequently carried a large display advertisement from George, detailing his inflated riposte to Sweatman's charge:

> In regard to the complaint against Brooks and George by Mr. Sweatman, I wish to give a few names who know I am not only the originator of 3 B flat clarinet playing, but were playing it before Mr. Sweatman: Harry Weber, Herman Weber, Ralph Dunbar, Tennessean Ten [*sic*], Western Vaudeville and Mr. Sweatman.
>
> I believe I am the only man in the country that really plays three clar [*sic*], three different to show.
>
> I am a master originator, not an imitator. Horace George.[26]

Sweatman's response is a masterpiece of putdown and self-promotion:

> . . . as for Mr. George saying that I am among the ones who know he is a "master originator", I can say this and verify it, when I was leader of the orchestra of the Grand Theater, Chicago, directing with a B flat clarinet, transposing violin parts, Mr. George was on hand trying to imitate me in every way, and when I left to go in vaudeville he got the job and tried to fill my place, but could not do it.
>
> When I was playing vaudeville he got his idea of trying to play more than one, and now I am making records for him to school by. [shades of Freddie Keppard!—MB]
>
> If he is a "master originator", he is the only one who knows it, and he should learn to play one well and then criticise. I planned and carried out the idea of playing two and three clarinets at once, had never seen or heard of anyone doing it, and therefore consider myself the originator and also started the jazz craze for the clarinet and am the originator of jazzing and slurring on that instrument, which quite a number of clarinetists have tried hard to imitate. Wilber C. Sweatman. The original and much imitated Rag-time clarinetist.[27]

Horace George made two records, issued on the OKeh record label in 1924, about which one can only say that they bear out perfectly Sweatman's comments concerning his playing ability!

CHAPTER 5

THE ANCHORAGE FOR THE WORLD'S MARVELS

⤙ The Minneapolis Years ⤚

ON HIS ARRIVAL IN MINNEAPOLIS, Sweatman wasted no time in forming a band—in fact, it is highly likely that he, along with cornetist J. Jeff Smith and drummer George Reeves, left the Mahara band with the prospect of a job already agreed. Smith was a star cornet pupil of P. G. Lowery who over several years worked sporadically with Lowery's sideshow band. Drummer George "Pippin" Reeves was one of the great early black jazz drummers, ranking alongside Charles "Buddie" Gilmore, Manzie Campbell, and Carl "Battle Ax" Kenny. One of the most difficult areas of Sweatman's career to document has been the time he spent in Minneapolis, for it has been well-nigh impossible to find any references to his activities in either local mainstream newspapers or the black press. A brief biography of Sweatman in the *Indianapolis Freeman* of October 8, 1910, provides us with the sole factual report of his years in Minneapolis: "When his second season [with Mahara's Minstrels] ended he went to Minneapolis and took charge of the first colored band and orchestra of that city. This was at the Palace Museum and he held that position for four years."

The "museum" or "dime museum" was commonplace in mid- to late-nineteenth-century towns and cities across the United States as a place of entertainment, amusement, and education. Though he is best known for his circus career, Phineas Taylor Barnum (1810–1891) was the central figure in the establishment of dime museums. After establishing his first in New York City in 1841, Barnum found a formula for success that entertainment entrepreneurs copied throughout the nineteenth and early twentieth centuries. Dime museums incorporated waxwork displays, menageries, automatons, pseudoscientific equipment (electric shock machines and laughing gas were great favorites with patrons), rope dancers, "living" statue tableaux, and musical and variety entertainment; but the dime museum's most significant contribution to the content of American popular culture was to "introduce and standardize the concept of the freak show."[1]

Two-headed babies, bearded women, Egyptian mummies, midgets and giants: all were staples of the dime museum, the most famous being the midget Charles Stratton, better known as General Tom Thumb. Barnum appeased those who were critical of his amusements on moral and religious grounds by expounding the educational benefits of his museum. He banned alcohol from his establishment, along with lewd language from performers on stage, in order to attract women and children. And by offering diverse entertainment (and changing his exhibits of curiosities often) he recruited patrons from all strata of society, many of whom attended again and again.

Another, less savory reason for the rise in popularity of dime museums was that less-than-scrupulous owners took advantage of a loophole in the law: that, as "museums," they did not have to meet the strict fire and safety regulations laid down for theaters. Likewise, they were free from the moral codes that city councils could and did use against "lewd" theater productions.

Aside from "freak shows" and the like, some dime museums opened their doors to black performers at a time when legitimate theaters and vaudeville houses were all but barred to them. Notable amongst these was Worth's Model Museum at 6th Avenue and 30th Street in New York, where, by the mid-1890s, in the words of James Weldon Johnson, it had "virtually become a Negro stock theater, the first place where a group of colored performers were able to gain anything approaching dramatic training and experience on the strictly professional stage."[2] Bob Cole, who later teamed up with Johnson to compose and write the first black musical comedy *A Trip To Coontown* (1897) and several other notable black musical shows, was both the resident playwright and stage manager at Worth's, succeeding another well-known black songwriter, Gussie L. Davis. Sweatman's tenure as orchestra leader at a dime museum demonstrates not only the variety of entertainment to be found at such places but also the relative openness to black performers, and casts light on an area of American popular entertainment that has not come under the scrutiny of jazz researchers.

The dime museum declined after 1900, in the face of competition from vaudeville and film; the last one in New York closed in 1916. But modern incarnations such as New York's Freakatorium, Baltimore's American Dime Museum, and the franchised Ripley's Believe It or Not are all direct descendants of the original concept, albeit focused on the more freakish and bizarre elements of the original.

Kohl, Middleton & Co's Palace Museum (THE ANCHORAGE FOR THE WORLD'S MARVELS—A SHELTER FOR NATURE'S ODDITIES, the signage running the length of the building boasted) was based in a three-storey building at the corner of Marquette and South Washington Avenues in downtown Minneapolis. As well as hourly performances featuring the "Illusions, Mechanical Wonders and Curiosities" that formed the backbone of such enterprises, the Palace also boasted a bar, "The Royal Bodega," and two theaters. It was presumably in one or both of these theaters that Sweatman and his orchestra performed. Amazingly, the Palace was photographed with remarkable clarity in 1896, seven years before Sweatman's sojourn, by Minneapolis photographer Arthur B. Rugg. The negative now resides in the Minnesota Historical Society collection, along with an extensive archive of other Rugg images that chronicle late-nineteenth- and early-twentieth-century Minneapolis life, and I am grateful for their kind permission to reproduce it here.

Whether Sweatman actually spent four years in Minneapolis as claimed in the *Indianapolis Freeman* in 1910 is debatable. What little evidence there is seems to point to him spending at least some of that time out of Minneapolis, possibly at other theaters, but almost certainly not with touring minstrel or circus sideshows. Touring groups were covered in remarkable detail in black newspapers such as the *Indianapolis Freeman*, acting as they did as conduits of information to, from, and about travelling performers and as poste restante mail boxes. Despite extensive searches of the *Freeman* and other black newspapers, it has proved impossible to find any references to Sweatman performing in that period other than in Minneapolis. Veteran minstrel and black vaudeville performer Tom Fletcher recalled that Sweatman in those years "had roamed around playing with different groups in different towns in Minnesota and Wisconsin."[3] He was certainly still in Minneapolis in 1905; Davison's Minneapolis City Directory for that year has him rooming at 1102 Washington Ave South and confirms that he was still playing at the Palace Dime Museum. But, interestingly, he is not mentioned in the 1908 directory.

Intriguingly, an advertisement that mentions Sweatman by name appeared in the *Indianapolis Freeman* in July 1904. The advertisement was placed by Jack Powell, leader of the Woodlawn Wangdoodle Pickaninny Band that appeared with the *In Old Kentucky* theatrical touring company, a hugely successful racially mixed show that toured for over a decade. Powell's advertisement states: "We are in need of clarionet [*sic*] and cornet players who can handle 3rd and 4th grade music. Must be small, not over 5 ft. 3 or 4 inches in height. Sweatman and Saulters write."[4] Sweatman's recorded height on his World War II draft registration card was 5' 5", certainly not tall and maybe just suitable for a "pickaninny band," despite being twenty-two years of age. It is unknown whether Sweatman responded to this advertisement, but it would seem a retrograde step to go from orchestra leader in one's own right, to mere clarinetist in a band full of juveniles, a role he had happily filled nearly ten years earlier.

What is known with a degree of certainty about this mysterious period is that Sweatman made his first recordings (also believed to be the first ever made by a black instrumental group) in about 1903, for the Metropolitan Music Company in Minneapolis. Initially located at 509-511 Nicollet Avenue and subsequently moving to 41-43 South Sixth Street sometime before 1907, Metropolitan Music was the largest music store in Minneapolis, selling a complete range of musical instruments, including holding the prestigious local concession for Steinway pianos. As well as retailing a broad range of sheet music publications, Metropolitan also published their own music, including several early cake walks and rags, notably Edmund Braham's "The Winner." Sweatman and his band recorded at least two titles for the Metropolitan Music Company on wax cylinders; Scott Joplin's "Maple Leaf Rag" and Kansas City–born white pianist and bandleader Edward Harry Kelly's languorous 1901 rag "Peaceful Henry." These, and possibly other titles, were presumably issued in very small numbers, bearing in mind it would only have been possible to duplicate by having a large number of cylinder recording machines in the studio, each recording a separate cylinder. Additional copies required the performers to repeat the process, and they were called back to make more, if the record proved popular. It is estimated that black singer George Washington Johnson, whose tune "The Whistling Coon" was one of the most popular cylinders on the 1890s, recorded the song over three hundred times including, allegedly, fifty-six performances in one day.[5]

Whether the cylinders of Sweatman's band proved popular with phonograph owners in Minneapolis is unrecorded, but their existence is not in doubt; when Sweatman was interviewed by Len Kunstadt in the 1950s, he produced the shattered fragments of the "Maple Leaf Rag" cylinder. Although it is nigh-impossible that playable copies of this or "Peaceful Henry" survive, one can live in hope . . .

CHAPTER 6

CHICAGO AND AN ENTERTAINMENT REVOLUTION

AS NOTED IN THE PREVIOUS CHAPTER, Wilbur Sweatman, according to a 1910 newspaper report, spent four years in Minneapolis—a very shadowy period of his life, with little factual information available. Tom Fletcher's previously quoted comment that Sweatman "had roamed around playing with different groups in different towns in Minnesota and Wisconsin" would seem to fit the period 1906–07—a baffling gap in Sweatman's career when there are no known reports of his activities in the black press.

The Minneapolis period gave Sweatman his first taste of leading a band in a theater, and by 1908 he had decided that the time was right to demonstrate his musical talents on a larger stage. In the spring of that year he moved to Chicago (Dave Peyton in the *Chicago Defender* of December 12, 1925, gives the date as 1906 but contemporary newspaper reports point to 1908 and Sweatman himself in an unpublished interview with Marshall Stearns in 1959 gives the date of his arrival in Chicago as 1908.[1] Journalist Carey Lewis, writing in the *Chicago Defender* in October 1910 noted that Sweatman "has been orchestra leader at the Grand Theater for two years. His versatility upon the clarinet is due to his original ideas and many people go to the Grand especially to hear 'Sweatman.' He transposes music and plays violin parts of standard overtures."[2]

Sweatman's decision to move to Chicago was prompted, no doubt, by the fact that, in the first decade of the twentieth century, Chicago vied with St. Louis and New York as the ragtime capital, with many of its finest composers and performers, including the likes of Scott Joplin, Louis Chauvin,

Joe Jordan, and Tony Jackson making their base there. More importantly, Chicago was increasingly becoming the creative epicenter of African
American entertainment with young, ambitious performers and musicians,
composers and songwriters, producers and managers creating a vibrant
and exciting artistic scene that was to prove vitally important to the early
development and popularization of both black theater and jazz and blues
music.

One of the chief attractions that Chicago offered to black musicians and
composers at the time was the vigorous and rapidly expanding black theater
and cabaret belt centered on South State Street and the notorious Levee
district—Chicago's own version of New Orleans's infamous Storyville red-
light district. Although the theaters and cabarets on the South Side, such
as the Pekin, the Grand, the De Luxe, and the Monogram, were predominantly owned by whites (the most notable exception being the Pekin, which
was owned and operated, until his death in 1911, by black entrepreneur
Robert T. Motts), actual creative and artistic control was usually in the
hands of black managers and producers, catering to predominantly black
audiences. In his study of Chicago jazz history, *Chicago Jazz: A Cultural
History, 1904–1930*, William Howland Kenney makes an important connection between the barring of entrepreneurial African Americans from most
political and corporate business activities and the rise of highly successful
black-owned or -managed entertainment enterprises:

> Jazz on Chicago's South Side was deeply woven into a fabric of economic
> and political activities designed to improve the standard of living and
> political power of the black community. South Side jazz . . . was closely
> allied with a dynamic pattern of entertainment enterprise which, given
> major racial constraints on black economic activities, played an even
> more important role in the South Side community than might otherwise
> have been the case.[3]

With such a concentration of black talent, free from the strictures of
white producers, directors, or managers and from the inherent racism of
white theaters and cabarets, South State Street became a fertile breed-
ing ground for new musical ideas. Noted authority on pre-jazz African
American entertainment Doug Seroff wrote:

> The Pekin, Grand and Monogram [theaters] were the first legitimate
> platforms in which black theater entertainment was provided for a black
> audience. That set the stage for black performers to bring forth a self-

directed, culturally distinctive brand of entertainment: jazz and blues. On State Street 1908–1910 Sweatman contributed his considerable talents to a critical moment in the advent of self-directed black stage arts. What was going on in Chicago in 1908 was a model that immediately spread throughout the Midwest and South as the fruition of black vaudeville.[4]

Theaters such as the Grand, the Pekin, and the Monogram were the first in the United States to provide a permanent base (rather than touring shows, tent shows, and the like) in which black entertainment was presented by black entrepreneurs for black audiences. These ventures received considerable publicity and promotion in newspapers with a black readership, such as the *Chicago Defender* and the *Indianapolis Freeman*, so Sweatman's arrival in Chicago, coming as it did shortly after the opening of these theaters, was hardly coincidental. News of the success of these Chicago theaters spread quickly by word of mouth and the black press, attracting black performers to Chicago from all over the country. Soon other theaters, run on the same model, opened throughout the South and Midwest, leading to an explosion of black vaudeville after World War I, which was aided by the formation of the Theater Owners Booking Association, established in 1920 by Nashville theater owner Milton Starr and a consortium of other prominent theater owners catering to black audiences.

Sweatman's initial employment in Chicago may have been as a member of the orchestra at Robert T. Motts's Pekin Theater, and he may have even acted as leader on occasion; but it has been impossible to trace any contemporary reports that could either confirm or deny this. The Pekin's regular leader from 1904 to 1912 was pianist, composer, and arranger Joe Jordan. However, Jordan was frequently involved in other ventures outside of Chicago and, in the summer of 1908, was in New York for rehearsals of Bob Cole and James Rosamond Johnson's musical comedy *The Red Moon*. That show opened in late 1908 and toured into the spring of 1909, followed by a second edition in the fall of 1909. Whether Jordan's involvement with the show carried on beyond preproduction is uncertain, but the show's musical director throughout its run was James Reese Europe.[5] It is known that Sweatman had connections with Motts—he was involved in the latter's funeral in 1911—but whether or not that connection was through his being employed by Motts at the Pekin can only be speculative.

Another connection with the Pekin can be found in the book *Blacks in Blackface*, where there appears a brief biography of comedian and singer Joe Simms. It states that "Simms . . . found himself with an engagement, three years later, at the old Pekin Theater, near 27th Street in Chicago. Among his partners during this period were Walker Thompson, who was a member of the Lafayette Players, Wilber Sweetman [sic], and Crickett Smith, the leader of a famous jazz band."[6] The possibility therefore arises that Sweatman and Smith, longtime musical acquaintances, worked with Joe Simms at the Pekin, either as a musical act or as members of the Pekin's resident orchestra. However, it has not been possible to substantiate whether this was the case or when such a partnership was likely to have occurred. An educated guess, based on Sweatman's subsequent and well-documented movements within the Chicago entertainment scene, would date it prior to Sweatman's sojourn at the Grand, before 1908.

Robert Motts's New Pekin Theater at 2700 South State Street was one of the largest theaters in the United States operated by a black entrepreneur for black theatrical productions. Motts himself was the new face of the black entrepreneur on South State Street at the turn of the twentieth century, with interests that encompassed politics, gambling, liquor selling, and entertainment. He was sufficiently astute to realize the economic necessity of attracting a certain sector of white customers with higher disposable income than the majority of his black patrons, the latter making up the bulk of his potential audience. Author William Howland Kenney notes: "The Pekin Inn and places like it therefore traditionally served the 'sporting fraternity,' an informal brotherhood of pleasure-seeking bachelors of both races. The sporting set included slumming young upper-class whites, who lined up at the bar and gathered around the gambling tables with downtown politicians, artisans, actors and immigrants to the city from many lands."[7]

As mentioned earlier, Motts was an astute businessman as well as politically active, and worked hard to ensure that Chicago's leading black intellectuals, activists, religious leaders, and fellow black entrepreneurs lent their support to his ventures. The Pekin was regularly given over at no cost to host charity events, such as a grand benefit for the Frederick Douglass Center and other fundraising events for black causes.[8] An early and historically important performance that took place at the New Pekin Theater shortly after its opening in March 1906 was the second appearance in Chicago of the black English composer Samuel Coleridge-Taylor, conducting his own works.[9] Wilbur Sweatman's old mentor Nathaniel Clark Smith rehearsed the Pekin Theater's orchestra and directed on the night of the concert.[10]

The chief form of entertainment at the Pekin was "tab" shows—condensed versions of revues or musical comedies performed by a stock cast of actors and actresses. Several well-known entertainers learned their craft in the Pekin stock company, most notably singer and comedian Arthur "Dooley" Wilson (1894–1953), best known for his appearance as Sam the pianist and entertainer in the classic film *Casablanca*. Motts had previously operated a cabaret, or music hall, in conjunction with his saloon at this site until it was severely damaged by fire. The original 1892 wooden building was extensively remodeled, transforming the saloon into a theater, which opened it doors on March 31, 1906.

The Pekin Theater orchestra's leader Joe Jordan often worked elsewhere for long periods, but it seems likely that Sweatman's first job in Chicago was as a member of his Pekin Theater orchestra. Joe Jordan, although almost forgotten except by musicologists and hardcore ragtime enthusiasts, was a major figure in the world of American musical theater, with a career extending from working with St. Louis ragtime pioneers Tom Turpin, Sam Patterson, and Louis Chauvin to providing music for Orson Welles's 1936 Federal Theater Project production of *Macbeth*.[11] Born in Cincinnati in 1882, the same year as Sweatman, he had studied in Jefferson City, Missouri, but by 1900 was working as a professional musician in St. Louis. By 1904 he was in Chicago, working as musical director at the Pekin Theater, having already worked in New York supplying some of the music for Ernest Hogan's show *Rufus Rastus.*

In 1905, presumably after the fire that destroyed the first Pekin Theater, Jordan was back with Hogan in New York, helping organize the Memphis Students, a group of singers and instrumentalists (none of whom were students or from Memphis). Many well-known names in the world of early-twentieth-century black entertainment were involved: James Reese Europe, composer Will Marion Cook and his soprano wife Abbie Mitchell, dancer Ida Forsyne, and dancing conductor Will Dixon. The show was a huge success at Hammerstein's Victoria Theater and in October a breakaway company, under the direction of Will Marion Cook and including Jordan, visited Europe. They appeared as the Tennessee Students at the Palace Theatre in London, and at the Olympia in Paris and the Schumann Circus in Berlin as the Memphis Students.

In 1906 Jordan was back at the Pekin as musical director, but the lure of travel never seemed far from his mind; later that year he was involved with another New York production by the Memphis Students, and in 1908 was in New York working with Cole and Johnson on their musical comedy *The Red Moon.* Following Robert Motts's death in 1911, Jordan had little involvement with the Pekin Theater and increasingly worked as an arranger, orchestrator, and composer, his most notable song being "Lovie Joe," written for Fanny Brice, with which she scored a huge success in the 1910 Ziegfeld

Follies. In 1910 and 1915 Jordan was again in Europe, his 1915 trip being particularly interesting because he was leading his own band, playing ragtime and proto-jazz on British music hall stages.[12] Jordan was also actively involved in property development and real estate in Chicago at this time and made and lost huge fortunes in his ventures.[13]

In about the fall of 1908 Sweatman was fortunate enough to secure the position of musical director of the Grand Theater, a small vaudeville and stock company theater owned by entrepreneur George Smith and situated just south of 31st Street at 3104 South State Street. The location of the Grand is often given as 3110-12 South State Street but this confusion arises from the fact that the Grand closed at the 3104 South State Street address in January 1911 and reopened a little further down the block on March 19, 1911.[14] Theatrical performers and pressmen alike used the terms "Old Grand" or "Little Grand" and "New Grand" to differentiate between the two—and to add further confusion, there were at least three other Grand Theaters in the Chicago area.

Sweatman's group at the "Old" Grand consisted of Sweatman himself, Dave Peyton at the piano, and George Reeves, the drummer from his Minneapolis band. Dave Peyton (1885–1956) was an immensely important and highly influential figure in Chicago musical circles for many years. He was a noted orchestral arranger, specializing in personalized arrangements, "patter choruses," and specialty material for such prominent vaudeville performers as Eva Tanguay and Al Jolson. Such personalized tailoring of songs for big-name performers conferred ownership of the song to the singer in the eyes of the public, making it stand out in comparison with other singers of the same material. Peyton was also a well-respected band booker and a successful music-store proprietor at 3109 South State Street, next door to the "New" Grand Theater. He later wrote a highly influential weekly music column for the *Chicago Defender* from 1925 to 1929 and, for most of the time from 1911 until the late 1920s, led his own band at the Grand and Regal theaters.

Peyton's reputation in Chicago entertainment circles as a fixer and organizer was second to none and, as a result he had unrivalled opportunities for organizing bands for both black and white venues. Only the much better-known James Reese Europe, based in New York and with prominent white socialite contacts, could boast of such influence at that time. Through his close working relationship with Ernie Young, a colorful vaudeville and cabaret booking agent and co-founder with Jules Stein of the Music Corporation of America, Peyton was able to provide work for black bands in many Uptown and Loop hotels and cabarets, venues that were otherwise closed to them because of the protectionist stance of the white Local #10 branch of the American Federation of Musicians.[15] Many well-known jazz musicians, such as King Oliver, Kid Ory, Baby Dodds, Zue Robertson, Lee Collins, Preston Jackson, Bob Shoffner, Darnell Howard, George Mitchell, Jasper Taylor, and Reuben Reeves worked for Peyton, and it is to be regretted that his own band only made one record, fronted by clarinetist and saxophonist Fess Williams, in 1928.[16]

Jazz history has, from its inception as a serious study in the late 1930s, been bound by available recorded evidence. From 1917 onward this recorded evidence is extensive, albeit in forms that have been honed and tailored to suit the needs of disparate and often conflicting groups and interests. Recording company executives, music publishers, theatrical entrepreneurs, and even bandleaders themselves all had a hand in what was recorded and how it was played, resulting in a form of musical censorship that distorts the actuality of a performance as it would have been given on the bandstand. There is ample evidence from musicians and onlookers that what a band recorded sometimes bore little resemblance to what they played on a job; George Wettling recalled that King Oliver's Creole Jazz Band played the best waltzes in Chicago and Louis Armstrong recalled that on his first day with the Fletcher Henderson Orchestra he was handed the parts for a medley of Irish waltzes. This over-reliance on recordings by jazz historians has meant that bands and musicians that failed to get on record have either been mythologized (Buddy Bolden, Emmett Hardy, the Creole Jazz Band, Benny Peyton's Jazz Kings) or disregarded.

Without the benefit of recorded evidence it is difficult to understand the impact created by Sweatman's little group; but, judging from contemporary newspaper reports and the reminiscences of those who heard them, the Sweatman trio was nothing short of sensational. Writing in 1925, Dave Peyton, by then a successful bandleader in his own right and a regular columnist in the *Chicago Defender*, paid the following tribute to Sweatman's pioneering role in jazz history, at the same time taking a swipe at what he saw as the hijacking of jazz by "white copyists" for their own gain:

> You have heard of Ted Lewis, Paul Biese, Isham Jones, Rudy Wiedoft [*sic*] and many other star players who originated the weird musical tones that have won favor the world over. This may or may not be true, but to my knowledge Wilbur Sweatman, the clarinetist, was the first one to do this kind of playing.
>
> In 1906 [*sic*] Mr. Sweatman played in a little picture house on S. State St., in Chicago, called 'The Little Grand Theater'. In the orchestra were

three players—piano, drums and clarinet. Mr. Sweatman led the band with the clarinet and was a sensation. White players would come to this little house from all over the country to hear Sweatman moan on the clarinet, and many of them would engage him to teach them how to do it.

His work at this house made it famous nationally, as all of the musical papers spoke of this peculiar clarinetist. Little did we think that Mr. Sweatman's original style of playing would be adopted by the great jazz artists of today; but it is and Mr. Sweatman can claim the honour of being the first to establish it.[17]

That Sweatman's trio was an important musical group in Chicago in the days before the migration of musicians from New Orleans and the Southern states cannot be doubted, and their popularity was remembered many years later by Harrison Smith, a black band manager and theatrical agent (and one time partner with Jelly Roll Morton in a music-publishing venture) who recalled that "they were the talk of the town long before the arrival of the Creole Band."[18]

The work was arduous: four shows daily accompanying acts and touring troupes, writing the music for tabloid productions (condensed musical shows of generally one or two acts) performed by the Grand's own theatrical company, and performing with the trio as an act in its own right. Many subsequently well-known black performers honed their skills before the flickering footlights at the Grand—Bill "Bojangles" Robinson, blues singers Mamie and Trixie Smith, the double act of Ollie Powers and Shelton Brooks (the latter best known as the writer of the evergreen "Some of These Days"), and famed operatic soprano Matilda Sissieretta Jones ("The Black Patti"), to name but a few. A report in the *Indianapolis Freeman* of January 29, 1910, noted that the Sweatman group played four shows and six overtures a day, and over a period of a little less than two years accompanied 576 acts the Grand Theater. However there were opportunities for moments of light relief: "Sweetman [*sic*], leader of the Grand Orchestra, paid his sister a flying visit at Kansas City, and arrived there on her wedding day. He had such a good time that Dr. Majors had to pump some of it out of him. Now he can't remember anything about his sister's wedding. He was met by the boys and a band, but when and how he left he will never be able to tell."[19]

The wedding day in question was that of Eva Sweatman, who married Alexander A. Moore in Kansas City on Saturday, June 19, 1909. However, the marriage was not a success, for by October 1913 Moore had remarried, to one Nellie Thomas. After their separation, Eva moved in with her sister Lula and aunt, Willa Bigby, setting up home at 2309 Tracy Avenue, Kansas

City, a racially mixed area popular with teachers. Whether by coincidence or not, their next-door neighbor in 1920 was Nathaniel Clark Smith and his family, Sweatman's mentor from the mid-1890s and celebrated music educator.[20] Lula herself married, sometime in the 1920s, to Beverly White, a bank porter, and Eva continued to live with them. According to the 1930 census, Lula was no longer working as a teacher, so no doubt Eva's teacher's salary was a welcome addition to the household income.

Audiences at the black-directed State Street theaters were highly critical of performers who they felt did not give value for their hard-earned money; an act being forcibly removed from the stage was a not uncommon occurrence. The *Indianapolis Freeman* reported in typically florid style how Sweatman, as leader of the Grand's orchestra, signaled the audience displeasure to both the performer and the audience:

> The Grand has a complete signal code that can't be beaten when an act falls flat, the leader of the orchestra, Mr. Sweatman by name, strikes up a sweet little rag, entitled "I'm Going to Exit" [a Joe Jordan song written for Ernest Hogan's Memphis Students in 1905], you will see Mr. Manager come strolling down the aisle. That's a plenty when you hear the orchestra strike up that little tune, "I'm Going to Exit" and end with "That's A Plenty." Go around in the alley and you will see the original packing up but no place to go.[21]

Sweatman's trio at the Grand Theater attracted much interest in the black press, which was always keen to promote the activities of African Americans who were "making good." In January 1910 *Indianapolis Freeman* journalist Simpson Johnson wrote an extensive feature on Sweatman, complete with a three-quarter-length photograph showing him in a smart suit, collar, and tie and holding a clarinet. The face is that of a confident, proud, good-looking man, definitely someone going places. The feature carries the headline "Wilber C. Sweatman. The Sensational Clarinet Player and Leader of the Famous Grand Theater, of Chicago," and the article was obviously based on an interview with Sweatman:

> Mr. Sweatman is one of the "stand-out hits" of the Grand Theater, regardless of who is on the bill. The people pack the house to hear the Grand Orchestra and "Sensational Swet" as he is usually called—to hear him play that clarinet. . . .
>
> Mr. Sweatman plays four shows and six overtures nightly on the same clarinet. All of this on the unruly B-flat clarinet. He has played five

hundred and seventy-six (576) acts in almost two years at the Grand, and has had but one complaint, and that actor in turn made an apology, as he (the actor) found that he himself was in the wrong and not the leader.[22]

It appears that the trio's work was not appreciated in all quarters: Sylvester Russell, the rather acerbic and opinionated theatrical columnist of the *Chicago Defender*, complained that "The singers at the Grand have been suffering from too much instrumental music lately. There was a time when the clarionet [*sic*] supported the voices, but now the voices support the loud, horrid squeak from the orchestra."[23]

The success of the trio brought Sweatman to the attention of notable figures, black and white, from the music and theater worlds, one such being the celebrated black composer and violinist Will Marion Cook. A conservatory-trained violinist, Cook (1869–1944) had studied violin at Oberlin College (his parents' alma mater) at the age of fifteen and in 1887 began two years at the Berlin Hochschule für Musik studying with the great violinist Josef Joachim, as well as with Joachim's former pupil, Heinrich Jacobson. From 1894 to 1895 he studied composition with Antonín Dvorzák at the National Conservatory of Music in New York, managing to fall out with the great composer in the process. However, racial prejudice and Cook's legendary belligerence made it almost impossible for Cook to make a career as a concert performer. Instead he devoted his efforts to advancing the cause of African American music through popular music and the musical theater, frequently working with the black poet Paul Lawrence Dunbar as his lyricist. He gained prominence through the scores he wrote for the productions starring Bert Williams and George Walker, most notably *In Dahomey* (1902) and *Bandanna Land* (1908).

Cook paid a visit to the Grand Theater in 1909 and was so impressed by Sweatman's clarinet playing that he offered him a verbal contract to lead the orchestra for Williams and Walker's 1909–10 season.[24] However it was not to be; Williams's longtime stage partner, George Walker, was suffering from paresis, a neuropsychiatric disorder affecting the brain and central nervous system, brought upon by syphilis infection. He started to show alarming signs of physical and mental deterioration through the latter part of 1908 and, despite struggling through performances of *Bandanna Land*, it was plain to see that he was unwell. Gamely, he carried on until, in February 1909, he could do no more and was forced to retire from the show. Amazingly, his part was taken over by his wife, Aida Overton Walker; but before long she too left the cast, to pursue a vaudeville career, and the show

closed. Walker lingered for two more years, dying in a Long Island sanatorium in January 1911. For the 1909 season, his first without Walker, Bert
Williams staged a new show, *Mr. Lode of Koal*, but the music was furnished
by composer and performer J. Rosamond Johnson, so Cook's offer came to
naught.

Another offer that came Sweatman's way in 1909 was more unusual—
even bizarre. He was offered a contract by an emissary of Nicaraguan president José Santos Zelaya to act as conductor and clarinetist for the national
orchestra on a tour of Central America. Born into a family of wealthy coffee
growers, Zelaya (1853–1919) had done much to modernize Nicaragua, developing rail and shipping infrastructures, improving coffee-growing methods (with a subsequent boom in production), and establishing a national
education system, but he was not averse to pocketing much of the country's
profits for himself and his friends. His expansionist views alarmed both
neighboring countries and the U.S. government, so when U.S. gunboats
appeared offshore, rebel forces were quick to overthrow him and send
him into exile. Simpson Johnson's *Indianapolis Freeman* article reports
Sweatman's response:

> ". . . the same day tickets came for Mr. Sweatman and another musi-
> cian, Secretary Knox put President Zelaya out of business. The ticket
> was lying on the table and Sweatman was reading the morning paper.
> He jumped up and began playing that old song "Take Your Time" [un-
> doubtedly a reference to "Take Your Time", written by Joe Jordan and
> lyricist Harrison Stewart, published in 1907 by Gotham Attucks Music
> Company]. His landlady wanted to know why he was playing that old
> song. "Sweat" pointed to the letter and morning paper and said "The
> South American Government will have to send their band to Chicago if
> they want me."[25]

The same article in the *Indianapolis Freeman* gives an interesting insight
into the direction Sweatman was considering for his future:

> He [Sweatman] declares he will not go on the road again unless there
> is a first-class Negro concert band organised, as good as Sousa's Band,
> which could be easily organised. That [sic] music-loving public has no
> idea how far advanced the colored musician is today in this country. . . .
> Mr. Sweatman thinks that the Negro musician is about the only profes-
> sional of the Negro race that has not had a chance to show what he really
> can do. The first good manager with proper financial backing who will

organise a first-class Negro band, regardless of salary, will reap fame and fortune.[26]

Such an orchestra did materialize in 1917, when Col. William Hayward, commander of the 15th New York Infantry Regiment, instructed James Reese Europe to form the best band in the U.S. army. Europe's military band played an enormously important morale-boosting role in France in World War I, and was instrumental in introducing jazz music to Europe. Europe's death in May 1919—he was stabbed to death by one of his bandsmen in his dressing room—robbed the black musical world of its leading spokesman, its supreme organizer, and a talented bandleader and composer who, had he lived longer, surely would have influenced greatly the directions of both jazz and African American entertainment.

As a successful and popular orchestra leader, Sweatman was well known as a man-about-town; his light skin, good looks, and stylish dress sense made him a favorite with the females in the audience. However, he had already lost his heart to the daughter of the family with whom he lodged at 3248 Wabash Avenue. Hazel Gilmore, known to her friends as Nettie, lived with her mother Nora and stepfather Andrew, a railroad waiter, who had moved the family to Chicago from Pennsylvania. As well as seeing each other at home, Nettie and Wilbur saw a lot of each other at the theater: she worked as the Grand's box office cashier.[27] A backstage romance ensued and on June 29, 1910, Wilbur C. Sweatman, aged twenty-six, and Hazel Venie Gilmore, aged seventeen, were married by Pastor Moses H. Jackson at the Grace Presbyterian Church in Chicago, followed by a reception at the apartment of Mattie Griffin in the Wellington Flats on Wabash Avenue.[28]

While on their honeymoon, Sweatman's role as leader of the Grand Theater band was taken over temporarily by another legendary name in the annals of early jazz—violinist Antoine Charles Elgar. Elgar had led the orchestra for P. G. Lowery's sideshow with the Forepaugh and Sells Brothers Circus for the 1900 touring season (two years before Sweatman's tenure with Lowery), and later led a star-studded big band in Chicago that made four memorable records for Brunswick-Vocalion in 1926.[29] The *Chicago Defender* reported Sweatman's return to the Grand with some enthusiasm: "Prof. Sweatman, the greatest clarionetist of his race, is back to his post at the Grand theatre. He has been away on a honeymoon, which came better late than never. It gave him a rest and he will be in fine fettle as a helpmate to the singers."[30]

As well as leading the Grand's orchestra, Sweatman as musical director was expected to provide compositions and arrangements for tabloid shows and acts as well as fill-in music for the musical interludes. Sweatman, with William H. "Billy" Dorsey and Dave Peyton, also ran a "song shop," providing a transcribing and arranging service for aspiring songwriters and performers. The *Indianapolis Freeman* said this about the endeavor: "William Dorsey, Sweatman and Peyton are the big trio that are doing all the music arranging around Chicago and points all over the country. If you have a song and think it can make good, send it to them and they will arrange it ready for the publisher. All of them are clever young musicians and have been very successful in their line. Read Dorsey's ad in the Indianapolis Freeman."[31]

This was a hectic period for Sweatman, composing, arranging, playing, and directing, with little or no time to capitalize on his compositions—most of which were, by the nature of his work accompanying acts, of a throw-away nature and seldom intended for any long-lasting purpose. Therefore it is not surprising that we know little of Sweatman's probably vast composing output at this time. One early composition, written in collaboration with Dave Peyton, was mentioned in Will "Juli Jones" Foster's *Chicago Defender* column "Oh You Dahomey" in May 1909: "Sweetman and Payton [*sic*], of the Grand Theater, have written a march song. 'Two Hundred Miles an Hour.' Words by Burlington route; music by Santa Fe. It's noisy enough to be called the Rocky Mountain."[32]

Joe Jordan, the great ragtime pianist, bandleader, and composer, held the position of musical director of Chicago's Pekin Theater contemporary to Sweatman's tenure at the Grand and the Monogram theaters, and in Rudi Blesh and Harriet Janis's *They All Played Ragtime* recounted his experiences of songwriting for black theaters at the time: "While there . . . I wrote all the music of the shows, but only a few things were published. In those days a colored writer only peddled his song for a few dollars and there it ended . . . you just skipped the matter."[33]

Sweatman did however find time to get one of his compositions from this period into print; fortunately for posterity it was the composition for which he is best remembered—"Down Home Rag," published in 1911 by Will Rossiter, the prominent Chicago music publisher. The *Indianapolis Freeman* of November 19, 1910, noted that Sweatman had sold the rights to "Down Home Rag" to Will Rossiter "for a neat sum."

In construction, "Down Home Rag" is a classic folk rag with little of the sophistication of Joplin or Joseph Lamb, but ideal for a string band or clarinet-led group. It bears structural similarities to Euday L. Bowman's "12th Street Rag" in the first and second strains and both share the "three over four" or secondary rag rhythmic pattern common in many folk rags.

Sweatman and Bowman are known to have been acquainted—Bowman (1887–1949) moved from his birthplace of Fort Worth, Texas, to Kansas City in 1897, and it has been suggested by a number of sources (including Sweatman himself) that Sweatman sold "12th Street Rag" to Bowman, although there is no evidence to substantiate this.[34] This is not as farfetched as it may seem; the two rags share similar rhythmic and melodic phrases in places, and several of Sweatman's other compositions bear strong resemblance to both compositions, among them "Old Folks Rag," "Boogie Rag," and "That's Got 'Em." Bowman's rag was initially self-published in August 1914, but was deemed to be unplayable until it was published in a slightly simplified form by the celebrated Kansas City music store and publishers J. W. Jenkins' Sons Music Company, nearly seven years after the initial publication of "Down Home Rag."

An interesting sideline in the puzzle of who wrote "12th Street Rag" is Bowman's apparent inability to perform with any degree of aptitude what is purported to be his own composition. Recordings of the piece he made for Gennett in 1924 and for the American Record Company in 1938 were both rejected for release. In 1948, riding on the phenomenal success of the Pee Wee Hunt version, Bowman personally financed the recording and release of his own version. The result, even allowing for his state of health (he died the following year), was hardly a competent performance. Maybe this is being unfair to Bowman; he had impeccable credentials as a rag and blues composer despite being a self-taught pianist (his "Kansas City Blues" was a big hit in 1919, its popularity in no small part attributable to the best-selling Columbia recording of the tune by Wilbur Sweatman), and the structure of "Down Home Rag" is not unique in rag compositions.

"Down Home Rag" was by far the most successful and best known of Sweatman's compositions. Sales of the piano solo sheet music were such that Rossiter rushed out an orchestral version arranged by Harry LaForest Alford, a noted arranger of the period. Thus "Down Home Rag" was readily available to the tens of thousands of professional and amateur bands and orchestras across America. The celebrated black orchestra leader James Reese Europe frequently featured the number at his Clef Club concerts in New York, and when he and his Society Orchestra made the first commercially issued records by a black band for Victor in December 1913, "Down Home Rag" was one of the compositions he chose to record. This performance, despite the poor balance, perfectly captures the folk roots of the tune, with its violin and banjo lead, and the shouts of encouragement from the band members to one another. Further contemporary versions of "Down Home Rag" were recorded by the Victor Military Band

(Victor, April 1913—predating the Europe version and using the Alford arrangement), The Six Brown Brothers, also for Victor (1915), Van Eps' Banjo Orchestra (Pathé, 1914, remade in 1916) and Van Eps' Trio (Edison, 1914).

The number even found its way to Britain by 1913, when the first recording anywhere of the tune was made by the London Orchestra, the studio band of the Gramophone Company's short-lived budget label, Cinch. In 1916 it was recorded again by the Gramophone Company, for issue on their prestigious 12" His Master's Voice label, this time by an authentic black American string band. The Versatile Four had arrived in England in 1914, fresh from accompanying dancers Vernon and Irene Castle in Paris. They quickly landed a plum job, playing for the Smart Set at the ultra-chic Murray's Club, a supper club located in London's Soho district. They soon found additional regular work on the music hall circuit, playing and singing mainly sentimental songs to a very different clientele to that at Murray's Club. They were extremely popular with music hall audiences—an indication of this is the number of song sheets of the period featuring a photograph of them—and made a comfortable living until their return to the States in the mid-1920s. Led by mandolin-banjoist, vocalist, and Clef Club stalwart Gus Haston, they turn in an extremely lively, nay, rowdy performance of "Down Home Rag" in a style that is a fascinating amalgam of country string band and Clef Club banjo orchestra, complete with shouted encouragements to both the imaginary dancers and to one another, and overzealous percussion from drummer Charlie Johnson. The wildness and abandon of the performance is capped by the shouted exclamation by Gus Haston of "Howww's that?" after the final cymbal crash.[35]

Possibly the most unusual version of "Down Home Rag"—certainly in terms of the location of recording and the personnel of the performers— was that recorded in Milan in December 1918, by the United States Army Ambulance Service Jazz Band directed by pianist and saxophonist Charles W. Hamp.[36] Originally a volunteer organization, the American Field Service provided volunteer ambulance services for wounded troops in France and Italy before the United States entered the war, its most notable member being Ernest Hemingway. On America's entry into the war in 1917, they were incorporated into the U.S. Army Medical Department and redesignated as the Army Ambulance Service, with over two thousand men and officers serving in Italy. The jazz band, sponsored by the YMCA as a morale booster for the Italian troops, in December 1918 recorded several sides for the Dischi Fonotipia record company—a company renowned for its almost exclusively operatic catalog, featuring the finest singers in Italy. "Hokum," a one-step medley, features "Down Home Rag" as the main portion of the performance, and the string band instrumentation and gentle swing lends it a genuine "down home" feeling.

Such was the success of "Down Home Rag" in its original, instrumental form that Sweatman's Chicago-based publisher Will Rossiter produced a vocal version in 1913. The lyrics by Roger Lewis are banal in the extreme:

> *When the summer's over and the frost is on the clover,*
> *Then you get an invitation down to Hemingway's farm;*
> *When you hear the joyous laughter floating gaily through the rafters,*
> *That's the time you should all gather at the old red barn.*
> *(Chorus)*
> *Oh, Si, put the chickens away,*
> *Oh, Hi, lock the mill for the day,*
> *Oh, Sue, get the candy and corn,*
> *And bring along some cider that will keep us warm.*[37]

An interesting racial shift took place between the cover illustrations of the 1911 and 1913 versions. The original cover shows a black boy and girl, their heads drawn inside cotton bolls, while the 1913 cover, with artwork by one of Will Rossiter's regular commercial artists Joseph Pierre Nuyttens, shows a country dance held inside a barn with white dancers in their best clothes, grinning animals peering in, and "old Josiah Perkins" fiddling away. Some copies feature the heading "Biggest Hit Since 'Turkey in the Straw'" and a photograph of the New Orleans–born singer Lee White who, together with her husband Clay Smith, scored a huge success in numerous revues on the London stage in the 1915–20 period. There is at least one other version that carries a photograph of Mae Curtis and Golden Wright, "The Girls from Songland."

The astonishing rise in popularity of social dancing, led by Vernon and Irene Castle, and James Reese Europe's groundbreaking Victor recording helped "Down Home Rag" reach even greater popularity. With such exposure, Rossiter issued a further version of "Down Home Rag" in 1914, appealing to dancing enthusiasts. The original 1911 cover artwork was retained, but with a photograph of dancing team Maurice Mouvet and Florence Walton masked over one the children's heads, above which was the bold boast "The Greatest 'Tango,' 'One-Step,' 'Trot' Of Them All" and a reference to Victor Record 35369 (Europe's recording of the number), leaving no doubt that the intended target audience of this edition was dancers.

In 1922 Will Rossiter assigned the copyright to fellow Chicago music publishers Melrose Brothers, who issued an orchestral arrangement penned by celebrated pianist, composer, and arranger Elmer Schoebel. Besides working as staff arranger for the Melrose brothers, Schoebel was holding down the piano chair and directing the New Orleans Rhythm Kings at the Friar's Inn, with a band that included several notable jazz musicians: trumpeter Paul Mares, trombonist George Brunies, clarinetist Leon Roppolo, and saxophonist Jack Pettis.

In view of the fact that Sweatman's work in black theaters usually occupied the earlier part of the evening, plus matinees, it would come as no surprise that he and his band found gainful employment in the numerous cabarets and "black and tans" in the notorious Levee district. The Levee was Chicago's equivalent of New Orleans's Storyville, a vice district on the South Side roughly bounded by 18th to 22nd Street and Wabash Avenue and Clark Street where, amid more than five hundred bordellos, there were over a thousand "concert halls." In 1912 Mayor Carter Harrison bowed to pressure from city reform groups and closed the Levee bordellos, forcing prostitution and gambling into other, less easily regulated areas of the city.

As one might expect, in view of the salacious activities that were the mainstay of the area, finding contemporary references to musical activities in the Levee is nigh impossible; the high-minded *Chicago Defender* would have balked at the thought of publishing reports of the musical goings-on in such a notorious area. However, an unlikely source of firsthand information comes from author and playwright Ben Hecht (1894–1964) who, in his short story "The Negress" published in his book *Gaily, Gaily*, provides a tantalizing glimpse of Sweatman's involvement in this demimonde:

> In that day, Negro aspirations were not considered newsworthy. The white world was implacably locked against Negroes of all shades and degrees of culture. Even its cafes were Negro-less. There was only one colored band playing in a white joint in Chicago—Peyton and Swetman's [*sic*] Dixie Group in Roy Jones' South Side cafe: and the city's guardians were a little fretful over the innovation of colored men playing music for white women to dance to.[38]

Roy Jones' Café, "one of the most notorious resorts in the levee district,"[39] was located in the heart of the district at 2037 South Wabash between East 21st and 22nd Streets. Its eponymous owner was a known associate of Giacomo "Big Jim" Colosimo, the Sicilian-born Chicago vice king and club owner who was gunned down on the orders of his nephew, Johnny Torrio, on May 11, 1920.[40] Violence and murder were not unknown at the café; in April 1914 gangster James "Duffy the Goat" Franche murdered Isaac Henagow on the premises. Despite its reputation, many other notable musicians also worked at Roy Jones' Café, among them Tony Jackson, the New Orleans–born pianist and entertainer, and pianist James "Slap" White, who were both there (albeit at different times) in 1913. Dating Sweatman's engagement at Roy Jones' Café with any degree of certainty is not possible; Hecht arrived in Chicago in 1910 at the age of sixteen and a half and went to work on the *Chicago Journal*, so his memories could date from then until the latter part of 1911, when Sweatman commenced working in vaudeville. However, Hecht does call them "Sweatman and Peyton's Dixie Group," which would point to a date before the beginning of 1911, when Sweatman left his position as leader at the Grand. Although no contemporary documentary evidence has been located that supports Hecht's assertion that Sweatman's group played at Roy Jones' Café, it is not unreasonable to assume that, after playing the evening performance at the Grand, Sweatman, Peyton, and Reeves were free to play late-night engagements elsewhere in Chicago.

In January 1911 (or possibly late December 1910) Sweatman left the Grand Theater to take up residency at the Monogram Theater at 3026-28 South State Street (on the west side of the street), taking drummer George Reeves with him. Like the Grand, there were "Old" and "New" Monograms; this was the Old Monogram, which had opened about 1910 and which, like the Old Grand, outgrew itself. In November 1913 the New Monogram opened at a new location, in the old Merit Theater building at 3453 South State Street, four blocks to the south and on the east side of the street.[41]

Sweatman's departure from the Grand allowed pianist Dave Peyton to take over leadership of the Grand's orchestra, and he remained there in that capacity until 1926, building for himself a reputation as a first-rate orchestra conductor and arranger. In place of Peyton the piano stool at the Monogram was occupied by Louisville-born pianist and arranger William Henry "Billy" Dorsey.[42] It is interesting to speculate whether Sweatman's move came about because of the impending closure of the Old Grand and the subsequent opening of the New Grand, a few doors away, or whether he was lured by the offer from the Monogram's owner of a higher salary.

Sweatman's move to the Monogram was first noted in the *Chicago Defender* in mid-January 1910, and two weeks later the *Indianapolis Freeman*—the same paper that had criticized Sweatman and his trio at the Grand for playing too loud—noted in a review: "The orchestra at this house [the Monogram], under the direction of Prof. W. C. Sweatman, the world's greatest colored clarionetist, since the coming of George Reeves, one of the cleverest of trap drummers, wins heavy encores after each selection."[43]

As to actual leadership of the Monogram Theater orchestra, there is room for debate. Contemporary press reports name both Dorsey and Sweatman as leader, and—both certainly had previous experience leading orchestras. Born in Louisville on October 5, 1878, Billy Dorsey had been musical director of the Florida Blossoms Company for their debut tour in 1906 and for the following season, and had been leader at the Monogram prior to the defection of Sweatman from the Grand.[44] Dorsey certainly was the orchestra leader at the Monogram after Sweatman left to try his luck in vaudeville in the autumn of 1911, and was soon to be an important figure in the popularization of black ragtime and jazz in Britain and Europe during the mid-1910s. He arrived in England in April 1915 as a member of Joe Jordan's Syncopated Orchestra, which was booked to appear in the London Hippodrome revue *Push and Go* by theatrical impresario and early champion of syncopated music in England, Albert de Courville. The Hippodrome engagement lasted barely three weeks, after which the orchestra played a couple of music hall engagements before most of the bandsmen returned to the States.[45] Jordan remained in England until May 1916, teaming up with black American drummer Louis A. Mitchell in a music hall act where they sang and accompanied themselves on piano and drums. Dorsey likewise stayed on in England, acting as musical director for a touring revue, *Darktown Jingles* (later renamed *Dusky Revels*) before forming his own band and also arranging for others, including the Versatile Three/Four.[46] His career was sadly cut short by tuberculosis, contracted while working in England. He returned to the United States in October 1919 to seek treatment and died in a sanatorium in Yuma, Arizona, in February 1920, aged forty-one.[47] Dorsey's obituary in the *Indianapolis Freeman* sheds interesting light on an important aspect of the group's success: "His [Dorsey's] leadership of the orchestra at the old Monogram Theater was memorial in that his three piece orchestra, Will Dorsey, pianist, Wilbur Sweatman, clarinet, and George Reeves, trap drummer, all crack musicians, was the beginning of high salaries being paid to colored musicians in Chicago."[48]

Contemporary reviews of the Monogram group demonstrate that they were very successful in their work. The *Freeman*'s normally prickly Sylvester Russell wrote in his "Regular Chicago Review": "There was a great demand for work in the popular little orchestra that holds State Street spellbound. Will Dorsey had the lighter work on the piano, but Sweatman, the clarinet expert, added charm to the singers, while Reeves' drum trappings were sweetened by labor and summer tears."[49] The *Chicago Defender*, in a similar vein, noted that: "W.C. Sweatman gave good variations on the clarinet, Will Dorsey's piano accompaniment was delicious and Geo. Reeves' trappings were unparalleled."[50]

It is interesting to note the use of the phrase "good variations," presumably to convey the fact that Sweatman was improvising; but, all in all, both reviews are a far cry from Russell's thoughts on Sweatman in July 1910.

The Monogram was right in the heart of the black theatrical district, known to its habitués as "The Stroll," and was one of the foremost black vaudeville houses in Chicago, albeit owned by white proprietor Henry B. Miller and managed by Martin Klein.[51] Throughout their history the Old and New Monogram Theaters played host to many jazz and blues performers—Sidney Bechet and Johnny Dodds played there with bands accompanying vaudeville acts in the late 'teens, and singers of the caliber of Ma Rainey, the Whitman Sisters, Laura Smith, and Ethel Waters frequently graced its stage. For all its fame as a black vaudeville house, the working conditions for performers were far from opulent. Ethel Waters in her autobiography *His Eye Is on the Sparrow* described conditions at the Monogram around 1917:

> Of all those rinky-dink dumps I played, nothing was worse than the Monogram Theater in Chicago. It was close to the El, and the walls were so thin that you stopped singing—or telling a joke—every time a train passed. Then, when the noise died down, you continued right where you left off.
>
> In the old Monogram you dressed downstairs with the stoker. The ceiling down there was so low I had to bend over to get my stage clothes on. Then you came up to the stage on a ladder that looked like those on the old-time slave ships.[52]

As at the Grand, the range of entertainment provided by the Monogram's producers and managers was broad, ranging from "single" acts—singers, dancers, comedians—through to "tab" (short for tabloid) productions. These were condensed versions of musical shows, generally performed by the theater's stock company. A flavor of this type of show was provided by the *Indianapolis Freeman*'s theater critic Sylvester Russell in his column:

> I waited for the second performance, as Prof. Sweatman was late, having gone to a picnic, and his clarinet gave able support to Miss Ethel James' rendition of "The Spirit Flower," quite a gem in exactness, which she mastered vocally. Miss Orleana James, who is now a most excellent contralto,

sang a ragtime song charmingly, and Cole and Johnson's "Big Red Shawl" made a splendid finale, even if Miss Ethel made a most effeminate Indian. Will Dorsey had played his piano quite loud, so that Geo. Reeves, the trap drummer, who was a little worried, could harmonize, but Reeves lit up with smiles at the coming of Wilbru [*sic*] Sweatman.[53]

Sweatman's three years in Chicago saw him climb from a relatively unknown clarinetist to a highly regarded performer, orchestra director, composer, and arranger. His tenure at the Grand and Monogram theaters coincided with an astonishing explosion of African American theatrical and musical creativity in Chicago, and Sweatman, at the hub of this activity in two of Chicago's best-known black theaters, regularly rubbed shoulders with some of the greatest names in the black entertainment world of the period. The success of "Down Home Rag" had brought him to the attention of key figures in Chicago's white-dominated world of music publishing, while his song-shop activities with Dave Peyton and Billy Dorsey enhanced his arranging skills and business acumen. He had also found a wife and many new friends, both in and out of the theatrical and musical worlds. As an African American performer, he had reached the pinnacle of what Chicago could offer—and it was now time to look further afield.

CHAPTER 7

THE ORIGINAL AND MUCH-IMITATED RAGTIME CLARINETIST

By the autumn of 1911, Sweatman, having spent three years accompanying traveling vaudeville acts and stock companies at the Grand and Monogram theaters, probably felt that the time was right to look for new opportunities and challenges. Throughout his professional career to date, he had been almost continually on the move; first with N. Clark Smith's Pickaninny band, then with the Lowery and Mahara circus bands, then roaming around Minnesota and Wisconsin. His tenure in Chicago had been the longest period he had stayed in one place and, although he put down roots in the form of his marriage to Nettie, one suspects that the urge to move on was, once again, starting to develop. His years of experience of stage and touring show work had taught him much of what audiences enjoyed and expected, and how to present it to them. Seeing the wide array of acts that passed across the stages of the Grand and the Monogram, some good, some bad, some indifferent, made him realize that it could be him on the stage rather than in the orchestra pit. Vaudevillian and entertainer Tom Fletcher recalled seeing Sweatman while at the Monogram and recognizing the potential he had as a vaudeville act:

> While laying off there in Chicago for a week I would meet "Sweat" after he had finished for the night and we would sit around and talk. . . . Ragtime was all the rage and still going strong. I said to Sweat: "Fellow, I have travelled around a long time and I have never heard anybody play

a clarinet the way you play one. Man, you have a novelty. Why don't you get an act just playing the clarinet?" When he revealed to me that he could play two, and even three clarinets at the same time I declared, "What are you waiting for?"[1]

Sweatman heeded Fletcher's advice and handed in his notice at the Monogram. His replacement as leader was pianist Billy Dorsey, directing a band that, by 1913, included Erskine Tate, violin, Harry Johnson, cornet, and George Smith, drums.[2] Dorsey left the position in 1914 and was replaced as leader by Sweatman's nemesis, the ubiquitous Horace George, who was evidently not held in the same esteem by the theater's management as had been Sweatman. A report in the *Indianapolis Freeman* noted: "The retirement of Horace George from the Monogram orchestra recalls the fact that Wilbur Sweatman not only brought trade to the house, but was the first leader who raised a musician's salary on State Street to anywhere near the size of the price paid to a white musician. Mr. George did not get so much money as Sweatman, and rather than have his salary cut, resigned from his position."[3]

Sweatman's first theatrical agent was Jo Paige Smith, who with Gene Hughes formed the Hughes and Smith management agency in 1909. Josephine "Jo" Paige Smith was a rarity in the white, male-dominated entertainment business of the day: a female talent scout and theatrical agent, highly respected by her peers for her ability to sound out and develop new acts. Other artists on the Hughes and Smith roster included a young song and dance act, Fred and Adele Astaire, and later the celebrated operatic soprano Rosa Ponselle.[4] Under Jo Paige Smith's management, in September 1911 Sweatman made his first vaudeville appearances, a sphere of activity that kept him in the public eye for over twenty years and took him from coast to coast and all points between. His first recorded vaudeville appearance was at the New Ruby Theater, Louisville, Kentucky, opening on Monday, September 18, 1911, to laudatory reviews. The normally prickly Sylvester Russell, in his column in the *Indianapolis Freeman*, wrote of his appearance: "Wilbur C. Sweatman, the expert clarinet player of the Monogram Theater, made his debut as a vaudeville artist at the New Ruby Theater, Louisville, KY., Monday, September 18. As a master of variety, Prof. Sweatman has no equal among all players of his race upon that instrument."[5]

It appears that he split his first week in vaudeville between theaters, as the *Indianapolis Freeman* of the same date carried a report of Sweatman at the Lyre Theater, also in Louisville:

W.C. Sweatman, billed as America's greatest ragtime clarinetist, was a sure knockout. Mr. Sweatman held the stage for twenty-two minutes, and this was going some. He created a sensation here and his act alone will no doubt draw packed houses every night. His selection on the saxophone was good. The playing of two clarinets at once was something the patrons had never before had the chance to witness, and they showed their appreciation by applauding him time and time again during the rendition of his ragtime selections. No manager will regret playing Mr. Sweatman.[6]

It is worth noting that this review mentions Sweatman playing saxophone. Reviews of this period and even later frequently mistake saxophones for clarinets and vice versa, but this reviewer makes the point of differentiating between Sweatman's performances on both these instruments, which makes this review the only known mention of Sweatman ever playing the saxophone; there are no other references, in print or on record, of him playing saxophone. However a degree of caution must be exercised, as Sweatman regularly featured bass clarinet in his act (and on record—he solos on bass clarinet on his 1924 Gennett and Edison versions of "Battleship Kate" and on the Edison recording of "It Makes No Difference Now"), and the similarity of shape (the curved bell and neck) may well have confused the writer of the review.

After only one week in vaudeville, Sweatman was receiving press reviews that would have gladdened the heart of a veteran of the business. The following review which appeared in the *Indianapolis Freeman* of September 30, 1911, of Sweatman's appearance earlier that week at the Crown Gardens, Indianapolis, is doubly interesting, for despite the florid prose, it sheds interesting light on black ragtime in vaudeville at the time:

The treat of the bill was the first appearance of Mr. Wilber C. Sweatman, the invincible clarionetist. Much had been heard of the great player before he reached these parts and that he fully came up to all that had been said of him in advance of his coming would be putting the circumstance mildly indeed. Great! Well, yes; the very greatest of them all, and then some! Without a peer this young man stands out a glorious representation of what the Negro can really accomplish in the field of instrumental music. This line of work is usually shied around by the "brother", and as yet we have been able to produce only a very indifferent representation in this line of stage craft. The brilliant success of this very capable young musician is sure to serve as an impetus to others, and who knows but ere long they shall take a more active part in this line of work, without doubt to the corresponding benefit of the profession so far as the Negro is concerned. Though somewhat diminutive in stature, Wilber C. Sweatman has a style and grace of manner in all of his executions that is at once convincing, and the soulfulness of expression that he blends into his tone is something wonderful. His first number was a medley of popular airs and "rags" and had everybody shuffling their pedal extremities before it was half over. The second number was the novelty number of the cast, in which Mr. Sweatman played two clarionets at the same time, rendering that beautiful song "The Rosary". This was followed with a bass clarionet solo, "Down In the Deep". He attempted to get away at the conclusion of his rendition of "Temptation Rag", an oddity in music, consisting of almost everything. He failed in his attempt, however, and was forced to respond to another encore and closed with one of his own compositions called "Cross The Way", which was also a medley of the clean-up variety. Mr. Sweatman is booked solidly for some time and doubtless will remain so; his act is one of the best of its kind on the stage today.[7]

The subject of black musical acts in vaudeville is a complex one. Many contemporary reviews of Sweatman's vaudeville act go out of the way to note that he worked in formal clothes, unlike the vast majority of other black vaudeville acts at that time. Sweatman may well have been the first black vaudeville performer not to appear in blackface—a moment of immense importance and significance in black theatrical history, and one for which Sweatman has never received due credit. In an interview conducted by pianist and ragtime historian Max Morath, veteran ragtime pianist, composer, and fellow vaudevillian Eubie Blake commented on the fact that he and his partner, singer Noble Sissle, did not wear blackface make-up when they formed their act in 1919: "*All* Negroes put on cork. Wilbur Sweatman was the first one that didn't put it on. But Wilbur Sweatman was an Indian."[8]

Vaudeville was the principal form of mass indoor entertainment in the United States from the 1880s until its demise at the hands of cinema in the late 1920s and early 1930s, and its importance in the development and dissemination of ragtime and jazz cannot be underestimated. Controlled by theater magnates with chains of theaters—some purely local, such as the Gus Sun chain of theaters covering the Midwest; and others, such as the Keith-Albee and Orpheum circuits covering the nation (and even Canada)—vaudeville houses provided cheap entertainment twice a day (three times a day with matinees). Performers were booked for circuits of theaters for weeks or even months in advance, playing whole weeks in larger towns but having to endure the dreaded "split weeks" in smaller localities. This entailed two or three days in one location, then a train journey (paid for by the circuit owners) to the next location for three or four more days. Such hopping about left little chance for performers to capitalize on any promotion of their work in the local press, because by the time a review of their performance had appeared printed in a local newspaper, they had more often than not moved to another town. The best one could hope for was that newspaper columnists and readers alike would remember an artist on their subsequent visit.

One of the reasons for Sweatman's success as a vaudeville artist is that his act was significantly different from the majority of black vaudeville acts, in both the type of act and the fact that he did not "black up." Vaudeville catered, by and large, to the lowest common denominator, and in most cases that meant that racial stereotypes were the rule rather than the exception. Jewish comedians (or "Dutch comedians," as they were frequently billed) were baggy-trousered, hook-nosed parodies, delivering thick-accented lines in a guttural argot (best exemplified by the comedians Joe Weber and Lew Fields). Italian acrobatic troupes just had to have center-parted wavy hair with luxurious waxed handlebar moustaches, while those few black acts that did manage to penetrate mainstream (white) vaudeville had to appear as though they had just walked off the plantation or the levee. The Original Creole Band, with such jazz luminaries as Freddie Keppard, Eddie Vincent, Bill Johnson, and George Baquet, met with notable success in vaudeville in the years 1914–18, but did so by following a well-established precedent of presenting what was in essence an "old-time plantation act." Dressed in overalls, straw hats, and bandannas, Keppard, Johnson et. al. were presented almost as a foil to comedian/singer Henry Morgan Prince, who, despite being black, appeared in burnt cork makeup. As Lawrence Gushee, author of the definitive history of the Original Creole Band, noted: "Much of what they [black vaudeville performers] were allowed or expected to do drew on venerable minstrel routines. . . . So the Creole Band's reliance on the Uncle Joe routine and the singing of 'My Old Kentucky Home' was almost to be expected, as also was their wearing of southern farmhand costumes and their blackface makeup."[9]

Such indignities of dress were not the sole preserve of black musicians; both Tom Brown's band and the Original Dixieland Jazz Band, pioneering white New Orleans bands who ventured north in 1915 and 1916, made vaudeville appearances in "rube" outfits, complete with false beards and corncob pipes. Such garb was deemed to be the most appropriate and "authentic" costume for southern musicians playing ragtime and proto-jazz in vaudeville. Many black acts chose to perpetuate such stereotypes by copying the routines of Bert Williams and George Walker, leading to the frequent charge by white critics that all black acts were essentially the same. The stereotypical view of white audiences toward black vaudeville acts is exemplified by a 1907 *Variety* review of the Four Georgia Belles: "The American public refuses to take the colored race seriously as entertainers. It wants them with a dash of comedy and consistently refuses to accept them in any guise than the jester's motley."[10]

How Sweatman singlehandedly broke through this demeaning stereotyping is a mystery;—despite reading hundreds of reviews of his act, I have not come across a single one that mentions him appearing in anything but normal dress clothes. The nearest to anything approaching specialized stage costume is a photograph of Sweatman in a white suit, wearing heavy (apparently) white theatrical makeup and wearing a white top hat, that appeared in the July 1918 Columbia Records monthly supplement.

His success in vaudeville was soon making Sweatman a favorite with managers and audiences alike. In October 1911 Sweatman played Chicago, where the *Chicago Broad Ax*'s reviewer noted: "Sweatman, the clarionettist [*sic*], is going like hot cakes over the Harding time. Looks like he can do better as his act is clean and novel."[11] Barely a month after Sweatman commenced vaudeville work, the *Indianapolis Freeman* in October 1911, noted of his appearance at the Pekin Theater in Cincinnati: "The one and only Sweatman was a lifesaver. He was booked in for two weeks, and it looks like we could use him for ten."[12]

Sweatman was back in Kentucky in November 1911. The *Indianapolis Freeman*'s review of his appearance at the Gem Theater in Lexington preserves details of Sweatman's repertoire at the time: "Wilbur C. Sweatman, sensational rag time reed bird, when he plays 'Some O' Dese Days [*sic*], 'Monkey Rag' and 'Do The Eagle Rock', the house gets up in a wonder. Three shows and standing room only."[13]

Sweatman's vaudeville career at first was confined to black theaters, such as those operated by Sherman H. Dudley, and minor white vaudeville circuits. But by the end of 1911, his reputation was spreading. After appearances at the Crescent Theater and the Palace Casino in Harlem in November and December 1911, he started to attract the attention of white booking agents, who regularly scouted black vaudeville houses looking for new talent or the latest novelty to bring to mainstream white vaudeville. One such agent was Charles Bierbower, who, after seeing Sweatman's act, booked him into major white vaudeville theaters, mainly on the Keith-Albee and Orpheum circuits.

Although white vaudeville chains offered far greater financial rewards, better coverage and publicity in the theatrical press, and a relative degree of stability, they were not without their downside. Any artist wanting to work on the B. F. Keith–E. F. Albee circuit of theaters, which dominated the vaudeville business in the East, or Martin Beck's Orpheum chain that stretched westward from Chicago to California, had to be booked through the United Booking Office (UBO). Better known as "The Syndicate," the UBO grew out of the Association of Vaudeville Managers of the United States, which Keith and Albee had set up at the turn of the century. In the summer of 1906 the UBO was booking acts for forty-five theaters; by the spring of 1907 the number had grown to over two hundred theaters. In exchange for the prestige and relative stability of the Keith-Albee and Orpheum circuits, artists had to pay a 5 percent commission of their pay, on top of any payments to their agents and managers. The UBO was all-powerful; in 1910 it was booking over 700 theaters nationwide, and in 1917 was booking over 7900 acts nationally. As historian H. Loring White noted:

> The UBO hired all artists; planned the weekly bills for every house on the various circuits; handed the artists their season itineraries; and set all the salaries. Everything was pre-arranged. No bargaining permitted. Refuse a billing, disobey a procedure or a theatre manager, and you were blacklisted. Anyone involved in organizing or unionizing the artists was blacklisted. The UBO determined who worked and who didn't. . . . Even theatre owners had to accept whatever set of acts that opened the weekly show every Monday.[14]

The UBO's power and authority even extended to what material performers could present and how it was presented—with a special emphasis on wholesomeness. It was generally accepted by managers and performers alike that headliners such as singer and dancer Eva Tanguay or Nora Bayes could bend the rules, but less stellar performers were rigidly controlled. Sophie Tucker, in her autobiography *Some of These Days*, recalled that Keith's theater managers assessed every act during the first performance of the week's engagement:

> Between the matinee and the night show the blue envelopes began to appear in the performers mailboxes backstage. . . . Inside would be a curt order to cut out a blue line of a song, or piece of business. Sometimes

there was a suggestion of something you could substitute for the material the manager ordered out. . . . There was no arguing about the orders in the blue envelopes. They were final. You obeyed them or quit. And if you quit, you got a black mark against your name in the head office and you didn't work on the Keith Circuit anymore.[15]

Vaudeville life for black performers at white-owned theaters at that time was far from rosy: segregated dressing rooms (if any), lower scales of pay, hostility, and frequently racist comments from white performers, segregated hotels, dismissal at the manager's whim, fines and "punishments" (canceled bookings) for the most minor misdemeanors—and all that before facing the audience! Robert Kimball and William Bolcom's *Reminiscing with Sissle and Blake* quotes Eubie Blake's memories of the conditions black artists had to endure: "Our dressing rooms were always the worst in the theater—usually on the top floor, a billion miles up from the stage, next to the dog act. Even when we were the most popular act on the bill we were treated that way."[16]

Racial prejudice even affected the position of black performers' acts on racially mixed bills, as they were put on usually as the dreaded opening act, while the audience were either still arriving and before the arrival of the theatrical press reviewers, or as the final act, when theatergoers were starting to leave the theater. Where an act was placed on the bill was crucial to their success in vaudeville; the next-to-closing position on a typical eight-act bill was every artist's dream. Audiences also understood the hierarchy of the bill and reacted accordingly:

The star system also emphasized the rewards of success through the placing of the bills. The top acts played the best houses, had the longest acts, and, most important, made the most money, a fact that was apparent from one's place on the eight-act bill and from discussions in the popular press. Vaudeville encouraged urbanites to enter a redefined race for success, transforming Horatio Alger into a consumer of material pleasure.[17]

For a black artist working in these oppressed conditions, with unappreciative (and frequently hostile) audiences and with little chance of newspaper or magazine publicity, it was necessary to have a novel effect, such as playing two or three clarinets simultaneously, to stand any chance of being noticed. It was through the dogged persistence of Sweatman, Sissle and Blake, Bill Robinson, Bert Williams, Miller and Lyles, Greenlee and Drayton,

Florence Mills, and many other black performers who, by determination and sheer talent, slowly but surely broke down the barriers of theatrical racism and paved the way for the black performers of today. Hopefully we can now take a more considered and contextual view of Sweatman's three-clarinet playing than that which many jazz writers have previously taken.

In late 1911 or early 1912 Sweatman and his wife Hazel, known to her friends as Nettie, moved from Chicago to an apartment in New York's burgeoning Harlem district, at 251 West 143rd Street. One of the earliest reviews of his playing a theater in New York appeared in the *New York Age* in December 1911, when Lester Walton, the *Age*'s music and drama editor, wrote of Sweatman's appearance that week at the Crescent Theater in New York:

> Wilbur C. Sweatman, who bills himself as "the sensational reed bird," can make such a reference to himself without becoming modesty, for he is a clarionet [*sic*] player of more than ordinary ability. There are times when Mr. Sweatman shows himself to be the complete master of his instrument, and while many musicians have some difficulty playing one clarionet, he demonstrates his abilities in one number by playing two at a time. This . . . is an act from the West and . . . should help elevate the colored theatrical profession.[18]

An indication of the novelty of his act and the immediate impact it made in New York can be gauged from the following week's *New York Age.* Among the pages of Christmas greetings from members of the theatrical and musical professions—and prominent on a page which includes greetings from Scott Joplin, Aida Overton Walker, Sissieretta Jones ("The Black Patti"), and Sweatman's old friend Crickett Smith, at that time working with the 6 Musical Spillers—was a large advertisement from Wilbur C. Sweatman. Billed as "The Latest Sensation of the East," it shows three photographs of a dapper-looking Sweatman, two with him wearing a soft hat at a rakish angle. In one he holds a single B♭ clarinet; in the next he appears playing two, and in the third is seen holding a bass clarinet.[19]

In 1912 Sweatman was on a tour of the hugely prestigious Keith-Albee vaudeville circuit that took him as far as Canada. Midway through his touring schedule, he was taken seriously ill in June (the nature of his illness is not specified in contemporary newspaper reports) and had to undergo an operation, which was carried out in a private hospital in New York. Sylvester Russell noted in his column in the *Indianapolis Freeman*: "Wilbur C. Sweatman, the clarinet expert, recently had to enter a hospital to undergo a serious operation. I am trying to locate his whereabouts. Although Mr. Sweatman is a C.V.B.A. [Colored Vaudeville Benevolent Association] it would be up to at least one of his musician friends, who he had helped to the front in Chicago, to aid him if necessary."[20]

After a period of convalescence he resumed his vaudeville tours in August 1912, starting at the Liberty Theater in Brooklyn for the week commencing August 19. He confined his activities for the rest of 1912 to engagements around New York and the East Coast states.

The position of black artists in vaudeville was constantly under discussion in the black press, primarily because of underrepresentation on the main, white-owned vaudeville circuits. Theaters controlled by vaudeville magnates such as B. F. Keith, E. F. Albee, F. F. Proctor, Marcus Klaw, Martin Beck, and A. L. Erlanger catered almost exclusively to a white audience, although black patrons were allowed into the balcony on a limited—and strictly segregated—basis. Vaudeville theater managers viewed the influx of black southerners to the big northern cities with alarm—reasoning that white lower-middle- and middle class patrons would stay away from their theaters if they were filled with black theatergoers as well. For this reason few black acts were booked on the mainstream vaudeville circuits, in the belief (and hope) that the absence of black entertainers would dissuade black theatergoers from frequenting their theaters. Lester Walton frequently raised this issue in his weekly column in the *New York Age*, the following being a typical example:

> Colored acts certainly have had hard trials and tribulations over the big circuits. Some booking agents say they are difficult to book because the majority of them are not box-office attractions, and yet there are times when complaints are registered that they draw too many people. Last season a certain colored act was one of the hits of the United Circuit. In one or two cities it was canceled because the act drew too many colored people.[21]

Whether the act in question was Sweatman is uncertain, but it shows the Catch-22 situation black artists found themselves in when playing white vaudeville: not getting bookings because they were not given enough publicity, but, if and when they did become popular, having dates canceled because they attracted too many black people to the theater.

Despite these obstacles, black vaudeville artists were increasingly to be found working in mainstream vaudeville, playing to black and white audiences. The number of black vaudeville acts, working in both the established

mainstream vaudeville circuits and the developing black vaudeville theaters, grew rapidly in the first two decades of the twentieth century. In a
1906 article in *Variety*, Ernest Hogan estimated that there were over fifty
black vaudeville acts, employing as many as two hundred artists.[22] By 1909
that figure, by a conservative estimate, had doubled, with over one hundred
acts employing between three and four hundred performers.[23] According to
a 1922 report in *Billboard*, that figure, swollen by the phenomenal growth
in black-controlled theaters (360 by 1922), had by then risen to over 600
acts.[24]

Sweatman's acceptance into the big time came in 1913 when he played
Hammerstein's Victoria at 7th Avenue and 42nd Street—"The Crossroads of
the World"—in New York. Built as a legitimate theater in 1899 by impresario Oscar Hammerstein, the Victoria Theater was the pinnacle of vaudeville
theaters from 1904, when it switched to two-a-day vaudeville, to 1915, the
year before it was substantially demolished and reopened by S. L. "Roxy"
Rothafel as the Rialto, New York's first purpose-built cinema.

Billed as "The Musical Marvel of the 20th Century," Sweatman played
Hammerstein's Victoria for the week of January 13, 1913, and again in May.
In August he was held over for two weeks and returned for one week in
mid-October, when the headliner was the celebrated English music hall
comedian Wilkie Bard. Another headline act on the bill was the legendary
ragtime pianist and early influence on George Gershwin, Mike Bernard
(1874?–1936). Bernard was then at the height of his success, having made
his name with the house orchestra at Tony Pastor's Music Hall in the late
1890s, and crowned "The Rag-Time King of The World" by adoring fans, an
accolade confirmed by his winning a ragtime piano competition sponsored
by the *Police Gazette* at Tammany Hall in January 1900. Sweatman's August
appearances at Hammerstein's Victoria Theater were a grueling schedule
of a matinee and early evening performances in the main theater, followed
by a more informal late night al fresco performance at the Roof Garden
Theater, where food and drinks could be enjoyed by its patrons. These two
August weeks must have been memorable for Sweatman; sharing the bill
with him were two of America's most colorful personalities, both notorious
in quite different ways.

Making her first professional stage appearance was Evelyn Nesbit Thaw
and her dancing partner Jack Clifford. Evelyn had achieved notoriety while
barely out of her teens by her marriage to millionaire Harry K. Thaw, the
"Pittsburgh Idler." The son of coal and railroad magnate William Thaw, Harry
Thaw was insanely jealous of Evelyn's previous relationship with America's
most celebrated architect, Stanford White. On the evening of June 25, 1906,

Thaw shot and killed White in full public view during the opening performance of Edgar Allan Woolf's musical revue *Mam'zelle Champagne* at the White-designed Madison Square Roof Garden Theater. In court Thaw was deemed to be insane and was incarcerated in the Matteawan State Hospital for the Criminally Insane, while Evelyn started to trade on her name and reputation. In August 1913, and coinciding exactly with Nesbitt's appearance at Hammerstein's Victoria, Thaw was smuggled out of Matteawan by persons unknown and driven across the border to Canada. It was suggested at the time that the escape was an elaborate publicity stunt organized by Willie Hammerstein—known for his promotion of "sensational" acts—to publicize Nesbitt's appearance at the Victoria. The fact that he placed an armed guard on Evelyn Nesbitt's dressing room—a fact widely reported in the press—shows that he at least knew how to use the situation to gain publicity for both his theater and his star.

Also sharing the bill was a young singer and dancer by the name of Mae West (though it was May West at that time), then at the threshold of a long and frequently controversial career. Sweatman remembered her performance and recalled to jazz writer Marshall Stearns that "She had that cute little shake!"[25]

A fascinating two-line comment in *Variety*'s "London News" column of March 21, 1913, provides the sole evidence to the tantalizing possibility that Sweatman may have visited England in 1913: "Wilbur Sweetman [sic], the flautist [sic], and the Kirksmith Sisters have been booked over here by Buckie Taylor."[26] If this trip did happen it would have been a short-lived affair, as Sweatman had a pretty full diary for 1913. As mentioned above, in January 1913 he was in New York at Hammerstein's Victoria and in Bridgeport, Connecticut, at Poli's Theater, and on January 28, 1913, played a benefit for veteran vaudeville comedian Sam Lucas at Young's Casino in New York. In February and early March he was in vaudeville billed as "The Original Ragtime Clarinetist."[27] In April and May toured Canada and was back in New York by May 15th, when he was booked for, but did not appear at, a charity dance organized by Aida Overton Walker at the New Star Casino.[28] In early June he was at Proctor's 5th Avenue Theater in New York, and in mid-July he appeared alongside James Reese Europe, Bert Williams, and Will Vodery at the summer Frolic staged by The Frogs, a fraternal organization that boasted among its members the cream of New York's black theatrical profession, Sweatman included.[29]

Sweatman's vaudeville activities from July to the end of October have been traced in detail, so the only time he possibly could have made a trip to England would have been from mid-June to mid-July or from

November 1913 to January 1914. Extensive searches of U.S. passport applications and theatrical trade magazines and newspapers on both sides of the Atlantic have found no documentary evidence that could substantiate the *Variety* report of his planned London visit. It is therefore likely that the *Variety* notice was a piece of theatrical hyperbole, a not-uncommon practice then as now, dreamed up by Sweatman's agent. Alternatively, an engagement in London and the English provinces may have been planned and organized by the successful and highly respected London theatrical agent W. Buchanan Taylor, but subsequently canceled for reasons now unknown.

Sweatman's arrival in New York happened shortly after the formation of the Clef Club, a musical association founded in December 1910 by James Reese Europe that operated as a trade union, booking office, and social organization for black musicians. At that time the American Federation of Musicians local New York branch would not accept black members, and the black-run New Amsterdam Musical Association (founded by Arnold J. Ford, later a Sweatman associate) was primarily interested in classically trained musicians. This left the growing number of black musicians working in restaurants and the increasingly popular nightclubs and cabarets unrepresented by a union, and consequently at the mercy of unscrupulous employers and agents. Europe, a consummate master of organizational skills, realized that the best way of both attracting new members and publicizing their fledgling operation (as well as providing income to pay for the staffing and renting of the Clef Club's West 53rd Street headquarters) was to put on a series of concerts featuring the talents of Clef Club members.

The first of these concerts, described as a "Musical Melange and Dance Fest," was held at the Manhattan Casino, at 155th Street and Eighth Avenue in Harlem, on May 27, 1910. It was a huge success, attracting both black and white audiences—so much so that they became semi-annual occurrences, culminating in an appearance in May 1912 at Carnegie Hall (twelve years before Paul Whiteman's famous premiere of Gershwin's *Rhapsody in Blue* there). The Carnegie Hall concert by the Clef Club Orchestra, and another in 1913, confirmed Europe's stature as the foremost black musical eminence in America; in the words of Eubie Blake: "He was our benefactor and inspiration. Even more, he was the Martin Luther King of music."[30] His Clef Club concerts were incredible affairs of symphonic proportions, often featuring over 120 musicians on stage, including 40-odd banjos and mandolin-banjos and eight pianos, playing a wide musical repertoire, ranging from formal classical pieces written by African American composers to popular songs and rags, including Sweatman's own "Down Home Rag."[31]

As far as can be ascertained by checking membership rosters, Sweatman was never a member of the Clef Club; he may well have thought it unnecessary, as he was a paid-up member of the Colored Vaudeville Benevolent Association, as previously noted, as well as other theatrical fraternal organizations. In common with many other theatrical performers, he was also a committed Freemason, attaining the level of 32nd Degree Mason. Sweatman and Europe certainly knew one another; not only did they share common friends, but they also appeared together at black theatrical events organized by the Frogs and other theatrical and Masonic associations of which they were members.

In February 1914 Sweatman received an unexpected offer—the position of orchestra leader at Harlem's Lafayette Theater. Opened on November 4, 1912, the 1500-seat Lafayette, situated at 132nd Street and Seventh Avenue in the heart of Harlem, was the scene of the first small, but significant, steps toward the desegregation of theaters in America. Despite being in the heart of the black district, the theater's white owners, a consortium led by Harlem liquor retailers Henry Martinson and Benjamin Nibur, deliberately booked purely white stage acts and employed white front of house staff. Black theatergoers, keen to support their local theater, were segregated into inferior seating in the balcony. Martinson and Nibur, popular figures among black Harlemites because of their generosity in supporting black charities and helping black businesses, were keen to reverse the seating policy, but were voted down by their fellow directors. Spurred on by inflammatory articles in the black newspaper the *New York Age* by its theater critic Lester Walton, picket lines soon formed outside the Lafayette. Martinson and Nibur, with the help of new investors, purchased the Lafayette in February 1913, and instigated a strictly desegregated seating policy. Within weeks state legislators were drafting a bill outlawing racial discrimination in public places of amusement, and in April 1913 it was passed by the New York state legislature. In reality little changed in New York's Broadway theaters and nightclubs, where de facto segregation was the norm for many years to come.

Despite its part in an important moral victory, the Lafayette's turbulent times were not over. In January 1914 Martinson rented the Lafayette to Jesse Shipp and Sam Corker, two well-respected and highly experienced personalities of the black New York theatrical scene. Shipp had stage-managed Williams & Walker's theater productions as well as writing songs for them, while Sam Corker had been business manager for Cole & Johnson's shows and in 1910 had managed Robert Motts's Pekin Theater. Their idea was to make the Lafayette New York's premier theater for both black performers and audiences in an effort to attract Harlem's burgeoning African

American community. The *Indianapolis Freeman* of February 7, 1914, mentions "Wilbur C. Sweatman, whose effort to secure a Chicago drummer reveals the fact that he will be the orchestra leader."[32] (Presumably the "Chicago drummer" was Sweatman's friend and musical associate of many years standing, George "Pippin" Reeves.)

Despite Shipp and Corker's extensive experience in theater management, the general depression in the theater business in the winter season of 1914 defeated their efforts to attract customers. writing in the *New York Age*, Lester Walton noted with alarm the poor attendance at Harlem's theaters: "The show business in Harlem is at a low ebb. The theaters where vaudeville is given are doing the smallest business in years."[33] For owner Martinson, enough was enough and by the end of February 1914 Shipp and Corker had been replaced by white managers.

Despite the change of management and the general air of gloom in the entertainment world, Sweatman retained the position of leader of the orchestra, and was apparently a success with both critics and audience alike. Shortly after Shipp and Corker's departure, the *Indianapolis Freeman* noted: "The new orchestra under the personal direction of the phenomenon, Wilbur Sweatman, which has recently been installed at the Lafayette Theater by the new managers, J. E. Johnson and Flugelman, received more applause than the acts on the bill. Now what d'ya think of that?"[34]

A clue to the identity of part of the personnel of the Lafayette Theater band can be found in the *Indianapolis Freeman* of April 25, 1914, which notes that "Wilber Sheatman's [sic] Orchestra" included trombonist Nappie Lee and his friend from the 1890s, the legendary trumpeter William Crickett Smith. Nappie (or Nappy) Lee was another circus band alumnus, famous enough among his colleagues for his permanently tousled hair that in 1903 Joe Jordan composed a rag, "Nappy Lee—A Slow Drag," in his honor. He went on to work with Ford Dabney's Band with *Ziegfeld's Midnight Frolic*, and recorded with the band for the Aeolian Vocalion record label in the 1917–19 period.

Sweatman's stay at the Lafayette was to be short-lived; on Sunday, April 26, 1914, after the evening performance, Johnson and Flugelman discharged the staff and orchestra and turned the theater's keys back over to Henry Martinson, on account of their inability to pay the rent. At this point the *New York Age*'s Lester Walton stepped in and, with his partner C. W. Morgenstern, took over the lease. They installed Hallie Anderson, a female violinist, to lead the orchestra, who in turn was later replaced by another woman leader, the celebrated trombonist Marie Lucas, who was to be a major musical influence on the young Fats Waller.

After the Lafayette fiasco, Sweatman returned to vaudeville on the Keith-Albee circuit via the United Booking Office, playing to predominantly—but not exclusively—white audiences. Perry Bradford's column in the *Indianapolis Freeman* of May 16, 1914, notes his appearance at the Temple Theater in Detroit, playing his latest composition "Old Folks Rag." Sweatman spent the next two years working solidly in vaudeville, travelling from coast to coast and even into Canada.

Sweatman's appearance at B. F. Keith's Theatre in Lowell, Massachusetts, for the week commencing November 2, 1914, elicited an insightful review of his act by the *Lowell Sun's* theatrical reviewer: "Wilbur Sweatman is the man who plays two clarinets at the same time and who also delivers a lot of funny stuff. He is an entertainer who is eagerly sought because of the polish of his work. No one knows better how to suit the tastes of an audience than he."[35]

December 1914 saw Sweatman's first appearance at Harlem's Lafayette Theater after the managerial fiasco earlier in the year. The *New York Age* review of his appearance is a glowing affirmation of his position as one of the foremost black vaudeville acts of the day:

> As the week before Christmas is regarded in theatrical circles as one of the dullest of the season, Morgenstern & Walton are seeking to keep business up to standard by putting on a bil [sic] chock full of entertainment. It is one of the best even seen at the Lafayette in a long time. The first half of the week every act scored strongly.
>
> Wilber Sweatman, clarionetist, occupied headline position, and won encore after encore at each performance. He is in a class by himself and has one of the best sin[g]les in vaudeville. Sweatman is versatile, playing "The Rosary" on two clarionets at one time, serious numbers on one instrument and ragtime medleys with equal skill. He also dressed the part and makes one lightning change that excites complimentary comment.[36]

The phenomenal rise in popularity of ragtime and syncopated music, fuelled by the dance craze headed by exhibition dancers Vernon and Irene Castle, meant that Sweatman was at his peak of success and popularity, as evidenced by full vaudeville rosters and glowing notices in the theatrical trade press and black newspapers. That being said, the position of an act on the bill was of enormous importance—too early and the audience would be still arriving and restless, plus the all-important newspaper reviewers would not be in the theater; too late and the audience were jaded and starting to leave. A 1916 *Variety* review demonstrated how even a "name" star could be affected by appearing too late—and also gives an early use of the word "blues" in a mainstream publication to denote a musical form rather than a song title: "Wilbur Sweatman was a bit too late on the program to wake them up with his clarinet and saxophone music. Even his combination of 'Blues' brought but little return and he bowed off to a rather quiet finale."[37]

In 1914, following on the heels of his hit with "Down Home Rag," Sweatman had published (by Jos. W. Stern & Company) a new composition, "Old Folks Rag." Much in the style of the better-known "Down Home Rag," it quickly found favor with dancers, and versions were rushed out by the major record companies to cash in on its success. On July 29, 1914, the Van Eps Trio, led by banjo virtuoso Fred Van Eps, recorded a 10" diameter version of "Old Folks Rag," arranged by Stephen O. Jones, for the Victor Talking Machine Company. However, the masters were judged unacceptable to the company, and the trio were brought back two days later for another attempt. They too were rejected by Victor's executives, and a third session was arranged for September 4, when a 12" diameter master, giving longer playing time, was made and eventually approved for issue. The result was a rather repetitive, stiff, and formal performance, dominated by drummer Eddie King's military-style snare drumming. The following month Van Eps waxed another version for Victor's bitter rivals Columbia, this time with the addition of his brother William on second banjo and Columbia's staff drummer Howard Kopp replacing King, and labeled as "Van Eps Banjo Orchestra."

Less successful for Sweatman was his 1915 followup, "Virginia Diggins," published by Chicago music publisher Will Rossiter, with whose company Sweatman had seen enormous success with "Down Home Rag," despite Rossiter's location outside the American publishing industry's nerve center of New York's Tin Pan Alley. It may seem strange, given that Sweatman was now firmly domiciled in New York, with his agent, manager, and publicists all being based there, that he should return to a Chicago music publisher. This may be due to a sense of loyalty on Sweatman's part, Rossiter having given him his first publishing hit, but Sweatman also may have felt a greater allegiance to his old friends and acquaintances in the bustling Chicago music scene than he did for those in New York. Of course Rossiter may have just offered him the best deal.

"Virginia Diggins" was published as an orchestral arrangement by Rossiter in 1915, with arrangement for Piano, 1st violin, 2nd violin, viola, 1st clarinet B♭, 1st cornet B♭, 2nd cornet B♭, cello, drum, flute, trombone, and bass by the well-known Chicago-based arranger Frank Klickmann (1885–1966), best known by his chosen professional name of F. Henri Klickmann. Klickmann was a longtime musical associate of pioneering saxophonists Paul Biese and Tom Brown. Brown's all-saxophone group, the Six Brown Brothers, were hugely popular in the 1910s and, more than any other musical organization, were responsible for popularizing the saxophone. His amazingly prolific career included scores of popular songs, many of the sentimental type, such as "My Sweetheart Went Down with the Ship" (written after the sinking of the *Titanic* in 1912), and rags, including the wonderful "Smiles and Chuckles," specifically written for the Six Brown Brothers; he even wrote a concerto for tenor saxophone. In later years he wrote and published many instrument tutorials, some of which are still in current publication.

Sweatman was to find more success with his 1917 composition "Boogie Rag," a composition very much in the same stylistic vein of both "Down Home Rag" and "Old Folks Rag" and one of the earliest (if not *the* earliest) uses of the word *boogie* in a musical context. The etymology of this word is as confused and complex as that for the word *jazz*—some sources claim its origin as African, others that it is Irish or Irish-American. It was certainly in use in the 1910s as African American slang for a rent party and also in general use as slang for a rapid departure or a rapid movement. It seems unlikely that the phrase *boogie woogie* was being used at that time in relation to a musical style, even as street slang, so it is not surprising that Sweatman's composition does not use the trademark "walking bass" that has for many years typified boogie woogie as a musical form. Far more likely Sweatman had in mind a rent party or, more likely given his use of minor key strains, a "boogie man." "Boogie Rag" was published in 1917 by top New York music publishers Shapiro, Bernstein & Co., and the sheet music cover (by one of the well-known English-born commercial artist brothers William and Frederick Starmer) was as bizarre as it was surreal—a faceless, spectral, imp-like figure is shown dancing, enticing hordes of croaking frogs to leave the mushrooms on which they are sitting to follow him! Sweatman regularly featured "Boogie Rag" in his vaudeville act at that time and made two recordings of it, both of which are discussed at length in the following chapter.

Although Sweatman's fame as a composer of popular dance tunes rested primarily on two compositions, "Down Home Rag" and "Old Folks Rag," he was considered sufficiently important by his peers in the music publishing industry to be admitted as a member to the American Society of Composers, Authors and Publishers (ASCAP) in 1917. Established in 1914 on the initiative of composer Victor Herbert and eight other founder members, including John Philip Sousa and Irving Berlin, ASCAP was initially founded to protect the copyrights of its members and to collect royalty payments for public performances. This role developed and expanded with the growth of the record industry and, even more importantly, the development of commercial radio, the introduction of sound films, and, eventually, television. Of the original 170 charter members, only two were African Americans—Harry T. Burleigh and James Weldon Johnson, both of whose fame rested on their arrangements of spirituals. Sweatman was the first African American composer working in the popular music idiom to become an ASCAP member, an indication of the esteem in which he was held within the music industry. By comparison, the much more prolific composer and publisher W. C. Handy was not admitted until 1924, Duke Ellington in 1935, pianist and publisher Clarence Williams in 1937, Jelly Roll Morton in 1939 and Scott Joplin in 1942, the latter twenty-five years after his death![38]

CHAPTER 8

EV'RYBODY'S CRAZY 'BOUT THE DOGGONE BLUES

IN DECEMBER 1916 A MUSICAL MILESTONE OCCURRED. What is astounding is that this event, a pivotal moment in black American musical history, passed virtually unnoticed at the time and has been subsequently overlooked by practically all jazz writers since. On the day in question Wilbur Sweatman visited the studios of the Emerson Phonograph Company at 3 West 35th Street in midtown Manhattan and cut the first jazz records. The Emerson recording ledgers, like those of many small record companies of the period, do not survive, so the December 1916 date is estimated from the catalog issue date. On the strength of his reputation in vaudeville, Sweatman was invited to the Emerson studios to record two numbers. One was a popular song of the day, "My Hawaiian Sunshine," on which he was accompanied by a studio band; the other title was his own "Down Home Rag," on which the accompaniment consisted of Emerson staff pianist and ragtime composer, the Georgia-born Malvin Maurice Franklin (1889–1981), pioneer saxophonist Nathan Glantz (1878–1945), and an unknown violinist. Let there be no doubt: jazz is heard for the first time on record on the latter title.

Tin Pan Alley songwriter L. Wolfe Gilbert's "My Hawaiian Sunshine" was a hit song from the Broadway revue *The Century Girl*, where it was featured by the popular vocal duettists Gus Van and Joe Schenck. It was just one of many popular songs of the period with a Hawaiian theme that emerged in the "Hawaiian song craze" that followed the hugely successful Pan-Pacific Exposition, held in San Francisco in 1915. The overall performance of Sweatman's version of "My Hawaiian Sunshine" is of a ragtime nature, but with Sweatman adding little embellished phrases throughout, especially in the final chorus. No doubt he found himself impeded somewhat by the rather stolid accompaniment provided by the studio band, which was somewhat grandiosely titled on the label as the Emerson Symphony Orchestra.

Fortunately no such inhibitions or dreary accompaniment mar the performance of "Down Home Rag." After Sweatman's initial statement of the first theme, he builds up the excitement via embellished phrases to an exciting final chorus where he wails and draws out the notes, backed by powerful bass figures from Franklin at the piano, Nathan Glantz's sax laying down harmonized figures, and even the violinist cutting loose with a countermelody. Sweatman's claim to have made the first jazz records is fully substantiated by his rendering of "Down Home Rag."

A number of reasons can be given that Sweatman's Emerson recording of "Down Home Rag" has not received the honor it deserves. Emerson was a minor record company, only incorporated in 1915, selling a cheap product indifferently recorded, in both 5" and 7" diameter disc formats. Despite winning a court case brought against them by Columbia in 1918 for alleged patent infringement, Emerson's poor sales and inadequate financing led them into receivership in December 1920.[1] In comparison to the major companies such as Victor, Columbia, and Edison, who issued 10" records with a playing time of between three and four minutes, Emerson's miniature discs had barely a minute and a half, giving little chance for thematic statement, development, and improvised choruses. Furthermore, Emerson executives were more interested in marketing their infant product at a low retail price rather than having a roster of well-known—and therefore expensive—artists. Thus they relied heavily on tried and trusted studio artists rather than big name performers.

The word *jazz* had not even arrived in New York when Sweatman waxed his Emerson records—nearly two months before the Original Dixieland Jass Band, having popularized both the word and the music in the nightclubs and cabarets of Chicago, opened at Reisenweber's Restaurant, and over four months before their first Victor record went on sale, placing the word "jass" on everybody's lips. A further reason for the dismissal of Sweatman's Emerson recordings by later jazz writers, critics, and record collectors is that they do not conform to the notional format of a jazz record of the period. Both titles are clarinet solos, one of them a rag, played in an identifiably jazz manner, but accompanied by non-jazz-playing studio musicians. Finally—and importantly—Sweatman does not fit the image of a jazz musician as espoused by a number of authors and critics. Sweatman was not from New Orleans—absolutely essential for recognition as a jazz pioneer by the majority of twentieth-century jazz writers—and he earned his money at that time performing in vaudeville. Sweatman always claimed that he made the first jazz records and this writer does not dispute that statement.

On Monday, February 26, 1917, five young white New Orleanian musicians who were making a big noise, literally, on the New York entertainment scene, went into the Victor Talking Machine Company's New York recording studio to cut two test records. The musicians in question were, of course, the Original Dixieland Jazz Band (ODJB). Victor executives were so pleased with the results of the tests that they were hurriedly assigned matrix numbers and sent to Victor's pressing plant in Camden, New Jersey, for immediate production. The finished records were issued on April 15, 1917 (not March 7, 1917, as has been generally reported).[2] However, what has escaped the eye of discographers and researchers for over eighty years is that two days after the ODJB's historic recording session, Wilbur Sweatman went into the same West 38th Street studio to cut a test record of his composition "Boogie Rag." The Victor studio logs tell us little about the session; there is no mention of accompaniment, even though all the other tests made the same day are noted as having piano accompaniment provided by Victor's Artist and Repertoire manager, Eddie King. The fact that King is not mentioned as accompanist in Sweatman's ledger entry leads one to suspect that Sweatman brought his own accompaniment—either a pianist or, as an outside possibility, a band.

It is interesting to speculate why Victor brought in Sweatman to record a test just two days after the ODJB. Perhaps they were hedging their bets—if, despite their success as the latest musical novelty at Reisenweber's Restaurant, the white group's coupling bombed with record buyers, they at least had another "jass" artist they could quickly offer to a dance-crazy public. As things transpired, the ODJB's recordings of "Livery Stable Blues" and "Dixie Jass Band One-Step" sold as no other dance record had sold before, leaving Sweatman's test record ignored and forgotten for ninety years.

Victor's dalliance with "Boogie Rag" did not end there; in November 1917 they recorded a version by Sergeant Markel's Orchestra, but decided not to issue it. Mike Markel eventually became a very successful bandleader, recording for both Okeh and Columbia throughout the 1920s.

With the astounding success of the Original Dixieland Jazz Band's recording of "Livery Stable Blues" for Victor, the rival record companies eagerly sought out jazz bands in an attempt to duplicate Victor's coup. Columbia, who had first auditioned the ODJB in late January 1917, but were so shocked and astounded at what they heard that they showed them the door, now relented. They hurriedly called the New Orleans men back at the end of May 1917 to record two pop tunes to capitalize on their success at Victor (amazingly, Victor had not tied them to an exclusive contract), knowing full well that the ODJB had effectively slipped through their fingers. But more about Columbia later. According to the ODJB's trombonist, Eddie Edwards, "Victor made the two sides as only novelties and didn't want us anymore. So we made another deal with Columbia to make another record. When it was released it was such a good seller that Victor called us back and made the series that are now so famous."[3]

Surprisingly, the first of Victor's competitors to issue their own jazz records were the normally unadventurous Edison and Pathé companies. Edison signed up the Frisco Jass Band, a West Coast band, most of the members of which had come to New York with the musical comedy *Canary Cottage*, which opened at the Morosco Theater on February 5, 1917. The band members included saxophone virtuoso Rudy Wiedoeft, trombonist Theron Ellsworth "Buster" Johnson, pianist Edvin Arnold Johnson (not related to Theron Johnson), and violinist and leader Marco Wolff. All were destined to go on to varying degrees of fame later—Wiedoeft as the premier virtuoso saxophonist of his age, Buster Johnson as trombonist in the early Paul Whiteman Orchestra and subsequently as a jazz pioneer in India and Southeast Asia, Arnold Johnson as a notable bandleader, and Marco Wolff, in partnership with his sister Fanchon, or Fanny, as a hugely successful West Coast theatrical producer. Between May and October 1917 the Frisco Jass Band recorded nine sides for Edison, some issued only on Blue Amberol cylinders, and two test records for Columbia. Their performances have little in common with the ODJB's polyphonic approach; usually they have a basic violin lead, with Rudy Wiedoeft weaving obbligato lines around the violin's melodic lead, sometimes on clarinet but more often on C-melody saxophone. Unfortunately his clarinet lines frequently jar with Wolff's violin lead, but on their most musically successful performance, "Johnson 'Jass' Blues," they manage to stay apart, creating a wonderfully laid-back, almost folksy performance.[4]

The Frisco Jass Band appeared from mid-March until the end of May at the Montmartre Café in the Winter Garden Building in New York, replacing the Original Creole Band.[5] The band subsequently spent some time in vaudeville, accompanying violinist Marco Wolff and his sister Fanchon in a dance act, and possibly also working with xylophonist Louis Frank "Frisco" Chiha, an association hinted at on the Edison record sleeve of "Johnson 'Jass' Blues." The band broke up in late 1917; Wiedoeft stayed in New York and worked for band contractor Harry Yerkes, Arnold Johnson moved to Chicago to work with saxophonist Paul Biese's orchestra, and Marco Wolff and Buster Johnson headed back to the West Coast.

For its part, the Pathé Frères Phonograph Company obtained the services of Wilbur Sweatman and his Jass Band. In 1917 Pathé were the new kids on the American record industry block. Although in Europe they had been pioneers of the industry in the 1890s, the record business in the United States was already crowded and tied up in internecine patent wars. At the top of the heap were Victor and Columbia, jealously guarding the right to produce lateral-cut records. Rather like the VHS/Betamax videotape-format war of the 1970s and 1980s, the recording industry of the pre-1920 era divided into vertical-cut and lateral-cut camps, depending on what patents one held. Columbia and Victor spent millions of dollars fighting one another over the right to make lateral-cut discs (where the grooves oscillated in a lateral, side-to-side plane) until they ultimately saw sense and pooled their patents to freeze out any Johnny-come-lately competition. From the outset, in France and other European countries in the 1890s, Pathé had produced vertical-cut cylinders and, because they produced three different-diameter cylinders, it made financial sense to make one master wax cylinder—a giant of 5 inches in diameter and 12 inches in length—and then copy it to master cylinders of the other diameters, using a pantographic mechanism, for subsequent processing and mass production. The same system was utilized when, in 1905, Pathé introduced flat disc records which, in true Gallic style, were produced in four different diameters, including a monster 20-inch concrete-backed disc. The problem with the Pathé system of pantographic copying was that it introduced mechanically-induced bass rumble into the copied recordings. Although inaudible at the time when played on low-fidelity wind-up gramophones, it is an obtrusive and occasionally alarming feature of Pathé discs when played on modern electrical equipment.

In 1914 Pathé moved into the American market; they opened a studio on New York's 42nd Street and, after a year of having their records pressed in France, opened a pressing plant in Belleville, New Jersey, before moving again to Grand Avenue in Brooklyn. Under the skilled guidance of recording manager Russell Hunting, a veteran of the recording industry both in his native United States and in Britain, Pathé gradually built an impressive roster of performers in all fields and styles of music. Being newcomers, they actively sought out artists unsigned by other record companies, which put less reliance on "studio" singers and musicians.[6]

The Pathé company's progressive policy is worth recounting in some detail. For three years, from 1917 to 1920, they established the first major catalog of black singers and musicians, recording more black artists in that period than all the other record companies put together. Their catalog included titles by the Eubie Blake Trio, Blake's Jazzone Orchestra, the Memphis Pickaninny Band, the Four Harmony Kings, singers Opal Cooper, Creighton Thompson, and Noble Sissle, Jim Europe's 369th U.S. Infantry "Hell Fighters" Band, Jim Europe's Singing Serenaders, and Wilbur Sweatman's Jass Band. Much of the credit for this degree of focused activity on Pathé's part must rest upon the efforts of James Reese Europe and his close friends and business associates, Noble Sissle and Eubie Blake, the latter running the Europe-organized Tempo Club's business activities while Europe and Sissle served in the army in the 1917–19 period. With the exceptions of Sweatman and the Memphis Pickaninny Band (about which nothing is known), all of the artists recorded were members of Europe's Tempo Club, though Europe and Sweatman were professionally acquainted.

The only other company to record black artists on anything like a regular basis was Columbia; as well as issuing several sides by Wilbur Sweatman and W. C. Handy's orchestra, the label had, beginning in 1901, sporadically issued records by a number of black performers. These included baritone Carroll C. Clark (both solo and duetting on one title with the black soprano Daisy Tapley), Joan Sawyer's Persian Gardens Orchestra, the Right Quintette, the Fisk Jubilee Singers, the Afro-American Folk Song Singers (directed by Will Marion Cook), and also private discs for sale by tenor Roland Hayes.

The biggest name in Columbia's catalog of black performers was undoubtedly the great black comedian Bert Williams. Starting in 1906, Williams was to be a best-selling feature of the Columbia catalog, continuing with regular issues until his premature death in 1922. Williams was unquestionably the best-known African American entertainer in the United States, with an illustrious career in black musical shows dating back to the end of the nineteenth century, and who, in 1910, made the great leap from black musical comedy and vaudeville to the pinnacle of white popular theater—the Ziegfeld Follies. He therefore was as well-known to white theatergoers and record buyers as he was to black audiences.

Pathé, on the other hand, tapped into the rich vein of black musicians and entertainers working in the cabarets and restaurants in New York under the auspices of James Reese Europe's Tempo Club booking office. Europe himself was actively engaged by early 1917 in organizing the 15th Regiment Band (including a trip to Puerto Rico in May 1917 to recruit clarinetists) and had increasingly turned over the management and administration of the booking office to his friend, the pianist Eubie Blake.[7] As mentioned previously, all of the artists concerned, with the exception of the Memphis Pickaninny Band, were well-known members of the Tempo Club. Although doubt has been cast on whether Blake's Jazzone Orchestra was directed by Eubie Blake (one writer cited the band as emanating from Richmond, Virginia), aurally it is typical of New York black syncopated music of the period, as comparison to the contemporary records made by Ford Dabney's band amply demonstrates.

Irrespective of whether Pathé approached Sweatman via Jim Europe or Eubie Blake or not, the six sides Sweatman recorded for them predate any other recordings by black artists for the label, and it is likely that the encouraging sales figures for Sweatman's issues prompted Pathé to locate and record other black artists.

Sweatman's Pathé recordings are most unusual, inasmuch as the "jass" band consists of Sweatman playing clarinet, backed by five saxophones, with no brass or rhythm section whatsoever. All of the saxophonists were accomplished, time-served musicians with extensive experience. Tenor saxophonist Clarence "Piccolo" Jones had, like Sweatman, worked in tent shows, most notably with the Florida Blossoms Company in the 1906-7 touring seasons. Baritone saxophonist Charlie Thorpe was, according to W. C. Handy, head of the "Harlem Musical Association."[8] The organization Handy was referring to was actually the New Amsterdam Musical Association, a black musicians' union founded in New York in 1904 to protect the interests of black musicians who at the time were not permitted to join the racially segregated American Federation of Musicians (AFM) Local 310 (later Local 802). Shortly after his spell with Sweatman, Thorpe's musical activity in New York was temporarily curtailed when he was drafted; he served in France as a member of the 807th Pioneer Infantry Band under its bandmaster, Will Vodery.

Previous discographical listings, based on Sweatman's own recollections, have credited the bass saxophone on these sides to Frank Withers, but this is questionable. Born in Emporia, Kansas (as was Crickett Smith) in 1880, Withers was better known as a trombonist, and it was in that capacity that he subsequently went to Europe with Will Marion Cook's Southern Syncopated Orchestra, and later worked in Paris as a member of Louis Mitchell's Jazz Kings. There he made a profound impact on local trombonists such as Leo Vauchant, who were anxious to learn about American jazz and who modelled their style on that of Withers. Although trombonists doubling bass saxophone are not unusual in early jazz (Keith Pitman and Jim Falco regularly recorded on both instruments), I have not been able to trace any references to Withers playing the bass saxophone. One also has to consider photographic evidence; a photograph of Wilbur Sweatman's Jass Band appeared in the May 1917 Pathé catalog, but the bass saxophonist is clearly not Withers. The photograph shows a tall, broad-faced man with a large moustache, whereas Withers was balding, clean-shaven, and thin-featured. Although the photographic evidence is no guarantee of the true identities of the performers on the Pathé records, it does at least cast doubt on Withers's presence thereon.

Best known of the Jass Band musicians was tenor sax player Henry Minton—but not for his skills as a musician. Minton was politically active and fought for the rights of black musicians to be represented by a union. Like Charlie Thorpe, Minton was a key figure in the New Amsterdam Musical Association, and was the first black delegate to the then whites-only AFM local #310 (later local #802).

In the late 1920s Minton made a career move to running nightclubs featuring high-quality music. His first venture was the Rhythm Club, a home-away-from-home for the cream of Harlem jazz talent of the day and celebrated in King Oliver's 1930 Victor recording "Rhythm Club Stomp." His policy of encouraging jam sessions attracted musicians anxious to test their skills or to challenge others, safe in the knowledge that Minton's union connections ensured they would not be fined by the union for participating in what was then a prohibited activity as far as the American Federation of Musicians was concerned. In 1938 Minton opened Minton's Playhouse, located on the first floor of the Hotel Cecil at 210 West 118th Street, and installed bandleader Teddy Hill as manager. Hill's experience and reputation as a leader attracted top-flight musicians to sit in with the little house band, and soon men such as Dizzy Gillespie and Charlie Christian were making regular appearances there. From these humble beginnings bebop could be said to have been born at Minton's and its celebrated after-hours jam sessions.

Sweatman's Pathé records were apparently recorded in two sessions: the first in late February or early March 1917 and a second in April 1917, almost certainly to remake an unsatisfactory "Dancing an American Rag." The release of four of the sides was announced in Pathé's *Record Bulletins for May 1917* and in the April issue of *Talking Machine World*. "Dancing an American Rag" and its backing "I Wonder Why" were allocated a lower catalog number, but were not released until June 1917. The May 1917 Pathé supplement shows a photograph of the band in formal dress clothes, which implies that this was a publicity shot of a working group, not one assembled by Sweatman for recording purposes.

The new "jass" music was a novelty that Pathé was keen to promote, demonstrating to prospective record buyers how up to date they were in recording the latest musical fads:

> Wilbur Sweatman, vaudeville artist and favorite, who can play a clarinet, and even two clarinets at the same time in a style all his own, and from which exudes both mirth and melody, is the owner of a "Jass Band", which has "out-jassed" all others. Devotees of the modern dance in the "400" and upper society set of New York City want nothing else to dance by. Sweatman's "Jass Band" is the sensation of the hour. The word "jass" is a negro coined word, meaning "strange harmonies and pep." Sweatman's Band knows its meaning. As a novelty it is the "last word" in dance music.[9]

It is interesting to note the implication that because Sweatman and his band were black, their understanding of jass was all the more authentic. Sadly, press coverage of Sweatman's appearances at the time gives no information as to whether or not he was working with the band in vaudeville, or where and when the "upper society set" danced to the group.

The six Pathé sides represent an interesting cross-section of material, some of which was undoubtedly forced on Sweatman by Pathé executives. They range from Jerome Kern's "I Wonder Why" (which also introduces, albeit uncredited, Raymond Hubbell's "Poor Butterfly," one of the major hits of 1917), to a fine spirited version of W. C. Handy's "Joe Turner Blues" which, as a bonus, also incorporates, again uncredited, a couple of choruses of Handy's "Hesitating Blues." Equally interesting is "A Bag of Rags," the best-known composition of black pianist and multi-instrumentalist William R. "Mac" McKanlass (1879–1937) who, like Sweatman, was a veteran of touring minstrel shows.[10] In the final chorus, with the saxes laying down a double-time riff, Sweatman takes off on a display of impassioned pyrotechnics that even now, over ninety years later, has the capacity to thrill. Bob Ward and Mort Green's 1916 composition "Dancing an American Rag" is an interesting precursor to Sweatman's 1920 clarinet tour de force performance of "Think of Me Little Daddy," in that he plays the third theme as an improvised flight of fancy, consisting mainly of a barrage of eighth notes, while the band maintain a steady 4/4 pulse beneath.

The dynamism and drive of these Pathé performances, coupled with Sweatman's improvised phrasing, leaves the listener in no doubt that here for the first time is the authentic voice of black orchestral jazz—not ragtime, but a rough-edged, rudimentary yet, at the same time, disciplined form of jazz. Even without the benefit of piano or drums, they manage to sustain a full sound and rhythmic momentum, if somewhat anchored by the two-beat oompah of the bass saxophone. The sound is akin to a supercharged version of the Six Brown Brothers (a white all-saxophone sextet who were extremely popular both in vaudeville and musical comedy, and who recorded extensively, notably for Victor), though with jazz clarinet lead and greater rhythmic fluidity.

A less well-known saxophone group, but equally important from the perspective of black musical history, were the Musical Spillers. Directed by William Newmeyer Spiller, and for a time including in its ranks Sweatman's old friend Crickett Smith, this group of male and female multi-instrumentalists were a great success in vaudeville, and a regular part of their act was their quintet of saxophones. Their musicianship was of the highest standard (they were dubbed a "travelling conservatory") and they toured in vaudeville in the States, Canada, Europe, and South America from 1906 until the outbreak of war in Europe in 1939.[11] Sadly, the Musical Spillers never recorded, but one can imagine that they probably sounded much like the Sweatman group, albeit without the clarinet lead.

Mention of the Six Brown Brothers raises an interesting question: who wrote the arrangements for Sweatman's Jass Band? By virtue of the lineup and potential for clashes of the overlapping harmonic ranges, Sweatman's Pathé performances are quite complex arrangements, with intricate patterns woven by the saxophones behind Sweatman's lead, which appears to be half arranged and half improvised or embellished. There were several talented black arrangers working in New York at the time, most notably Will Vodery, James "Tim" Brymn, William Grant Still, Will H. Tyers, and Ford Dabney, all of whom were capable of producing arrangements of the quality and complexity of those used on the Pathé records. One arranger particularly adept at writing for saxophones was the aforementioned William Newmeyer Spiller, and he is an equally likely candidate for the arranger. Like Sweatman, Spiller had worked with W. C. Handy's band at the turn of the twentieth century, and they probably knew one another well through both working on the Keith-Albee and Orpheum vaudeville circuits.

One other possible candidate for consideration is the Chicago-based arranger and composer F. Henri Klickmann. Klickmann was a talented composer, pianist, and trombonist with several excellent rags to his name ("Knock Out Drops" and "Delirium Tremens Rag," to name just two), but he is best remembered as an arranger. He regularly provided arrangements for

Chicago-based publishers Will Rossiter, McKinley Music and Frank Root, including the orchestral arrangement of Sweatman's "Virginia Diggins" for Will Rossiter just two years earlier. Starting in 1916 he wrote and arranged for the Six Brown Brothers, the most celebrated saxophone sextet of the day. His compositions specifically written for them included "Smiles and Chuckles" and "The Ghost of the Saxophone."[12] Certainly, the overall sound of the Pathé recordings is akin to the Six Brown Brothers, but with more drive and urgency.

W. C. Handy relates an interesting anecdote concerning Sweatman and his Pathé recording of "Joe Turner Blues" in his autobiography:

> It was difficult to get "Joe Turner" recorded. I came to New York for that purpose and while walking down Broadway I met my old friend Wilbur Sweatman—a killer diller and jazz pioneer. He invited me home with him and his wife Nettie prepared a lovely dinner. While dining she turned on the phonograph and lo and behold it played "Joe Turner Blues," which Sweatman had recorded not only on Pathé but Emerson records also.[13]

Handy's mention of an Emerson version of "Joe Turner Blues" by Sweatman is at variance with what was actually issued on Emerson; their issued version was by the Emerson Military Band, a studio orchestra—although it is not beyond the realm of possibility that Sweatman may have recorded "Joe Turner Blues" for Emerson and possessed a test pressing that for some reason was not issued.[14]

Sweatman's own composition "Boogie Rag" was also recorded by Pathé. Like his later "That's Got 'Em," this composition bears a remarkable similarity to "Down Home Rag," albeit played at a considerably more relaxed pace than the usual frenzied tempo one normally associates with performances of the latter piece.

Three titles from the first Pathé session were rejected. —One of them was almost certainly "Dancing an American Rag," but the titles of the others are lost, as the Pathé recording ledgers disappeared many years ago. However there are clues to the possible titles recorded and rejected. Some copies of "Dancing an American Rag" are mislabeled "Down Home Rag," raising the possibility that this was one of the titles recorded—and possibly even remade—but withheld at the last minute after an issue number had been allocated and labels had been printed (Pathé at that date did not print matrix numbers on the label). Pathé already had a version of "Down Home Rag" in their catalog by Van Eps' Dance Orchestra, recorded in 1916, and would not have been the first company to mistakenly record a title already in catalog. Another possible candidate for one of the missing matrices is Handy's "Memphis Blues," which Sweatman recalled recording—he thought for Edison—when interviewed in the 1950s by Len Kunstadt. However careful examination of the Edison company's weekly recording reports for 1916 and 1917 reveals no sessions by Sweatman. It is a distinct possibility that Sweatman's memory was at fault, that in fact he had recorded it for Pathé, and that it was one of the rejected titles.

By the spring of 1918 Sweatman, along with his vaudeville appearances and private engagements, had started to involve himself in booking and managing bands, a venture that was to become increasingly important to him in the 1920s. The *Chicago Defender* in March 1918 noted: "Wilbur Sweatman, the famous clarinetist is playing vaudeville in and around New York and at the same time is booking a couple of bands that he has organised and rehearsed."[15] In all likelihood he would have made appearances at nightclubs or cabarets with these bands after his evening of vaudeville work was over, and it was probably from the ranks of these groups that he picked the musicians heard on his Columbia records.

Mention was made earlier of Columbia's search for suitable jazz bands to mount an offensive against Victor, who not only had issued the ODJB's massive hit "Livery Stable Blues" (in the meantime, the ODJB had left Victor for the new Aeolian Vocalion record company, over the "Livery Stable Blues" court case and litigation from Joe Jordan over their uncredited use of his "That Teasin' Rag" in their composition "Dixie Jass Band One Step") but had also signed up Earl Fuller's Famous Jazz Band, led by an up-and-coming clarinetist and entertainer, Ted Lewis. Columbia's Director of Artists and Repertoire Ralph Peer searched far and wide for new talent, recording tests of the Frisco Jass Band, Earl Fuller's Famous Jazz Band, Arthur Stone's Jazz Band, and others. According to the ODJB's Nick LaRocca, hardly the most impartial or reliable observer, Peer spent three weeks in New Orleans listening to local bands. Peer's trip was apparently fruitless, culminating in a telegram allegedly sent by Peer from the Crescent City back to Columbia's New York offices: "No Jazz Bands in New Orleans." This infamous telegram was first quoted in H. O. Brunn's hagiographic *The Story of the Original Dixieland Jazz Band*, but Brunn does not provide evidence for its authenticity or the source of his information.[16] The source of Brunn's information is apparently a letter from the ODJB's cornetist and self-proclaimed leader, Nick LaRocca, to the French writer and broadcaster Jean-Christophe Averty, written on May 23, 1956. LaRocca, besides his overzealous promotion of the ODJB as the creators of jazz via a stream of letters to jazz magazines and writers, was well-known for his absolute disavowal of any black involvement whatsoever in the birth of jazz. Even Averty himself questioned the veracity of LaRocca's statement about Peer's telegram, likening it to the Holy Grail.[17] If Peer had travelled westward to Chicago he would have found the Windy City awash with New Orleans jazz bands, black and white, that had fled New Orleans because of the big money to be earned in northern cabarets and dance halls.

Jazz flourished in the hotel bars and cabarets of New Orleans, and Peer would have easily found both black and white jazz bands to audition. The New Orleans *Times-Picayune* in November 1917 reported the work of one such band, complete with a photograph:

> "Original Jazz Band" at the Cave. The complete success of the "Original Jazz Band" and the reception it received from the New Orleans dance world has justified the belief of the Hotel Grunewald management that the good dance music would make a hit in the city. . . . The Cavemen are real jazz players, so real in fact that the crowd keep them playing four extras at the end of each number.[18]

The band in question was led by celebrated white cornetist Johnny De Droit and included on clarinet the young Tony Parenti, later a bandleader in his own right and an important figure in the New Orleans revival movement of the 1940s and 1950s.

In June and August of 1917 Columbia made audition records of Wilbur Sweatman's Original Jass Band (in all likelihood the same all-saxophone group that had recorded for Pathé in April 1917), but for reasons unknown, possibly because of contractual obligations to Pathé, no action was taken at the time to sign Sweatman to record.

Eventually Columbia obtained the services of Handy's Orchestra of Memphis, as they were billed by Columbia, which Peer brought to New York from Memphis in September 1917 for a week's hectic recording. It is unclear whether Peer heard the band on his alleged tour of the South in the summer of 1917, or whether he heard Handy's band on one of its regular eastern tours, or whether Handy's publishing partner, Harry Pace, had tried to sell the band to New York record companies on his numerous trips east. Handy, in his autobiography, was vague on the subject, merely stating that "the Columbia Phonograph Company sent me a contract to bring twelve musicians to New York to make a dozen records as a result of Pace's previous build-up."[19]

Although of significant historical importance in being the first nationally available recordings of a black band based outside of New York, Handy's

Columbia records are somewhat disappointing as jazz records to modern ears, even though at the time they were considered the very epitome of jazz. The band is laden with violins and on many sides a very prominent xylophone, and although such well-known names as Darnell Howard and Jasper Taylor are among the musicians present, there is little syncopation or improvisation. The listener is left with the overwhelming feeling that the band was under-rehearsed and unhappy with both the material and arrangements. Add to this the records being badly balanced and poorly recorded—a continually recurring problem with Columbia records at the time—and it is difficult to deal with them objectively, over ninety years after they were recorded. However, comparing them with, for instance, the Europe's Society Orchestra sides from 1913, also poorly balanced and recorded, one is left with the feeling that the Handy sides lack rhythmic cohesion—no doubt heightened by the absence of a strong rhythm instrument such as a banjo or guitar, or a bass instrument. Handy's regular band used a string bass, played by Archie Walls, but the primitive recording equipment of the period was simply unable to record the subtlety of the instrument. To get around this technical problem, most bands of the pre-electric recording period used a brass bass player when making records, but the Handy sides are devoid of any bass instrument. To be fair, Handy encountered enormous logistical problems in putting his band together for the Columbia sessions. In his autobiography he makes it clear that the majority of his regular bandsmen were either unwilling or unable to make the trip: "it was impossible for me to get more than four [musicians] who were able and willing to make the trip. Some must have doubted my ability to advance their fares to and from the big town, pay their expenses while there and pay them a large salary."[20]

In desperation, and with his four regular musicians, he journeyed to Chicago and hired seven musicians willing to travel, including violinist Darnell Howard and drummer and xylophonist Jasper Taylor, and when he arrived in New York added local clarinetist and saxophonist Nelson L. Kincaid to the band. So, instead of a "Memphis Blues Band," Handy had effectively brought to New York a band of three parts, none of which knew the work of the others. Handy admits in his autobiography that the band was underrehearsed and that the sessions were postponed to allow the newly drafted musicians time to rehearse the numbers to be recorded. Clarinetist and violinist Darnell Howard also recalled the problems encountered at these sessions, some of them caused by the musicians' unfamiliarity with the acoustic recording process:

They used three horns to pick up the sound and they had me stand-ing very close. On my account they had to stop quite a few times for I couldn't stop my violin bow from striking the horn. The first time I did it the engineer played it back and it did sound terrible—a real loud thud. I remember just one title from the sessions—Fuzzy Wuzzy—as the violin part was difficult for me at the time and I had to go into another room to run over it a few times.[21]

In view of the mountain of problems that beset Handy's first recordings, it is hardly surprising that his own memories of the sessions were less than enthusiastic. "To my way of thinking the records were not up to scratch. Our band was capable of better work, but the Columbia people seemed satisfied."[22]

Columbia did indeed seem satisfied, and gave the Handy records maxi-mum promotion. They declared a "Handy Week" at their dealers across the country and heavily promoted the Handy records in local newspapers on their release in January 1918:

Old Mr. Jazz has been outjazzed! The trick has been turned by the newest note in novelty, the last word in wizardry, the big sweeping sensation of the hour, the most delirious dance music of the day. The muffled boom of the tom-tom flirts with the crash of barbaric cymbals; the hollow moan of weirdly swept strings is overwhelmed as jungleland's wild symphony swells to its maddest height. Through it all the fierce rhythm, the fren-zied swing of a super-syncopation that is sweeping the dance world into a vortex of new delight. The Jazz Dance Blues are here! W.C. Handy of Memphis, Tenn. is the originator and composer of these famous "Blues" successes. The Handy Orchestra of southern negro musicians plays "Blues" dance numbers as no other orchestra ever could. This unique organization makes records exclusively for Columbia. You want its Jazz Dance Blues records for your party—they'll make it a success. You will respond to these records whether you dance or not—they're great![23]

The fact that Columbia had recorded and issued "blues" compositions by its "house orchestra" under the direction of Charles A. Prince from as early as 1914 was conveniently forgotten.

Despite healthy sales figures for the Handy records (exact figures do not survive, but the records are still relatively common and some remained in catalog until Columbia's switch to electrical recording in 1925), Columbia was still without a jazz band that could compete with the phenomenal sales success of the ODJB's first record for Victor. In March 1918 they called Sweatman back to record two sides with a band that included his regular pianist, Dan Parrish, and drummer, probably Zeno Lawrence, along with established black New York–based musicians such as Sweatman's old buddy from the 1890s, Crickett Smith.[24]

This time the results were issued and sold extremely well. The two sides made at this session, "Regretful Blues" and "Ev'rybody's Crazy 'Bout the Doggone Blues, But I'm Happy," are in many respects the best sides Sweatman recorded in his two years at Columbia, from both the musical and technical points of view. Recording technology in 1918 had barely improved since the late 1890s; the sound was captured via large metal horns alone (with no electrical amplification whatsoever) and focused onto a mica or glass diaphragm to which was attached a cutting stylus. This etched the vibrations of the diaphragm onto a rotating tablet of beeswax which had been warmed sufficiently for it to be easily cut into by the stylus. The recording lathe was also non-electrically powered; a falling weight-driven motor gave a more constant speed than potentially unreliable electrical motors of the period (and even less reliable consistency of voltage supply). Such lathes were in use into the 1940s. Balancing the different instruments of a band was part art form, part science, and part luck: too loud and the resulting grooves would "blast" and quickly wear on repeated playing on steel-needled gramophones. Too soft and all detail and volume would be lost. Some instruments, such as the double bass, were impossible to record, its range being mainly beyond the limited frequency band of the acoustic recording process. With the louder, brass instruments at a distance from the recording horns and the piano and stringed instruments almost inside them, any sense of natural positioning or staging was technically impossible.

When the engineers did get it right, the acoustic recording process yielded remarkable results; such performances possess a warmth and mellowness that electronically amplified recording and overuse of microphones fail to capture, the results of which frequently reproduce as harsh and unrealistic. The music critic R. D. Darrell, harking back to the introduction of electrical recording in the mid-1920s, some years later wrote that "the old process, then at its height, oftentimes put the crudities of the new to shame. One thought shrieking string tone and sour woodwinds inseparable from the new method, and more than one verbal tear was cast over the passing of the cool, dark beauty of the old at its best."[25] The recording engineer and his assistants at Sweatman's first Columbia session skillfully balanced the instruments against one another—the studio ambience has a naturalness, the sound has warmth, depth, and richness, and the speed is nigh-on correct for modern reproduction at 78 rpm. (more about speed later).

As for the performances, Sweatman and the band play with the confidence of musicians who know one another's strengths and weaknesses, which leads one to suspect that this was not just a pickup band organized for the session. One is also led to think that the ODJB-like polyphony of the performances is not something recently picked up and mastered; there is a tremendous degree of empathy and subtlety in these performances. By comparison, contemporary recordings by such bands as Earl Fuller's Famous Jazz Band emphasize the madness and raucousness of the new music and, although rhythmically exciting on a basic level, lack the refinement and subtlety of the Sweatman performances.

Unlike their main competitor, Victor, who invariably issued only one take of a performance, Columbia until 1922 (and less frequently thereafter) regularly issued multiple takes of performances, which provides the opportunity of comparing the performances and the degree of improvisation and embellishment. Two takes of "Regretful Blues" and three of "Ev'rybody's Crazy 'Bout the Doggone Blues, But I'm Happy" were released, and by comparing the various takes we can hear that the band, and Sweatman in particular, did indeed improvise. In fact, the second master of "Regretful Blues" has an extra half chorus, inserted by the musicians as the tempo was slightly faster than the first take, and more space was thus available on the record.

Mention of the word *improvise* brings us into difficult territory; spontaneous improvisation on a harmonic and chordal sequence in jazz was a development that was to come several years later. Many of the great recorded solos considered to be masterpieces of jazz were worked out in advance of a recording, or in the studio itself, and merely embellished or elaborated on from one take to another. Embellishment here is the key word: up until the mid-1920s ensemble playing predominated, with few solo passages for the musicians to explore the melodic line and its harmonic structure. Thus out-and-out collective improvisation beyond embellishment was practically impossible, as the musicians would tend to get in the way of one another.

Throughout jazz history musicians have stored useful phrases in a mental reference file for subsequent retrieval during a performance, and this storehouse of phrases, added to the embellishment of the base melody and chordal progression, forms the foundation of most early jazz recordings. What we hear on the records by Sweatman and all his contemporaries is a basic arrangement, either written or memorized (the difference

is irrelevant), which is then further embellished by the musicians bringing their own ideas to bear on the piece. The jazz trumpeter and author
John Chilton, in his biography of Coleman Hawkins, *The Song of the Hawk*,
writes:

> At this stage of his career (and for years afterwards) Hawkins rarely at-
> tempted any startlingly different variations if called upon to record a
> second or third take. On a whim he occasionally improvised steadfastly
> for each succeeding take, but he mostly chose to make only small embel-
> lishments on the shape of his solo. This was a deliberate plan, as he made
> clear in one of his first interviews when he said, "the repetition is not so
> much memory as method."[26]

Sweatman's Columbia records are important and early examples of a
style of jazz performance reliant to some degree on scored arrangements,
with space for improvisational embellishment, and are thus very different from contemporary recordings by the Original Dixieland Jazz Band or
black bands such as those of Ford Dabney or James Reese Europe. Europe's
1913–14 Victor recordings have been analyzed at length by musicologist
Gunther Schuller in his groundbreaking book *Early Jazz*.[27] The Europe
Victors are heavily scored but show no attempt at dividing the orchestra
into separate sections—by and large the melody is carried in a collective
ensemble, with even the five mandolin-banjos duplicating the melody.
The only attempt at varying the performance comes from the drummer
Buddy Gilmore, who varies his beat and degree of syncopation within the
framework of the performance. Ford Dabney's 1917–19 Aeolian Vocalion
recordings are more complex structurally, with a greater preponderance of
brass and woodwind instruments and less reliance on stringed instruments
than the Europe Victors. However, they still rely heavily on nearly everyone
but the trombonist, tuba, and drummer playing the melody. Trumpeter
Crickett Smith occasionally breaks out of this musical straitjacket but, for
the most part, chorus follows chorus with little attempt at building excitement by the use of dynamics or variation.

The most obvious candidates for critical comparison with Sweatman's
Columbias are the Original Dixieland Jazz Band's records of the 1917–18
period, but even then there are more differences than similarities. The
ODJB adhered to a very simple polyphonic structure—cornet lead, trombone counterpoint, clarinet obbligato/embellishment—the whole performance committed to memory and repeated more or less note for note, as
comparison between their Victor, Aeolian Vocalion and English Columbia

recordings of "Tiger Rag" or "At The Jazz Band Ball" clearly demonstrate. Only clarinetist Larry Shields, the band's most technically competent musician, makes any attempt to vary his routines, both within a performance and on subsequent recordings.

The Sweatman Columbias have a richer and more complex pattern and texture. The lead frequently alternates between trumpet and clarinet (and occasionally even trombone and clarinet), so a typical pattern would be clarinet lead on the first verse with a harmonized trumpet counterpoint (or occasionally even duplicating the clarinet), followed by a chorus following the same pattern. The repeat chorus would have the lead switch to trumpet while Sweatman's clarinet plays an improvised or embellished obbligato. As often as not, there would follow an interpolated chorus from another tune with the lead switching back to Sweatman, followed by another chorus of this interpolated tune where the lead switches back to trumpet, followed by a final chorus where Sweatman tends to make the most of the opportunity to demonstrate both his technique and improvisational abilities.

This switching of roles from lead to embellished or improvised obbligato was a microcosm of Sweatman's live performances. On the vaudeville stage he was usually accompanied by a pianist and drummer or, earlier on in his stage career, by the theater pit orchestra. Thus, opportunities for polyphonic interplay with other front-line instruments (trumpet, trombone, etc.) were nonexistent. Consequently, it was imperative that Sweatman craft his performance into a form whereby the melody was stated in a relatively straightforward manner followed by choruses of variations, building to a climactic finish. A good example of this on record is his version of "Joe Turner Blues" (Pathé 20167), where, after a relatively straight statement of the verse and a chorus, subsequent repetitions of the chorus become increasingly embellished and exciting, demonstrating what Dave Peyton called Sweatman's talent as "a sensational, rapid, clever manipulator of the clarinet."[28] Such a pattern, worked from a basic written arrangement, would be enhanced and developed in the 1920s by arrangers such as Don Redman, Benny Carter, Duke Ellington, and Bill Challis, and would provide the musical form of most jazz performances by larger bands for the next thirty years. Sweatman was one of the first to put it into practice, albeit in a somewhat scaled-down and simplified form.

Given that Sweatman's name, on account of his reputation as a vaudeville performer, was the draw that helped sell his Columbia records and that in his vaudeville work there was no other lead instrument to work with (or against), there is a surprising amount of latitude given to the trumpet and trombone players. The latter in particular fills an important role in the Sweatman Columbias, providing a deeper-voiced counterpoint to the melody and even, on occasion, such as on "Rock-A-Bye Your Baby with a Dixie Melody," carrying the lead for a chorus. What with the lead switching from clarinet to trumpet and back again, this was pretty advanced stuff in 1918!

Posterity has not recorded who was responsible for the arrangements used on any of Sweatman's records, but those of the 1918 period are almost certainly by his pianist Dan Parrish. What is all the more remarkable is that many of the arrangements of Sweatman's Columbia performances must have been written or worked out on the day of the recording session. At about this time Columbia, in agreement with a number of music publishers, instigated a policy in its production of dance records of interpolating one or more tunes into a performance, making them medleys. As Columbia only had to pay one royalty providing all the tunes originated with the same publisher, they could both save money and hedge their bets as to whether a tune would be a hit or not. Likewise, the publishers got several of their tunes, including the poorer sellers, into Columbia's prestigious and well-publicized catalog, thus giving a boost to sales of sheet music.

While such practice was beneficial to both Columbia and the publishers, it did mean that the resulting performances could be both disjointed and under-rehearsed, as it is likely that the musicians only found out what they were to record on the day of the session. A good example of this is Sweatman's recording of "Has Anybody Seen My Corrine?" which introduces not one, but two other tunes into the performance. The trumpeter in particular seems uneasy with the material and the overall performance is both lackluster and uninspired. By comparison, the Little Wonder version does not introduce other tunes into the performance, and, with the likely presence on this session of Sweatman's old friend, the powerful and inventive trumpeter Crickett Smith, the resulting recording is both exciting and cohesive. Despite having to work around the restrictions brought about by Columbia's medley policy, a considerable degree of freedom is apparent in the 1918 arrangements, which the musicians seized when the opportunity arose. The two takes of "Oh You La La!" are substantially different though retaining the same basic structure and tempo, while the two takes of "Regretful Blues" from his first issued Columbia session are taken at completely different tempi, the slower of the two being a half chorus shorter.

Sweatman's 1919 Columbia recordings are particularly interesting, inasmuch as they were made with what was in all likelihood a contingent of Will Marion Cook's New York Syncopated Orchestra, a large quasi-symphonic group who, with the notable exception of clarinetist Sidney Bechet, were all sight-reading musicians.[29] Cook's orchestra were cooling their heels waiting for contractual problems to be resolved prior to their groundbreaking 1919 visit to Britain and Europe and, during this time, the band, or sections thereof, made several concert appearances on the Eastern seaboard. Thus some of Cook's musicians were available to Sweatman for record dates.[30]

These 1919 Columbia recordings, made with a larger, more schooled band of musicians, are very different in feel, sound, and orchestral texture, and one suspects that the arrangements are by someone used to writing for a large ensemble. This may well have been Cook himself, or possibly Cook's close associate Joe Jordan, a friend of Sweatman from his time in Chicago and a well-known arranger and orchestrator. These sessions feature much tighter and less freewheeling arrangements that give little opportunity for improvisatory freedom. A good example of this is apparent in the two takes of "Kansas City Blues": apart from the clarinet and piano breaks, the two issued takes are virtually indistinguishable from one another. "Rainy Day Blues," of which there are also two issued takes, has slightly more opportunity for embellishment and, indeed, Sweatman makes the most of it. "That's Got 'Em" and "A Good Man Is Hard to Find" stand out for their improvisation—both generate primitive excitement, in part due to some rudimentary swinging violin, probably played by George Smith.

Sweatman's association with Columbia proved lucrative for both parties. Columbia now had a jazz band led by a nationally known performer whose records could be promoted by Sweatman's vaudeville performances across the States, and Sweatman benefited from the publicity that Columbia put out via their dealers and in extensive newspaper advertising. An example of Columbia's publicity for Sweatman and his jazz band appeared in a 1918 monthly supplement, which is interesting for its stereotyping of jazz, associating it with gyrating musicians and acrobatic drummers:

We saw Sweatman and his jazz experts record their dance coupling of the month. There were times we bet ourselves the drummer would never get his stick back from the ceiling in time for the next "drum"—but he did! Our photograph was taken in the Columbia Recording Laboratory and shows the Sweatman jazz experts "in action" and partially explains the "action" to be found, in their Columbia dance recordings! The Sweatman crowd are surely saturated with syncopation. While playing they swing and beat time with their entire anatomy. It is their thorough feeling of the music that enables them to play such rag riots of jazz pyrotechnics as "Good-bye Alexander" and "Darktown Strutters' Ball."[31]

The accompanying photograph, taken at the May 28, 1918, recording session, shows Sweatman and his "jazz experts" in a typical sort of pose that was de rigueur for jazz band photographs of the time and for several years after. The horn players are kneeling on the floor in a group, with their instruments pointing to the ground, while Palmer Jones, one of the two pianists, has one hand raised above his head and the drummer has a stick poised in mid-air. A second photograph taken at the session is more conventional—Sweatman and the trombonist are standing, trumpeter William Hicks is seated, trumpet to his lips, the pianists are poised to play but the drummer has one arm held high, shaking a tambourine, while one leg is poised in mid-air! This was several years before the school of naturalistic photography entered the world of jazz.

The Columbia records by Wilbur C. Sweatman and His Original Jazz Band sold extremely well (see Appendix Four) and even today may occasionally turn up in antique and junk shops, usually well worn—an indication of their popularity at the time. Never before had a black musician been the subject of such intensive advertising campaigns. Only Ziegfeld Follies comedy star and America's best-known black performer Bert Williams, another exclusive Columbia recording artist, was given as much promotion by a record company at that time.

Even so, Sweatman was made to know his place in the order of things. In 1919 he was approached by composer and performer Perry Bradford to see if he could persuade Columbia to record Bradford's vaudeville partner, Jeanette Taylor, singing his song "Crazy Blues" (then known as "The Harlem Blues"). Bradford had been knocking on record company doors for months trying to get his bluesy songs recorded by a female blues singer, but racial prejudice and the total lack of comprehension on the part of the record company executives of the fact that there was a black record-buying public ensured that he got the same answer every time—there was no demand for a black blues singer. At Bradford's behest Sweatman approached Columbia to see if they would record one side by his band with Jeanette Taylor. Bradford recalled:

> Sweatman rehearsed my vaudeville Jeanette and went downtown and tried in vain to sell her to Columbia, singing vocals with his jazzband. Although Sweatman had a large following, a Columbia executive nailed the lid down tight on him with this little hammer: "You don't need any help because your records are very big sellers for Columbia; why slow down your sales by experimenting?" Which caused Sweatman to cry out, "This girl will help, not hinder my sales. Let's make one side with her

and see what happens. I know what the results will be and Columbia won't be buying a 'pig in the bag,' for I played for her when I was direct-ing my jazz band at Chicago's Grand Theater in 1912 where she stopped the show at every performance singing jazz songs." The same executive snapped back, "But Columbia wouldn't think of recording a colored girl at this time.[32]

Why would Columbia not record a black female singer at that time? One reason that has been suggested was that to do so might risk the boycot-ting of their products below the Mason-Dixon line. Such attitudes would linger for many years to come in the entertainment industry; as late as 1968 Columbia Pictures allegedly vetoed film director Carol Reed's choice of black British singer Shirley Bassey to play the major role of Nancy in the film *Oliver!* (based on Lionel Bart's musical adaptation of Charles Dickens's *Oliver Twist*) on the grounds that a black Nancy would alien-ate white filmgoers in the American South. A much more likely reason is one already discussed—that the record companies did not believe that there was a demand for records from the black population. Bradford had to wait until February 1920 before he could persuade the then-struggling minor record label OKeh to record Mamie Smith singing his composition "Crazy Blues." The phenomenal sales success of that record—and especially its popularity with black record buyers—turned the industry upside down. Soon, every record company, from industry giants Victor and Columbia down, were vying against each other to sign up black female blues sing-ers as fast as they could be found and recorded. Jeanette Taylor eventually made records in 1927, when as Jeanette James (she had married performer Seymour James, and worked in vaudeville as Seymour and Jeanette) she recorded some vaudeville blues for Paramount with her regular accompa-nists, John Williams's Synco Jazzers, featuring on piano a youthful Mary Lou Williams.

Several problems are encountered in understanding and appreciating very early jazz records and placing them in the context of what followed. First, the acoustical recording process was purely mechanical, with no microphones or electronic amplification used to capture the sound. The frequency range of the acoustic process was severely limited, covering a band from approximately 150 Hz to 4500 Hz, and what signal was recorded tended to suffer from horn resonances in the midrange. The present-day amplifier has a built-in industry-standard response curve, known as the RIAA curve, whose characteristics are totally unsuitable for reproducing acoustic records. The RIAA curve has a steep bass lift, which rolls off at about 250Hz, below which the signal on acoustic recordings is severely diminished, serving only to emphasize bass rumble. The RIAA curve is virtually flat where the acoustic response should be lifted, leaving midrange voices and instruments sounding shallow and thin. These problems can be remedied with a graphic equalizer, or a specialized pre-amp with built-in acoustic curves.

The greatest problem for the modern-day listener is that the recording speeds of many of these records were below 78 rpm, most notably on Columbia and Victor. Although the drop in speed may be only 2 or 3 rpm, the difference that makes to the performance is highly significant—at 78 some of Sweatman's Columbias sound like a shrieking babble. However, if played at the correct speed (in most cases 76 or 77 rpm) the performances come sharply into focus, the sound becomes fuller, and the instruments sound as if they are being played by human beings. One theory for this drop in recorded speed against playback speed is that it was a deliberate act on the part of the A&R men of the day to make jazz bands sound even more frenzied and wild than they actually were, and this theory can be borne out by examining the four sessions following Sweatman's first two issued Columbia sides. The products of these four sessions lack the cohesiveness, flow, and richness of the first two sides, and it is my suspicion (and that of composer and sound engineer Ron Geesin) that the recording executives had a greater hand in these sessions, and probably not only dictated the repertoire, which is of a more popular nature than the foregoing sides, but also ordered the musicians to play in a wild, abandoned manner. Another, more practical, theory is that recording technology was still very much in its infancy when jazz first appeared on record, and such problems as speed variation were everyday hindrances to the engineers of the day.

I have spent many hours ascertaining the correct speeds and keys for Sweatman's records. With the invaluable assistance of two of the foremost experts on vintage recording and remastering (and both fine musicians to boot), Ron Geesin and the late John R. T. Davies, the key and speed of every available Sweatman record has been verified and are noted in the discography that follows. Ron Geesin has very kindly contributed a short discourse on the speeds of the Sweatman Columbias, which is to be found in the appendices.

As well as recording for Columbia in the 1918–20 period, Sweatman's band can be heard, albeit anonymously, on the Little Wonder record label. These 5.5-inch-diameter single-sided records were introduced in 1914 by Henry Waterson, president of music publishers Waterson, Snyder and Berlin. Originally conceived by Columbia's then–chief recording engineer, industry veteran Victor Hugo Emerson, they were cheaply made, with no artist credit, and pressed on inferior quality material. They sold for ten cents in dime stores such as Woolworth's, McCrory's, and Kresge's, and in mail-order catalogs such as Sears, Roebuck & Company. The records were manufactured under Columbia patents and pressed at its Bridgeport plant in great secrecy. Little Wonder's pricing policy caused shock waves in the industry. None of the established companies would admit to having any connection with this venture, but it was clear to anyone who took the time to read the minute address line, showing the company based in the Woolworth Building—as was Columbia—and the stamped patent details on the blank reverse, that Columbia was heavily involved in their production.

Although initially owned and operated by Waterson, it soon became apparent that Columbia executive Victor Emerson was personally profiting from the venture, hastening his departure from Columbia and his decision to form Emerson Records in 1915. Columbia, seeing the fantastic opportunities to be realised in selling low-price records (or perhaps fearful of it), took over Little Wonder in about 1917 and slowly, but steadily wound it down, issuing its final records in 1923. The heady days of January 1915, when 4.5 million Little Wonders sold in one month, were over by the time Sweatman recorded for the label, and post-1918 issues are remarkably scarce.[33]

It was long thought that the performances found on Little Wonder records were edited versions of the same titles on Columbia. This however is not the case; in most instances different artists were used (for instance, none of the titles on Little Wonder that duplicate titles recorded for Columbia by Ted Lewis are in fact by Lewis). Where the same artist was responsible, as was the case for many of Sweatman's records, aural comparison proves that not only do the performances differ but, in at least three cases, the Little Wonder sides appear to be products of different sessions from the Columbia recordings of the same titles. Further research may well establish that many, if not most, of the Little Wonders were the products of separate sessions.

It is interesting to note that Sweatman apparently had no idea that the Little Wonders he recorded were commercially issued. In an interview with Len Kunstadt at which Kunstadt produced some examples of Sweatman's Little Wonder recordings, he said that he thought they were test records; the engineers had told him to play numbers of a minute or so duration! How much credence can be put on this one can only surmise, bearing in mind that the performances would have to have been rearranged to fit the much shorter playing time. However it would go some way to explaining how Little Wonder achieved such a low selling price and gives rise to speculation that the anonymity of the records was intended to shield the identity of the performers not only from the public, but also from the artists that made them!

When compared to Sweatman's Columbia performances, the Little Wonders show marked differences in the style of playing by both Sweatman and his sidemen. Not having the full three minutes to develop and enhance a theme, the Little Wonders tend to consist of "busked" performances, with Sweatman taking a much more clearly improvised obbligato role to the trumpet lead. This is most marked on the Little Wonder of "Has Anybody Seen My Corrine?" The Columbia recording is a rather fussy, overcomplicated performance, with two other numbers being interpolated into the arrangement, leaving little scope for creative thematic development. The recording balance favors Sweatman's clarinet, and this, together with an overly prominent tuba, leaves the trumpet vainly fighting to be heard. By comparison the Little Wonder, recorded with a smaller group and with none of the balance problems of the Columbia, sticks to a verse and a chorus and a half chorus, giving Sweatman ample opportunity to work an exciting improvised countermelody to the trumpet lead throughout. Could the Little Wonders be the authentic sound of Sweatman's band, freed from the strictures and demands of the Columbia recording executives? I, for one, tend to think so—they are much more relaxed and, despite their hasty assembly and arrangement, are looser, yet at the same time more cohesive performances.

The Sweatman Little Wonders are very difficult to find nowadays, mainly for two reasons. First, most jazz records were sold with one purpose in mind, and that was for buyers to dance to them (even the legendary King Oliver Gennett recordings of 1923 have the legend "Fox Trot" or similar after the title of the piece). The era when people sat down and assiduously studied every nuance of the performance was a long time in the future; besides, it made little sense for a record buyer to purchase a record for the purpose of dancing which barely lasted ninety seconds. Second, most jazz record collectors never considered that any worthwhile jazz items came out on the label, and subsequently they were left to deteriorate in junk shops.

The four known exceptions to the rule that all the Sweatman Little Wonder titles that duplicated those on Columbia are also by Sweatman are "Lucille" on Little Wonder 1169, "Rainy Day Blues" on Little Wonder 1107, "Hello, Hello!" on Little Wonder 1234, and "Indianola" on Little Wonder 778. "Lucille" has long been reported as being by Sweatman; aural examination shows it instead to be by Yerkes's Jazarimba Orchestra. The fact that it is labelled as by Jazzarimba [sic] Orchestra has not deterred reports that it is by Sweatman. "Rainy Day Blues" is also by Yerkes's Jazarimba Orchestra. Little Wonder 1234, "Hello, Hello!", although not by Sweatman, is an important discovery. This performance is actually a previously unreported recording by the Louisiana Five, featuring the fine New Orleans–born clarinetist Alcide Nunez, and is doubly interesting for the presence of fellow New Orleanian and multi-instrumentalist Bernhard "Doc" Berendsohn, here playing cornet. Berendsohn was better known as a clarinetist, his fluid, woody-toned playing being featured on several recordings with Lanin's Southern Serenaders, Ladd's Black Aces and Lindsay McPhail's Jazz Orchestra of Chicago, but his playing on the two records made with the Louisiana Five show him to be a driving, exciting cornetist as well. No copy of "Indianola" has been found to confirm it as a Sweatman performance or not, but the issue number suggests a late 1917 recording date, much earlier than Sweatman's own recording of the number. It is almost certainly by Prince's Band, the Columbia house orchestra, which recorded a 12-inch version of the number on December 10, 1917.

Sweatman's Little Wonder version of San Diego–based composer and publisher Will Nash's composition "Lonesome Road" is unique: Columbia saw fit to reject Sweatman's 10-inch recording, but the Little Wonder was mastered and issued, and a very fine and relaxed performance it is, too! Interestingly, the sheet music for "Lonesome Road," published by Pace & Handy (presumably they had bought the publishing rights from Nash, along with his "Snakey Blues" which Handy had recorded for Columbia in 1917), shows a photograph of Sweatman seated on a bench playing three clarinets beneath which is the cryptic legend "Featured by Sweatman's Jazz Band on Columbia Record." This seems to imply that the 10-inch recording was scheduled for release by Columbia but at the last minute withdrawn for unspecified reasons. Usually this situation arose because of failure on the record company's part to obtain copyright clearance, but in this case, with the publishers actively promoting the forthcoming Columbia release (albeit somewhat prematurely, given the vagueness of any proposed issue number), that seems unlikely.

Chapter 9

Rainy Day Blues

In 1918 war was raging in Europe, and the United States had been drawn into the fray despite Woodrow Wilson's attempts to keep the country neutral. American troops started to arrive in France in June 1917, but were not involved in combat until October 1917. By early 1918 tens of thousands of U.S. troops were arriving weekly in France—and they were needed: on March 21, 1918, the Germans launched Operation Michel, the start of their final offensive of the war and a last-ditch attempt to break the stalemate of trench warfare.

As part of the preparedness for war, every U.S. man, whether native-born, naturalized, or alien, was registered for the draft. The Selective Service Act 40 Stat. 76 was passed by Congress on May 18, 1917, on the nation's entry into World War I. The act gave the president the power to draft men for military service. By the end of World War I about 24 million men had registered for the draft, and some 2.8 million were inducted into military service.

There were three draft registrations between June 1917 and September 1918, totalling over 24 million names of all men between the ages of eighteen and forty-five. The first registration, on June 5, 1917, was for all men between the ages of twenty-one and thirty-one. The second, on June 5, 1918, registered those who attained the age of twenty-one after June 5, 1917. A supplemental registration was held on August 24, 1918, for those becoming twenty-one after June 5, 1918. Finally, on September 12, 1918, a third registration was held for men aged eighteen to forty-five. These draft registration cards provide an invaluable source of information for genealogists and researchers alike, and their importance is only now starting to be appreciated by researchers into early jazz history.

On September 12, 1918, Sweatman duly completed his draft registration card, thereby confirming to posterity his baptismal (middle) name of Coleman (although it is shown as Coleman, the *e* has clearly been obliterated, but by whom is not known) and at the same time sowing the seeds of confusion by signing his forename as Wilber, although that appears to have been his choice of spelling at the time. He gave his date of birth as February 7, 1882, that he was a native-born Negro, and that his address was 251 West 143rd Street in New York City and that his nearest relative was his wife, Nettie, who shared the same address. It is particularly interesting that he gave his employment as "vaudeville performer" and that his employer was Bruce Duffus of the Putnan [*sic*] Building, 1493 Broadway, New York. Reading this at face value, as was no doubt intended, it seemed that he was working for Bruce Duffus in a nonspecific role as a vaudeville performer. It is important to bear in mind that the purpose of the draft registration was to ascertain the number of men suitable to send to the Western Front, and many used any ploy available to defer or delay being called up. If Sweatman had entered on the card that he was a self-employed musician, there would be a much greater likelihood of his being called for a medical examination.

British-born Harold Bruce Duffus was a partner, along with brother Lennox Duffus and Louis Wesley, in the Wesley Office, a theatrical management business based on the fifth floor of the Putnam Building, a well-known base for businesses involved in all aspects of vaudeville and theater management.[1] Also located in the Putnam Building was the theatrical agency headed by veteran vaudevillian Pat Casey, who later on acted as Sweatman's vaudeville booker. It seems likely that the Wesley Office was booking Sweatman on the Keith-Albee and Orpheum vaudeville circuits, so to call Duffus his employer was not stretching the truth too far.

By the beginning of 1918 black regiments (under the command of white officers) were completing basic training at army camps throughout the country and being readied to make the Atlantic crossing to France—but not to engage the enemy. Practically all black American troops spent their active service undertaking a variety of menial but essential logistical roles; transport, trench digging, road repairing, pioneering, stevedoring at English Channel ports, and the like. The solitary exception to this was the New York–raised 15th Regiment (later the 369th U.S . Infantry), nicknamed the "Hellfighters," who, under the command of Col. Arthur Little and with their famous band directed by Lt. James Reese Europe, were seconded to the 16th Division of the French army. The Hellfighters were in the thick of the fighting in eastern France, including action in the Argonne and Marne offensives.

Back in New York many concerts were staged for the benefit of black troops, by black and white performers alike. Sweatman was an enthusiastic supporter of these concerts and frequently participated in them. On July 27, 1918, he appeared at a benefit for the Colored Men's YMCA at Keith's Alhambra Theater, 7th Avenue and 126th Street. Sharing the bill were some of the top black and white performers of the day, including Sophie Tucker, Bert Williams, Eddie Leonard, Miller & Lyles, Irving Berlin, and Eddie Foy.[2] Another benefit concert at which Sweatman appeared was held on October 27, 1918, at the Century Theater, New York City, for the 367th Infantry Regiment (the "Buffaloes"). The star-studded bill of performers who along with Sweatman gave their services for free included Bert Williams, Eddie Cantor, Abbie Mitchell, Marilyn Miller, Eddie Leonard, Irving Berlin, David Bispham (the celebrated operatic bass), Belle Baker, Ford Dabney's Syncopated Orchestra, and the Clef Club Orchestra and Singers, conducted by Will Marion Cook. Another example of Sweatman's willingness to support good causes came a few years later when, in May 1927, he appeared along with Bill "Bojangles" Robinson and the casts of many of the Harlem nightclub revues at a benefit held at the Lafayette Theater in aid of the victims of the dreadful Mississippi River flood of that spring.[3]

The years 1918–20 were in many respects the pinnacle of Sweatman's career; his records were selling extremely well and the resultant publicity made him a desirable attraction in the leading vaudeville houses. He also appeared at numerous Sunday Concerts at the Eltinge and Lafayette theaters in New York. At that time New York's entertainment venues were governed by the so-called "blue laws," which prevented theatrical entertainment on Sundays, and such one-off concerts were a way of circumventing the law. They also offered an opportunity for bookers, press agents, and the theatrical press, with some degree of leisure, to apprise performers apart from the normal hurly-burly of the midweek hustle.

One such concert held at the Eltinge Theater on April 20, 1919, and another, a week later, billed Sweatman's group as "The Largest Jazz Band Ever Assembled" that played "Syncopation and Blues, Songs, Classics and Ragtime." Press advertisements for the concert listed the artists performing, including Dan Parrish, Walter Hunter, Seth Weeks, Charlie Sims, Isaac Hatch, Will Farrell, and the That's Got 'Em Quartette, though it does not stipulate whether they appeared singly or as members of the band.[4] Dan Parrish was Sweatman's regular pianist who, just a month later, sailed for Paris with Louis Mitchell's Jazz Kings and blazed the trail for the French love of jazz, staying there for many years. Seth Weeks was a well-known mandolin virtuoso who had recorded several solos for the Berliner Gramophone

Company in England as early as 1900, including a cake walk. Ike Hatch was a banjoist and well-known vocalist who, like Parrish, made his home in Europe, and Will or Billy Farrell was a songwriter, drummer, and onetime partner with stride pianist James P. Johnson in a music publishing venture. Walter Hunter and Charlie Sims's instruments—if they were in fact musicians—are not known; Hunter's name appears from time to time in the contemporary black press as master of ceremonies at Harlem dances.

Sweatman's high profile in the world of black music and entertainment brought him into contact with many musicians on the lookout for regular engagements or casual gig work, and doubtless many of these found their way onto Sweatman's Columbia records. The personnel for the 1919 recordings, in particular, changes almost from session to session, giving future generations of researchers and discographers their share of headaches. Bearing in mind that Sweatman generally only used piano and drums as accompaniment in vaudeville, it is not surprising to find that the Columbia sessions from this time were made up of men picked from Sweatman's roster of available musicians from the bands he booked, plus the odd musician befriended over a drink. One such ad hoc participant was the nineteen-year-old trumpeter Arthur Briggs, destined to become one of the most important and influential African American musicians working in Europe in the inter-war years.

James Arthur Briggs (1899–1991) was born in St. George's, on the Caribbean island of Grenada, on April 9, 1899, the youngest of ten children of a father from St. George's and a mother from Barbados. He arrived in the U.S. in 1917 and lived in Charleston, South Carolina, but despite previous assertions that he studied music at the famous Jenkins Orphanage, there is no evidence whatsoever that he was a pupil there. The Jenkins Orphanage Band, often billed as a "pickaninny band," made regular fundraising tours of the northern states beginning in 1895, and made appearances in Britain in 1895, 1904, 1914, and 1929.[5] Upon U.S. entry into World War I, Briggs enlisted in the 15th Infantry Regiment as a member of James Reese Europe's celebrated band, probably on the recommendation of bandmaster F. Eugene Mikell, who had taught at the Jenkins Orphanage. Too young to be sent overseas, Briggs remained in New York, and in early 1919 joined Will Marion Cook's New York Syncopated Orchestra. Cook took his orchestra to Europe in 1919, where Briggs stayed, making his home in Berlin and later Paris. He toured with his own band throughout Europe and recorded prolifically in Germany in the mid-1920s, his style at that time owing much to that of Red Nichols, whose records with his Five Pennies were readily available in Europe. As records by leading black American jazzmen such as Louis Armstrong and Duke Ellington percolated through to European buyers in the late 1920s and early 1930s, Briggs's style took on much of the bravado and brilliance of Louis Armstrong's, as is amply demonstrated on his records with pianist Freddy Johnson's Orchestra, recorded in Paris in the mid-1930s. In 1940 Briggs was interned by the Nazis, but continued to play, forming a band at the Saint-Denis internment camp. He was liberated in 1944 and resumed his playing career, but increasingly devoted more time to teaching music, becoming a professor of music in 1964. After a long and varied life, Briggs died in Paris on July 15, 1991, aged ninety-two.

In early 1919 Arthur Briggs recorded with Wilbur Sweatman's Original Jazz Band, filling the second trumpet chair on at least one and possibly four Sweatman sessions—his first recordings, prior to sailing to England with Will Marion Cook's Southern Syncopated Orchestra. Apparently Briggs was a friend of Sweatman's regular pianist Dan Parrish, and it was through Parrish that Briggs, and maybe other members of Cook's orchestra, came to be on Sweatman's recordings of early 1919. When interviewed by Dutch researcher Ate van Delden, Briggs recalled that he recorded "Ja-Da" and "Weary Blues" with Sweatman for the OKeh record label and that the sessions were held after touring with Will Marion Cook's New York Syncopated Orchestra.[6] Another confirmation that Briggs recorded with Sweatman at this time comes in a letter from American writer and researcher Warren Plath to his German counterpart, Rainer Lotz. Plath details a number of meetings with Arthur Briggs:

> Had several meetings with Arthur Briggs and his family though we never do seem to get down to talking about jazz. However, this year I did ask him about his first recording date (this is always a good way to start an interview!!!) and he said it was with Wilbur Sweatman and that one tune was "Ja-Da" and the other "Sister Kate". He also said he played second trumpet to Willie Lewis (not the sax man) and the trombone was Frank Withers. This does not jibe with Rust's data [the discography *Jazz Records 1897–1942*, by Brian Rust], though maybe Arthur is talking about an unissued session which shows only "Ja-da". The issued "Ja-Da" is in my possession and in good condition, though I really cannot tell if there is one or two trumpets.[7]

Although Sweatman recorded "Ja-Da" for Columbia (not OKeh), he did not record either "Weary Blues" or "Sister Kate." It is likely that Briggs confused the titles and that he actually played on "Ja-Da" and "Rainy Day Blues," recorded by Sweatman on January 17, 1919. Three takes of "Ja-Da" were recorded, none of which were acceptable to Columbia executives. The Columbia file cards show that take 1 was "Too confused," take 2 "Out of tune" (or "Out of time"), and take 3 "Wrong tempo." "Ja-Da" was recorded again on February 5, along with "Lonesome Road" and "A Good Man Is Hard to Find." On February 8 the band recorded Sweatman's composition "That's Got 'Em" and probably versions of "Lonesome Road" and "A Good Man Is Hard to Find" for issue on Little Wonder records. The Willie Lewis that Briggs refers to is probably the same William Lewis listed as a trumpeter in the 1929 American Federation of Musicians Local #802 Directory, living at 205 West 137th Street in Harlem. The lead trumpet work on all these sessions, although poorly recorded and badly balanced, appears to be by the same musician, in all probability Willie Lewis, with Briggs playing second trumpet on "Rainy Day Blues," "That's Got 'Em," and possibly on "Kansas City Blues" and "Slide, Kelly, Slide," both of which have two trumpets present. It is difficult to state with any degree of certainty whether there are two trumpets on the session of February 5, 1919, which produced the issued version of "Ja-Da" and "A Good Man Is Hard to Find." The recording quality is poor and badly balanced, with drums, tuba, and piano overly prominent and the resulting sound very muddy. Also, the concept of arranging for separate sections was a year or two in the future, so the musicians indulge in a free-for-all ensemble, with no attempt at structuring the performance beyond a simple "head" arrangement.

Although Arthur Briggs is almost undoubtedly present on the first of the Sweatman Columbia sessions of early 1919, there is a logistical problem to resolve with his presence on the February sessions. Briggs, trombonist Frank Withers and saxophonist Mazie Mullins were, by late 1918 or early 1919, members of Will Marion Cook's New York Syncopated Orchestra, which in early 1919 toured theaters in Eastern seaboard towns and cities. On February 5 the orchestra appeared at the Mishlar Theater in Altoona, Pennsylvania. On February 8 they were in Cleveland, appearing at Engineers' Hall. Of course, there exists the possibility that Briggs, and possibly other members of the orchestra, did not complete the whole tour, and thus could have recorded with Sweatman on those days.[8] The logistics of the March sessions are less problematic, as the New York Syncopated Orchestra were working in and around New York City. There are two trumpets to be heard on the March 22 session, probably Willie Lewis and Arthur Briggs.

Rumors have abounded for years that Sidney Bechet played for a while with Sweatman. Since Bechet was also a member of Will Marion Cook's New York Syncopated Orchestra, it is not beyond the realm of possibility that Bechet found temporary work with Sweatman at that time—although unfortunately not on record. However, it is highly likely that other New York Syncopated Orchestra musicians recorded with Sweatman in the early months of 1919, because the sound of the band on the records from this period is completely different from those sides immediately preceding and following them. Frank Withers, by Briggs's identification, is the likely candidate for being the trombonist on these sides, and the violinist may be fellow orchestra member George Smith, a Clef Club veteran who had recorded as early as 1913 with Europe's Society Orchestra. The identity of the saxophonist on a number of these sides is difficult to establish, but it must be noted that Frank Withers's wife, Mazie Mullins, was both a talented saxophonist and a member of the New York Syncopated Orchestra.

There is strong evidence to suggest that Sweatman was involved to some degree in the formation of Mitchell's Jazz Kings, the black group led by drummer Louis Mitchell that went to France at the end of May 1919 and became a profound influence on musicians and writers alike in Paris. Mitchell was no stranger to Europe, having made his first trip there in the summer of 1914 and, apart from a seven-month spell in the States in late 1914 and early 1915, spent the ensuing years working in Britain and France. In January 1919 Parisian theatrical producer Leon Volterra sent Mitchell back to the United States to organize a band of black musicians, over fifty in number, to be featured at the Casino de Paris.[9] *Jazz* was the buzzword in the nightclubs, dance halls, and cabarets of post–WWI London and Paris. James Reese Europe's army band had wowed doughboys, tommies, poilus, and civilians in France with their syncopated rhythms.

American soldiers brought over to France copies of the Original Dixieland Jazz Band's first recordings and, in April 1919, the ODJB themselves arrived in London, lured by the promise of big money and fame by theatrical impresario Albert de Courville. Despite the initial setback of being removed from the de Courville revue *Joy Bells* after just one night at the insistence of its star, the comedian George Robey, the ODJB soon found an eager following among both the rich, at such supper clubs as Rector's, and with the general public through their appearances at the London Palladium and the Hammersmith Palais de Danse. Their fifteen-month tenure in England had a profound influence on local musicians, many of whom tried to emulate the ODJB's success. By comparison to the ODJB, the local bands in London and Paris, black and white alike, did not sound very exciting. Volterra and Mitchell both knew that they had to have a jazz band in Paris—and quickly.

What should have been a brief trip home for Mitchell eventually lasted five months, due to a variety of difficulties. Passport requests were turned down, musicians were already booked for engagements, both at home and overseas, and work at home was relatively plentiful. He eventually assembled a large aggregation, including such prominent names as Crickett Smith, Herb Flemming, Sidney Bechet, and Dan Parrish; but, just as he was ready to start organizing the group's passage to Europe, he received a telegram from Volterra requesting Mitchell's return—alone. Mitchell in essence ignored Volterra's telegram and left for France at the end of May 1919. However, he had gambled away all the money Volterra had advanced him, and returned with a considerably smaller band, the traveling expenses for which (according to Dan Parrish) were paid for by the band's saxophonist James Shaw out of his own pocket.[10]

The connections between the group Mitchell finally assembled to go to Paris and Wilbur Sweatman are more than just tenuous; the pianist of the Mitchell group was Sweatman's regular pianist, Dan Parrish. Frank Withers, the band's trombonist, had allegedly recorded on bass saxophone with Sweatman in 1917, and, according to Arthur Briggs, on the early 1919 Columbias as trombonist. Mitchell's star player was trumpeter Crickett Smith, another Sweatman associate of many years' standing, and other members of the group may also have had Sweatman connections, possibly even appearing on the enigmatic recordings made in the spring of 1919.

Dan Parrish's immediate replacement as Sweatman's pianist is uncertain, but is thought to have been Bobby Lee, who is mentioned by name in January 1920 (along with drummer Herbert King) both in the *Chicago Defender* and *Variety* in connection with Sweatman's vaudeville work. Although Sweatman's vaudeville act had been frequently mentioned in press reports through 1919, the identity of his accompanists was never revealed. A typical advertisement from August 1919 for Sweatman's appearance at the Royal Theater, New York, merely mentions that he was "Assisted By Two Supreme Jazzists." Interestingly, the same advertisement gives a clue to the type of material that Sweatman and his act featured at the time: "Sweatman Blues," "Down Home Rag," "Boogie Rag," and "That's Got 'Em" are all named as being featured by Sweatman in his act.[11] Lee and King are also named in an article in the *New York Age* in June 1920 in connection with a "Midnight Revue" held by the Temple Club of Hiram Lodge at the Lafayette Theater in Harlem, at which the cream of Harlem's entertainers appeared, including Bert Williams, W. C. Handy's Band, featuring pianist Fred Bryan and drummer and xylophonist Jasper "Jazzbo" Taylor, songwriter Maceo Pinkard, pianist Luckey Roberts, and vaudeville vocal duettists Chappelle and Stinnette. The article states: "Wilbur Sweatman claims the distinction of being king of jazz clarionetists [sic]. He was accompanied to Harlem by several booking agents from down town, so Wilbur knew he had to exert himself a bit to shine in the limelight, and so he did. Assisted by Bobbie [sic] Lee at the piano and Herbert King on traps, he made a record during the performance for encores."[12]

While Sidney Bechet's association with Sweatman is unconfirmed, another legendary New Orleans musician definitely did work with Sweatman in 1919 but, sadly, not on record. Cornetist Freddie Keppard had come north with the Original Creole Band, but left under mysterious and somewhat farcical circumstances on a station platform in Boston in April 1917.[13] He played for a while in Chicago alongside Sidney Bechet in Lawrence Duhé's Band at the Dreamland Cafe, before leading his own band at the De Luxe Gardens. How and why Keppard came to New York is uncertain; it has been suggested that the arrival of Joe "King" Oliver in Chicago in early 1918 had dented both his pride and his reputation as the hottest cornet player in town, but this seems an unlikely or irrational reason to leave Chicago. More likely he had received sufficient exposure in the music business around New York to have work opportunities thrust at him on a regular basis. Drummer Jasper Taylor recalled seeing Keppard with Tim Brymn's orchestra at the Cocoanut Grove in New York in 1919, and he apparently found work with Sweatman for a summer engagement at the Brighton Beach Hotel at Coney Island. When interviewed by Len Kunstadt and Bob Colton, Sweatman produced a canceled check with which he had paid Keppard during this engagement. The veteran Philadelphia trumpeter Charlie Gaines recalled in an interview with Russ Shor that Keppard at this time was working freelance, hiring himself out to bandleaders who wanted to liven up their bands and to learn the New Orleans style.[14] In an article on Charlie Gaines in *Storyville* magazine, Shor quotes Gaines's recollections of working with Keppard in Charlie Taylor's Orchestra at the Danceland in downtown Philadelphia: "We all tried to sound like him but he was a stuck-up sort of guy and wouldn't show you anything."[15]

Sweatman was adamant that the fine trumpet on his 1924 Edison recording of "Battleship Kate" was Keppard, but aural comparison with Keppard's known work shows that this is patently not so (a full discussion of this session precedes the entry in the discography). It has also been suggested by Larry Gushee that Keppard's presence on Sweatman's 1920 Columbias cannot be entirely ruled out; to my ears, this is the work of a competent sight-reading musician, which Keppard was not. A far more likely candidate would be Charlie Gaines who, by the time of the recordings, was working in Atlantic City with Charlie Johnson's Orchestra.

Sweatman's popularity and high public profile at this time brought him useful contacts in the music publishing industry. One was Joe Davis, a white Jewish music publisher who ran the newly formed Triangle Music Publishing Company with partner George F. Briegel, a professional trombonist and arranger for the Pelham Navy Band. Joe Davis's influence loomed large over African American music for many years; he was a good friend to many black composers and performers, and arranged both publication of their material and record dates for them. Fats Waller, Andy Razaf, Spencer Williams, Rosa Henderson, Josie Miles, Viola McCoy, and a host of other female blues singers worked with and for Davis. His slight, balding figure was a familiar sight at smaller recording companies such as Gennett, Ajax, Emerson, and Edison. Sweatman placed his composition "That's Got 'Em" with Triangle (with lyrics subsequently supplied by Davis) and recorded a best-selling version for Columbia, giving Davis and Briegel's fledgling company both publicity and much-needed income. The sheet music for "That's Got 'Em" is notable for the cover illustration by legendary film cartoon animator Myron "Grim" Natwick, the creator of Betty Boop and later lead animator on Walt Disney's *Snow White and the Seven Dwarfs*. Natwick's cover features a grotesque, fat-lipped, top-hatted black male character dancing with a smartly dressed black woman, whose face is all but hidden by a large red hat with a peacock feather. Although racially offensive by today's standards, it was no different from the bulk of sheet music covers and theatrical posters of the period in its portrayal of black men.

Sweatman enhanced his relationship with Joe Davis and Triangle by recording George Briegel's own composition, "Slide, Kelly, Slide"—not surprisingly, given the connotations of the title, a trombone novelty specialty piece. Backed with white jazz band the Louisiana Five's recording of "I Ain't 'En Got 'En No Time to Have the Blues," "Slide, Kelly, Slide" provided Sweatman with one of his biggest-selling records, earning Davis and Briegel a considerable amount of money in royalties and sheet music sales. The success of "Slide, Kelly, Slide" did not go unnoticed in the theatrical trade press: "Wilbur Sweatman, the jazz artist, who records for Columbia, has made a wonderful success with his latest recording Slide, Kelly, Slide. It is a novelty trombone one-step, and is full of pep and everything that keeps the feet a-jazzin'. Triangle Music Publishing Co. has issued orchestrations of the number."[16]

Sweatman continued his professional relationship with Davis for their mutual benefit for several years but, after he formed his own publishing company in 1924, never again used Triangle to publish his compositions.

In mid-February 1919 Sweatman was in the middle of a hectic schedule—two recording sessions for Columbia and a full diary of theater dates—when he received news that his mother, Mattie, was dangerously ill. He canceled his appearance at Proctor's Theater in Newark, New Jersey on Friday, February 21, and caught the first available train to Kansas City, to be at his mother's side. Strangely, despite the urgency, he found time to stop in Chicago and visit the *Chicago Defender*'s offices, to meet Tony Langston, the *Defender*'s show business columnist.[17] Mattie Sweatman did not survive her illness, so after organizing the funeral arrangements and consoling his sisters, Sweatman returned to New York. By early March he had resumed his heavy vaudeville schedule over the Keith-Albee circuit, playing mainly East Coast states, with occasional forays into Pennsylvania and Ohio. Vaudeville engagements took up much of Sweatman's calendar for 1919 and the first half of 1920, but he had contractual commitments to Columbia to fulfill, so February and March of 1919 saw several visits to the Columbia studios for a busy month recording with an enlarged group.

The 1919 Sweatman recordings differ in many, often subtle, ways from the 1918 Columbias. The style and instrumentation of the 1918 sides are strongly influenced by the Original Dixieland Jazz Band and other small "dixieland" groups of the time, but with the addition of a bass player and with the heavily syncopated rhythmic phrasing of black musicians of the period. However, the 1919 Columbias draw from other inspirational sources: the influence of the large black "syncopated orchestras," such as those led by Ford Dabney, Tim Brymn, Jim Europe, and Will Marion Cook, is strongly in evidence. The reason for this is not difficult to surmise; the end of the World War I saw the return to the United States in early 1919 of Jim Europe, Tim Brymn, and other black regimental bandleaders, and with them were hundreds of what were, as a result of their army service, well-trained, disciplined black musicians, all looking for work. Europe, Brymn, and Cook all assembled colossal syncopated orchestras, capitalizing on the availability of schooled, disciplined musicians, and took their bands on nationwide (and in the case of Will Marion Cook, international) tours. Jazz and jazz-inspired music was only part of the repertoire of these overblown orchestras; "serious" music by African American composers was featured, along with spirituals and descriptive novelties. Members of these orchestras were also featured as vocalists, either as soloists or in groups, as well as solo spots by "comic" trap drummers and banjoists.

The sheer size of such orchestras (often forty-plus musicians) led to the need for tight arrangements, with few opportunities for embellishment or improvisation. These syncopated orchestras were enormously popular in the period immediately after WWI, and it stands to reason that Sweatman, ever watchful of musical trends, would incorporate these influences into his performances, at least on his recordings. As previously suggested, the influence of these large orchestras on Sweatman's own Columbia recordings may have been more direct than mere imitation, inasmuch as he employed trumpeter Arthur Briggs, trombonist Frank Withers, and almost certainly other members of Will Marion Cook's New York Syncopated Orchestra on some of his 1919 recordings.

The instrumentation on the 1919 Sweatman sides usually includes violin, sometimes saxophone, and, on one session, banjo and three mandolin-banjos. The performances themselves are more elaborately arranged, which tends to restrain the musicians' improvisational abilities but occasionally, as on Sweatman's own composition "That's Got 'Em" (Columbia A2721), they rise above the confines of the arrangement and play with real swing and abandon. From the same period came his recording of Euday L. Bowman's "Kansas City Blues," which was to be Sweatman's biggest-selling record. Like "Slide, Kelly, Slide" it was coupled with a Louisiana Five recording—the hit tune "The Alcoholic Blues" (the Volstead Act had already been passed and the country was preparing for the introduction of nationwide Prohibition in January 1920). The resultant recording of "Kansas City Blues" issued on Columbia A2768, sold like hotcakes—certainly the numbers of copies shipped from Columbia's Bridgeport pressing plant indicate that to be the case, as does the frequency of its discovery in junk shops even today. Over 180,000 copies were shipped to dealers nationwide, a substantial number for the period. No doubt the coupling with the Louisiana Five, who were then riding on a wave of popularity, and the public's liking of "The Alcoholic Blues" accounted for the impressive sales figures.

Sweatman's recordings of "Lucille" and "I'll Say She Does" from this period are of note for the presence of four banjo and mandolin-banjo players, a lineup more akin to the prewar Clef Club orchestras of James Reese Europe and which, due to their plectrum style and adherence to the melodic line, give these sides a somewhat archaic sound, quite unlike anything else Sweatman recorded.[18] One of the mandolin-banjoists on these sides, Arnold Joshuah Ford, was a fascinating character, prominent in Harlem musical, political, and religious circles in the first three decades of the century. A classically trained bassist and banjoist, Ford was politically active from the early 1900s when, seeing firsthand the difficulties black musicians faced when trying to join the American Federation of Labor's Musicians' Union, founded the New Amsterdam Musical Association. Catering exclusively to classically trained black musicians, the NAMA had an elitist attitude toward New York's many black musicians working in the fields of popular music in the various cabarets, nightclubs, and hotels, who were consequently attracted to Europe's rival Clef Club upon its formation in

1910. Ford was also a practicing Jew, became a rabbi, and founded the Beth B'Nai Abraham synagogue in Harlem, as well as being a prominent member of Marcus Garvey's Universal Negro Improvement Association in the early 1920s.[19]

The Columbia issue of Sweatman's recordings of "Lucille" and "I'll Say She Does" sold very well—over 135,000 copies—despite suffering from very obvious technical problems; the sound is thin and the battery of mandolin-banjos and banjos are so heavily recorded that the recording engineers must have torn their hair out trying to obtain a reasonable balance.[20] Columbia file cards for the session tell of the difficulties encountered—comments such as "poor tone," "do not use" and, most tellingly, "blasting banjos." Before full-scale production was started, test pressings of musically acceptable performances were pressed and subjected to intensive wear tests—continual playing using a steel needle for up to a hundred plays to ensure that the chosen performances would hold up to regular use without the grooves breaking down. However, the banjos are so over-recorded on these two sides that it is virtually impossible to find copies of this coupling that do not suffer from excessive blasting due to groove degradation.

We can glean an impression of Sweatman's vaudeville act of this time from a review of Sweatman's Jazz Trio, comprising clarinet, piano, and drums, when they appeared at the Harlem Opera House in early June 1919. His fourteen-minute act consisted of an opening number of a medley of gypsy tunes, followed by part of a Tchaikovsky symphony and a medley of jazz numbers, and concluded with his specialty of "The Rosary" played on three clarinets simultaneously. Two encores were requested by the audience and for one of them he played a medley of blues numbers, which the reviewer thought should be incorporated into the main act.[21]

For the week commencing November 3, 1919, Wilbur Sweatman and His Jazz Band appeared at the Fifth Avenue Theater in Boston and featured "Hot Coffee," a composition by Chicago-based pianist James "Slap" White. A review of the act in *Variety* states that the "jazz band" consisted of Sweatman and a pianist and goes on to state, in a rather telling manner, "His specialty seemed to be the same as ever with jazz instruments that he played long before jazz was jazz."[22] The implication of this statement seems to be that, to the reviewer's ears at least, Sweatman was playing the same sort of musical style that he had been employing for some years in his vaudeville act, and that this particular style, although now called jazz, was no different from what he had been serving up on vaudeville stages for years.

By late 1919 the style and personnel of Sweatman's Columbia recording band had changed again, reverting to a lineup of trumpet, trombone, clarinet, and rhythm, but with different musicians, creating, to my ears at least, a more melancholic sound. The identity of the trumpeter on these late Columbia sides—a much more florid and expressive player than William Hicks or Russell Smith—is something of a mystery. Several eminent authorities have suggested that it is the great New Orleans cornetist Freddie Keppard heard on these recordings.[23] While it is beyond doubt that Keppard did work for Sweatman that summer at the luxurious Brighton Beach Hotel at Coney Island, he did not appear on Sweatman's issued records. Keppard possessed a readily identifiable style and tone, and these distinctive attributes cannot be heard on any of Sweatman's issued records. A much more likely candidate is Philadelphia-born trumpeter Charlie Gaines, who was known to be associated with Sweatman around this time.[24] In the case of the pianist and drummer on Sweatman's Columbia records of this period, concrete evidence can be found in several contemporary press reports and advertisements. One example is a report in the *Chicago Defender* of March 20, 1920, under the headline "Stoppin' 'Em": "Wilbur Sweatman, the celebrated clarinetist, and his company of three, including Bobby Lee at the piano and Herbert King at the drums, is stopping all shows at the Majestic Theater, Chicago, Ill., this week. This act is the surest fire on the big time and works the year round."[25]

Philadelphia-born pianist Bobby Lee is something of a shadowy figure on the New York musical scene of the period. He is thought to have been a member of W. C. Handy's Memphis Blues Band in 1919 prior to joining Sweatman's vaudeville act. In 1922 he made a few incredibly rare records for the Chappelle & Stinnette record label, accompanying black vaudeville husband-and-wife singing team Thomas E. Chappelle and Juanita Stinnette. On the same label he made two sides featuring his own band, as Bobby Lee and His Music Landers, and one with the band accompanying singer-songwriter Clarence Williams. Later in the 1920s he led a band featuring trumpeter Adolphus "Doc" Cheatham and trombonist Juan Tizol, later to be an outstanding contributor to the sound of the Duke Ellington orchestra.

Sweatman, Lee, and King spent the first four months of 1920 on a tightly packed schedule of vaudeville work with full diary dates on the Keith-Albee circuit. Their itinerary started in Ohio in January, wheeled north to Chicago for two weeks, then dropped back to Ohio and Pennsylvania. Mid-March saw them return to the Majestic Theater in Chicago before crossing the border into Canada, where they played the Grand Opera House in London, Ontario. They made more appearances on either side of the Canadian border in early to mid-April, including Buffalo and Toronto, before heading back to New York via more engagements in Ohio and Pennsylvania, finishing with a plum engagement at the Palace Theater in New York for the week of April 17 and, by popular demand, again for the week of Saturday May 1.[26] Sweatman then took a well-earned rest from his hectic vaudeville schedule, but still found time to perform for CVBA benefits and Masonic lodge entertainments.

Lee apparently stayed with Sweatman until the summer of 1921, when he was reported to have been with W. C. Handy's Band.[27] Lee's replacement was Bill Hegamin, the husband of the vaudeville blues singer Lucille Hegamin. An advertisement in the *New York Age* of May 13, 1922, for the following week's presentation at Harlem's Lafayette Theater shows Sweatman, billed as "The Acme of Syncopation," topping the bill, and names his accompanists as Bill Hegamin and drummer Buddy Edwards. The identity of Buddy Edwards is something of a mystery, but it is thought to be John L. "Junk" Edwards, a comedian and drummer who worked with P. G. Lowery's company in 1913–14 and who was recalled by Garvin Bushell as being the father of his friend, also called "Junk" Edwards, and that he had worked as a drummer with Wilbur Sweatman.[28] Interestingly, lower down the bill at the Lafayette that week were Clarence Williams and Eva Taylor with Chappelle and Stinnette's act, and acting as musical director for "Harper and Blanks' Revue" was James P. Johnson.

Sweatman spent a goodly part of June 1920 in the Columbia studios, trying to get records made that Columbia would find acceptable for release. His busy vaudeville commitments earlier in the year had meant that he had fallen behind in his contractual commitments to Columbia, whereby he would have almost certainly been contracted to make twenty-four useable recordings. However, tastes were changing, and one suspects that, with the rapid developments in dance music away from out-and-out jazz bands to smoother-styled dance orchestras, Sweatman was fighting an already lost cause. In September of the previous year Columbia, amidst great publicity ballyhoo, had brought Art Hickman's Orchestra from San Francisco, in a private Pullman car, to their New York studios for a frenetic two weeks of recording, sufficient for a year of monthly releases. Such was their success that the Hickman band returned in May of the following year for a twenty-week engagement with the Ziegfeld Follies and more Columbia recording sessions. What made the Hickman band different was its smooth dance rhythms and the use of two saxophones in a dance band environment, something completely new to most listeners. Professor emeritus of philosophy, bandleader, and author Bruce Vermazen, who has studied the role and impact of the saxophone in early-twentieth-century syncopated music, outlined the reasons for Hickman's enormous success, both on record and in the Ziegfeld Follies:

New York in 1919 was primed to welcome the Hickman Orchestra for many reasons. One was that the jazz craze had gone on for a long time, and the dancing public was looking for something new. Another was racial politics. In his biography of James Reese Europe, Reid Badger has documented the dominance, in the mid-'teens, of African-American groups in New York's dance-band field, and the perception, on the part of white musicians, of a threat in the popularity of those groups. The proliferation of mostly white jazz bands, along with the temporary absence of many African-American musicians who were fighting in the European war, substantially changed the relative market shares of the two ethnic groups, but the jazz bands were still too wild, noisy, and sexy for many older and richer customers who tended to think of wildness, noise, and sexiness as more "colored" than "white." New York's affluent whites, as well as its white dance musicians, whether they knew it or not, had a psychological niche ready for the new music from California.[29]

Sweatman, whose adrenalin-fuelled Columbia recordings were the antithesis of everything Hickman and his band played, was suddenly passé, and Columbia did their best to both change the style of Sweatman's performances, at the same time making it as difficult as possible for Sweatman to turn in acceptable performances. Columbia's medley policy, of introducing one or more tunes into a performance, absent for most of Sweatman's 1919 recordings, was reintroduced with a vengeance; all but two of the seven titles recorded in June 1920 were medleys. On June 10 Sweatman recorded two titles, "In Gay Havana" (a "tango fox trot," according to the Columbia files) and Irving Berlin's little-known "But," the actual title of which was "But! She's a Little Bit Crazy About Her Husband." Although take 2 of "In Gay Havana" was originally designated "OK" by Columbia, it was never released—a great shame, as it would have been one of the earliest recorded examples of the fusion of jazz and Latin rhythms. "But" was found to be acceptable to Columbia's executives and two takes were released, although take 1 is extremely rare.

Sweatman and his band were back at the Columbia studios on June 15 to record three titles, and it appears from comments in the Columbia files that it was a day fraught with technical problems. Three takes of "Think of Me Little Daddy" were made and all were rejected. "Poor balance" was the reason given on the file cards and, although take 2 was originally considered for issue, it was ultimately rejected. "Sunbeams (Introducing "Rose of Bagdad [I Love You So])" and the interesting-sounding "Su Ez A" were similarly rejected on the same grounds of poor balance, even though one take of each was originally considered for issue. Sweatman's run of bad luck with Columbia continued a week later, when on June 22 he and his band paid another visit to the studios. Two more takes of "Think of Me Little Daddy" were made, both of which were issued, even though take 5 was originally designated "store." Copies of take 5 are extremely rare and one suspects that either it was used at a different pressing plant from Columbia's main plant at Bridgeport, or was substituted for a broken-down master. Three takes of "Never Let No One Man Worry Your Mind (Introducing 'I'm Gonna Jazz My Way Right Straight Thru' Paradise')" were waxed and, although take 3 was originally deemed acceptable for issue, it was again rejected at the last minute by Columbia executives.

Sweatman's final recording for Columbia was "Pee Gee Blues" or, more accurately, "Pee Gee's Blues," a fitting title for a tribute to his employer of nearly twenty years earlier, Perry George Lowery. "Pee Gee's Blues" was composed by cornetist H. Qualli Clark, who himself spent nearly ten years on Lowery's payroll. Sadly, the world was to be deprived of the chance to hear Sweatman's personal tribute to the great cornetist and bandleader; yet again Columbia's executives rejected all three takes, two of them being described as "edgy," whatever that might mean.[30]

In the summer of 1920 Sweatman's contract with Columbia expired and the option to renew was not taken up by the company. There are a number of reasons that could be put forward for this, all of which to some degree possibly contributed to Columbia's decision. First, and most obvious, is the possibility that Sweatman's record sales were falling. Certainly this is not borne out by either the Columbia figures of copies shipped to dealers or the ease of finding the later titles—they appear to be no rarer than the earlier ones. In fact, many of the 1918 sides turn up less frequently than the 1919–20 records. For instance, the figures for copies shipped to dealers of his last Columbia coupling show a healthy 97,300 copies shipped—more than the equivalent figures for his second and third Columbia releases back in 1918. What the shipping figures do show is that Sweatman's records apparently sold very quickly on release, then dropped off dramatically.

Second, jazz was getting bad press in 1920, due to its associations with loose morals and illicit nightclubs. The introduction of Prohibition in January 1920 coincided with a wave of moral righteousness in the press; jazz, with its associations of booze-fuelled nightclubs and parties, was a soft and highly visible target. A direct result of this was the rise in popularity of the smoother, less raucous style epitomized by the bands of Art Hickman, Paul Whiteman, Vincent Lopez, Isham Jones, and others, who did all they could to disassociate themselves from the more spontaneous and less "musically correct" playing of Sweatman, the ODJB, Earl Fuller, The Louisiana Five, and other early jazz bands. Whiteman and Hickman in particular did everything possible to distance themselves from both the word *jazz* and the music itself (despite both being billed as "The King of Jazz"), as dispensed by the numerous small jazz bands that proliferated in New York's cabarets and nightclubs. In a 1920 interview with the *San Francisco Examiner*, Hickman made plain his feelings about jazz and its practitioners in New York (the reference to a top-hatted clarinetist is an obvious snipe at Ted Lewis):

> People [in New York] thought who had not heard my band . . . that I was a jazz band leader. They expected me to stand before them with a shrieking clarinet and perhaps a plug hat askew on my head shaking like a negro with the ague. New York has been surfeited with jazz. Jazz died on the Pacific Coast six months ago. People began to realize that they were not dancing, that the true grace of Terpsichore was buried in the muck of sensuality. If I can make New Yorkers appreciate the true spirit of the dance I will be happy and I will be glad that I came to the Ziegfeld Roof.[31]

The primary element of this change of style was the introduction of the saxophone section to dance music, popularized by Art Hickman's Orchestra via its appearances in the Ziegfeld Follies and on its Columbia records. The instrument's inherently sweet tone was not suited to the free-for-all of a small jazz band, and it was some time before players such as Coleman Hawkins and Sidney Bechet revealed the hidden facets of its capabilities (although the now almost forgotten white Chicago saxophonist and bandleader Paul Biese was experimenting, both rhythmically and stylistically, with the tenor saxophone in the late teens and early twenties). The fact that larger bands were considered the way forward was to impact directly on Sweatman's subsequent career. From his Chicago days in the early 1910s through the early 1920s, Sweatman had generally worked his vaudeville act with just a pianist and drummer; this trio format was universally popular in dance halls, theaters, and silent movie houses. With the arrival in New York of the five-or-more-piece jazz bands in 1917–18 and, slightly later, the first large dance bands, many of whom (including such luminaries as Paul Whiteman, Vincent Lopez, and Art Hickman) played vaudeville theaters, musical acts such as Sweatman's had to move with the times. In 1919 his act was billed as Sweatman's Jazz Trio, but the reviewer for the *New York Clipper*, seeing the act at the Harlem Opera House in June 1919, clearly saw the way forward: "Sweatman would do well to get one or two more musicians and turn out a big time jazz act."[32]

The final reason for the end of Sweatman's career as a Columbia artiste was that in the autumn of 1919 Columbia secured the services of clarinetist Ted Lewis, then at the threshold of national success and at the start of his long career as a popular bandleader and entertainer. Although less than a year had elapsed since Lewis's departure from Earl Fuller's Famous Jazz Band, his career had advanced by leaps and bounds—he had already headlined at the Palace Theater, was starring in the Greenwich Village Follies and Ziegfeld's Midnight Frolic, and was appearing at his own nightclub. Here was a very marketable white musician and entertainer who not only had a ready-made public following, but could also blend the styles of both the jazz band and the dance band. Add to this his half-sung, half-spoken vocals and his considerable personality, and it was obvious to Columbia executives that here was a highly saleable product. His signing with Columbia in the fall of 1919 was the start of a fifteen-year relationship that saw Lewis become Columbia's biggest-selling and highest-paid artist, his records outselling those of both Al Jolson and Paul Whiteman.

It was stated earlier that Sweatman achieved his biggest record sales when his recording of "Kansas City Blues" was issued back-to-back with a recording by white jazz band the Louisiana Five. Whatever the boost given to Sweatman's Columbia sales figures by the white group pales when one considers the impact of the arrival of Ted Lewis on the scene. The number of copies shipped of the Sweatman/Louisiana Five coupling on Columbia A2768 was a more than respectable 180,358; Ted Lewis's first Columbia record, "Wond'ring," was also coupled with a recording by the Louisiana Five, and shipped a hefty 231,275 copies! The true reason for Sweatman's departure from Columbia was no doubt a combination of all of the above reasons. Sweatman was not a saxophonist, his recording group was not fashioned along the lines of the newer, smoother-sounding groups, nor could he sing as far as we know; thus he was not in a position to follow the prevailing tastes of musical fashion.

Ironically, Columbia were overly hasty in their desire to remove Sweatman and all other vestiges of jazz bands from their catalog. In August 1920 Mamie Smith, a black singer with extensive experience in tent shows and cabarets, recorded "Crazy Blues" for the fledgling OKeh record label. Unwittingly, OKeh, Mamie Smith, and her manager, Perry Bradford, tapped into the previously ignored but potentially huge market within the black community for records by black artists, and thus kick-started the "blues craze." Columbia were wrong-footed—a situation that took nearly three years to change, and one in which Columbia lost ground to newer, smaller, more aggressive rivals OKeh and Paramount. The irony, of course, is that it was the same Perry Bradford who, in 1919, had cajoled Sweatman to get a black female singer to record that very song (although it was called "Harlem Blues" at the time) with his band, an idea that Columbia executives had dismissed outright.

As a postscript to this period of Sweatman's recording career, it may be noted that, in an interview with Len Kunstadt, he recalled making some records for the Lyric label. Lyric was the label name for the Lyraphone Company of America, a minor New York–based recording company formed in 1917 and apparently working under tight budgetary constraints. Most of the artists they used were freelance performers who made the rounds of the other small record companies, such as the various bands under the direction of band contractor Harry A. Yerkes and a newcomer to the bandleading business, Ben Selvin. Other bands on Lyric included the exotic sounding Bal Tabarin Jazz Orchestra—in fact Harry Raderman's Jazz Orchestra, who were playing nightly at the Bal Tabarin cabaret—and, according to contemporary Lyric press advertisements, Handy's Memphis Blues Band. If, however, Handy did indeed record for Lyric, the resulting records were never released; the issue numbers quoted in trade magazine advertisements were subsequently used for other artists, including the Raderman group. Lyric ceased issuing records in May 1921 and their records are now quite scarce. It has proved impossible to locate any Lyric records by Sweatman, either as actual copies or as titles advertised in catalogs or trade journals, and it may well be that Sweatman recorded some test sides for Lyric but, due to his contractual obligations with Columbia, they were never issued.

"The Acme of Syncopation"—Wilbur Sweatman
playing three clarinets, ca. 1925. Author's collection.

P. G. Lowery's Band and Sideshow with
Forepaugh & Sells Brothers Circus, 1902.
Seated on stage center is Sallie N. Lee.
Orchestra, standing left to right: Wilbur
Sweatman, P. G. Lowery, Thomas May.
Seated, left to right: William May, rest
unidentified. Author's collection.

The Palace Museum, Minneapolis, 1896.
Sweatman led the orchestra here from
1903 to probably 1907. Photo by Rugg.
Courtesy Minnesota Historical Society.

The first edition cover of the sheet music of "Down Home Rag," Sweatman's best-known composition. Author's collection.

The Metropolitan Music Company, 41–43 South Sixth Street, Minneapolis, ca. 1907. Sweatman made his first recordings, on wax cylinders, for the company in about 1903–04. Courtesy Paul Merrill.

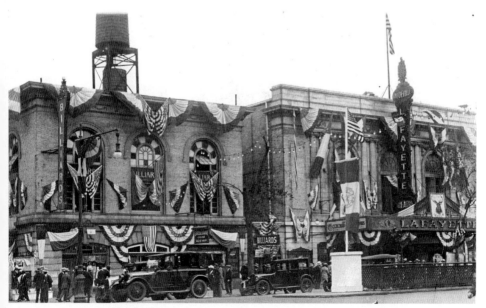

The Lafayette Theater in Harlem, decorated for a 1923 Elks Convention. Sweatman regularly appeared here from 1912 onward and in 1914 was leader of the theater's orchestra. The famous "Tree of Hope" can just be discerned on the extreme right. Courtesy Frank Driggs Collection.

Sheet music cover of Sweatman's "Boogie Rag," which he recorded both for Pathé and as a test recording for Victor in 1917. Author's collection.

Wilbur C. Sweatman's Original Jazz Band in the Columbia recording studio, May 28, 1918. Left to right: Wilbur Sweatman, William Hicks, Palmer Jones, Dan Parrish, Arthur Reeves, George Bowser. Author's collection.

Trumpeter Arthur Briggs, who, after making his first records with Sweatman in 1919, became an important pioneer of jazz in Europe. Author's collection.

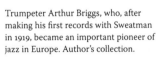

Sheet music cover for Sweatman's 1919 composition "That's Got 'Em" featuring artwork by celebrated cartoonist and animator Grim Natwick, creator of Betty Boop. Author's collection.

Sheet music cover for "Lonesome Road," which, despite being promoted as being recorded by Sweatman for Columbia, was only issued anonymously on the Little Wonder record label. Author's collection.

The Real Jazz Kings, Paris 1923, featuring Sweatman's longtime friend and associate, trumpeter Crickett Smith, along with other Sweatman associates trombonist Frank Withers and pianist Dan Parrish. Author's collection.

Wilbur Sweatman and His Acme Syncopators with singer Flo Dade on stage at the Lafayette Theater, Harlem, March 1923. Left to right: Maceo Jefferson, Ralph Escudero, Duke Ellington, Sweatman, Flo Dade, Sonny Greer, John Masefield, Otto Hardwick. Courtesy Steven Lasker.

Another photograph of Wilbur Sweatman and His Acme Syncopators taken on stage at the Lafayette Theater, Harlem, March 1923. Same personnel as previous but without Flo Dade. Note that Sweatman is playing a bass clarinet. Courtesy Frank Driggs Collection.

Cornetist Leslie Davis and trombonist Earl Granstaff, "Exponents of Ragtime," ca. 1916. Both were P. G. Lowery alumni; Davis is almost certainly the fine trumpeter heard on Sweatman's 1924 recordings. Author's collection.

Ramón Hernández (left) and Percy Green, both members of Sweatman's band in 1923 and 1924. Courtesy Frank Driggs Collection.

On stage at the Emery Theater, Providence, R.I., May 1926. Left to right: Harry Batcheldor, Wilbur Sweatman, Percy Arnold, Walter Hall. Courtesy Frank Driggs Collection.

Wilbur Sweatman and His Orchestra, 1929. Left to right, top row: Henry Doarch/Dortch, Emmanuel Cassamore, Edward "Wash" Washington, William "Cozy" Cole. Middle row: Charles "Bubia" Bowier/Bowyer, Eddie Gibbs, Revella Jentes, Teddy Bunn, Henry Green, Rudolph Toombs. Seated: Hazel Vanverlayer, Wilbur Sweatman, Ida Roberts. Front: Inez Seeley. Courtesy Frank Driggs Collection.

"Sweatman fired the devil out of me because I couldn't play nothin'—I had a beat but I couldn't read!" Cozy Cole, ca. 1940. Author's collection.

Wilbur Sweatman's Orchestra and Famous Sepia Entertainers, 1933. Probably taken aboard one of the Hudson River night boats that Sweatman worked on in 1932 and 1933—note the bulkhead step in the floor. Sweatman is seated on right wearing a white suit, others are unidentified. Author's collection.

Wilbur Sweatman at a privately produced recording session in 1950. Left to right: Bill Hegamin, Henry Turner, Wilbur Sweatman, Delphine Carmichael, Herman Bradley. Not shown is guitarist Eddie McLean. Author's collection.

A selection of Wilbur Sweatman records. Author's collection.

CHAPTER 10

THE RAGTIME DINOSAUR

BY THE EARLY 1920S it seemed that Sweatman's recording career was over. New bands, both black and white, were changing the whole approach to jazz. On one hand there were the "symphonic jazz" bands such as Paul Whiteman and Vincent Lopez dispensing a form of dance music that, to the casual dancer or record buyer of the time, was the epitome of modern jazz music, but to subsequent generations of collectors and critics plumb the very depths of banality. On the other hand, black musicians such as Johnny Dunn were riding the crest of the "blues craze" wave, which started with Mamie Smith's recording of "Crazy Blues" for OKeh in the autumn of 1920. Dunn arrived in New York around 1920 with Handy's Memphis Blues Band and made a name for himself with his "freak" trumpet style, making much use of various mutes. Dunn joined Mamie Smith's backing group, the Jazz Hounds, and appeared with her, both on record and her sellout tours, until she and manager Perry Bradford had a falling-out in the summer of 1921. Bradford approached Columbia, who were desperate to capitalize on the craze for records of blues singers, and offered them the services of singer Edith Wilson, Johnny Dunn, and most of the former members of Mamie Smith's Jazz Hounds, plus Bradford himself, as supplier of blues songs and talent scout.[1]

Sweatman, no doubt, eyed the competition with not a little degree of envy, and took steps to bring both himself and his act up to date and to appeal to a new, younger audience. In April 1922 the *New York Clipper* reported that "Wilbur Sweatman 'The Clarinet King' and his 15 piece orchestra, now playing the Keith Circuit have been signed to make a series of novelty records for Vocalion. Sweatman claims credit for having made the first so-called jazz records '10 years ago.'"[2]

The reference to making records for Vocalion (Aeolian Vocalion, to be accurate) is intriguing. While he was to make four sides that appeared on the Vocalion label in 1935 (by which time the label had gone through two changes of ownership), the possibility exists that he did make some records for the label when it was in the hands of the Aeolian Company, which, for whatever reason, were never issued. However, the Aeolian Vocalion recording ledgers for the period no longer exist, so it is impossible to verify whether he did make records for them or not, or whether this was simply a case of journalistic hyperbole.

Sweatman spent much of the 1920s vacillating between leading large bands with a full complement of featured singers and dancers and working with a backing trio or quartet. Despite his disappearance from the Columbia catalog, his popularity was apparently undiminished. He was extremely popular with fellow black musicians and performers, not least because of his wide experience in a business that, at that time, was not known for its benevolence to black musicians and performers. He was working as regularly as ever in vaudeville, as well as looking after his music publishing and band contracting interests from his office at 1547 Broadway. This, along with club and radio work with his own band, ensured a full diary. The various groups that Sweatman led in this period were frequently rostered with younger sidemen who subsequently went on to greater fame, most notably Duke Ellington and Coleman Hawkins. Other notable musicians who later achieved renown and who worked with Sweatman in the mid twenties included drummer Cozy Cole, pianist Claude Hopkins, trombonist Herb Flemming, and saxophonist Jimmie Lunceford, the latter working for him in 1926 during college vacations. With the rage for female blues singers at its height in the early 1920s after the phenomenal success of Mamie Smith's OKeh record of "Crazy Blues," Sweatman regularly featured female blues singers and dancers in his vaudeville and club work. These included Princess White, Zaidee Jackson (who made a successful career as a theater and cabaret performer in Britain in the late 1920s and 1930s), Ada "Bricktop" Smith (later a celebrated club owner and hostess in Paris), Tressie Mitchell, and Flo Dade. He even made a record with one of his singers, probably Hazel Vanverlayer, on his 1929 Grey Gull record of "Battleship Kate."

Sweatman's engagements in vaudeville kept him continually on the road, mainly on the Keith-Albee and Orpheum circuits, covering the East Coast, Chicago, and the Midwest, returning to his New York base at the end of a booking run. However, in February 1921, he had to cancel all his vaudeville engagements due to a throat ailment and influenza. It seems that either his illness was of a long duration, or that he was "punished" by the B. F. Keith office for his cancellations, as his act is not reported again in the press until the end of March, when he was appearing at the Lyric Theater in Fitchburg, Massachusetts. Sweatman once again had a full diary of vaudeville engagements through the summer and fall of 1921, but still managed to find time to appear at black theatrical fundraising events. On Thursday, July 28, 1921, he made an appearance at a benefit for the Dressing Room Club, an organization of "Colored Actors, Authors and Allied Professions," held at the Manhattan Casino, 158th Street and Eighth Avenue. Along with Sweatman, those who were going to "Ramble Around the Town in the Morning, Give a Hot Show in the Evening and Give a Dance All Night" included celebrated stage actor Charles Gilpin, composers and singers Henry Creamer and Turner Layton, Joe Simms and Charlie Warfield, and stride pianist James P. Johnson.[3]

As mentioned earlier, Sweatman's own band was usually comprised of pickup musicians, and among the bevy of unknown or unfamiliar names that graced the bandstand with Sweatman, every so often a well-known name appears. One such occasion was when Sweatman was working at the Lafayette Theater in Harlem for the week commencing Monday, March 5, 1923. Wilbur Sweatman and his Acme Syncopators were performing twice daily with a midnight show on Friday. Sunday saw a continuous performance of the featured acts, from 2:00 p.m. to 11:00 p.m. Sweatman realized the importance of diversification and keeping his stage act up to date, and for his 1923 season planned an altogether bigger and more varied act. Seeing the huge sales of blues records by female singers such as Lucille Hegamin, Edith Wilson, Sara Martin, and Mamie Smith, he brought into his stage act a blues singer by the name of Flo Dade.

Little is known about Flo Dade and her professional career. Aside from her 1923 appearances with Sweatman's band, references to her appearances are few and far between. In August 1922 she appeared at the Lafayette Theater in Harlem, as one half of the song and dance act Malinda and Dade, and in December 1922 she was a cast member of the touring "creole revue" *Follow Me*, which starred blackface comedian Billy Higgins. The revue played a one-night stand at the Sixth Street Theater in Coschocton, Ohio, on December 29, before opening in Pittsburgh on New Year's Day 1923. The show was enthusiastically reviewed in the local Coshocton newspaper, which noted that Flo Dade sang the current blues hit "He May Be Your Man." In the fall of 1928, Flo Dade was apparently working as a member of the regular company at one of the scenes of Sweatman's early triumphs, the Grand Theater in Chicago.[4] There she appeared in "tab" musicals presented by Joe Simms, such as *Harlem Flappers, Pullman Porters,* and *Dancing Days*; in the latter she was described in a review in the *Pittsburgh Courier* as "a fairly good soubret" [*sic*].[5] By this date the Grand's orchestra was led by the well-known pianist and composer Clarence M. Jones, and included in its ranks "novelty" clarinetist Vance Dixon.

In line with his new, expanded stage show, he enlarged his accompanists from the usual pianist and drummer to a six-piece jazz band, which included three musicians fresh to New York from Washington: saxophonist Otto Hardwick, drummer Sonny Greer, and a young pianist by the name of Duke Ellington. The *New York Age* reviewed the Lafayette's bill of that week:

> A real all-star vaudeville program is being presented at the Lafayette this week. The show is headed by Wilbur Sweatman and company with Flo Dade, and includes the following: A classy acrobatic act by two colored performers, Well(s) and Wells; Walters and Farrell, in some of the latest songs, "Husbands Three," an interesting revue with a cast of 20; "The Story Book," a well-acted revue; and Joyner and Foster, two well-known colored comedians, who kept the house laughing continuously throughout.[6]

It appears likely that Sweatman had first heard Sonny Greer, and possibly Ellington, while playing with his act at the Howard Theater in Washington, where Greer worked as a drummer with Marie Lucas's resident orchestra. Certainly he appeared regularly at the Howard, Washington's foremost African American entertainment venue, which had opened in 1910 in the predominantly black neighborhood close to Howard University. By 1922 the Howard had been leased from the white-owned National Amusement Company by black theatrical performer and entrepreneur, Sherman H. Dudley, who transformed it into one of the country's leading theaters catering to African American audiences. Many of the twentieth century's greatest black performers graced the Howard's stage, and it is fitting that the Howard is to be restored to its former glory as a working theater.

According to Ellington, Sweatman initially wanted only Greer for his band to replace his existing drummer but, after some persuasion on Greer's part, took Hardwick and the Duke as well. Ellington, with family and band-business commitments in Washington, got cold feet and initially turned down the opportunity to go to New York with Sweatman. According to Greer, he and Hardwick would write the Duke weekly, telling him of the great time they were having and begging him to reconsider his decision.

In early March he did join Sweatman, his first engagement with the band being the week commencing March 5 at the Lafayette in Harlem.

The Washington trio's time with Sweatman was not particularly happy. Ellington recalled that it was spent mainly in vaudeville, working the dreaded split weeks—half a week in one location, then having to pack bags and instruments and move to another venue, often in another town, for the rest of the week. Otto Hardwick recalled that "we rehearsed for a while and rehearsed some more—but nothing much really happened."[7]

Sonny Greer recalled the time with Sweatman as "horrible" and remembered one particular engagement on Staten Island as "a weekend of grief."[8] Greer also was horrified by Sweatman's insistence that they use makeup to lighten their faces.[9] Despite the racist connotations this implies, it was almost certainly the first time that Greer and Ellington had worked on a theater stage, and they were unused to theatrical makeup, which is essential in the glare of stage lights. All along—and unbeknownst to Sweatman—the main reason for the Washington trio joining Sweatman was that it afforded them the opportunity to savor the Harlem nightlife and, in particular, to hear the many bands and pianists at work after they finished their theater work with Sweatman. When the time came for Sweatman to carry on his pre-booked engagements on the Keith-Albee circuit, which would take him and his band out of town for several weeks, Ellington, Greer, and Hardwick gave their notices to quit. Their tenure with Sweatman is difficult to ascertain with any degree of certainty, but it was probably longer than Greer, in particular, liked to intimate to later interviewers. As Greer recalled: "he had an engagement in Chicago or somewhere, but we wouldn't go. Said no, we ain't leaving New York, so he got somebody else."[10] However, a report in the *Chicago Defender* notes that Sweatman "with his assisting Syncopators" was appearing at the Grand Theater in Philadelphia for the week commencing April 28, 1923, and, while the identity of the Syncopators is not revealed, it seems likely that the Washington trio were still with the band at that stage.[11] They stayed in Harlem for a few more weeks, Greer and Ellington rooming with one of Greer's aunts and Hardwick rooming with one of his own aunts a few doors away. After a few weeks of hustling for work without much success, Ellington allegedly found an envelope on the street containing fifteen dollars, enough to pay the trio's train fare back to their homes in Washington—at least for the time being.

Ellington's short stint with Sweatman has been unfairly misrepresented over the years in a variety of books, and should be put into context. Sweatman was an established, middle-aged black musician with a long and honorable career behind him, who had been in the public eye, in one form or another, since before the turn of the century. Due to changing musical tastes, he was finding himself being swept aside by younger, more technically skilled musicians, but still needed to earn money. His workplace for the previous thirteen years had been in vaudeville theaters, and it would be fair to say that in that time he had learned what his vaudeville audiences wanted, and was unwilling to experiment too much with what had developed into a sharply honed act. Mindful of the need to keep his act up to date and to reflect the contemporary public tastes, he engaged blues singer Flo Dade and the trio of young Washington-based musicians on the strength of Sonny Greer's reputation as a drummer and entertainer. Ellington, in particular, was unused to the rigid regime of vaudeville work, but it was an experience that was to serve him well in the ensuing years. In his autobiography, *Music Is My Mistress*, he gives appropriate credit to Sweatman (while also intimating that that they played further afield than merely Greater New York, as has often been suggested):

> Then Sonny Greer came up with the opportunity to work for Wilbur Sweatman, who was playing three clarinets at once in a vaudeville show. He had been making records for a long time, and I think he was famous for "The Barnyard Blues." We joined him in New York and played some split weeks in theaters. It was another world to us, and we'd sit on the stage and keep a straight face. I began to realize that all cities had different personalities, which were modified by the people you met in them. I also learned a lot about show business from Sweatman. He was a good musician, and he was in vaudeville because that's where the money was then, but I think things were beginning to cool off for him, and soon we were not doing so well.[12]

Ellington may well have already been known to Sweatman. Greer alleged that he, Ellington, Hardwick, trumpeter Arthur Whetsol, and banjoist Elmer Snowden visited New York in March 1921, two years prior to their documented visit, and they may have come to Sweatman's attention at that time. Ellington's involvement with Sweatman may not have finished in the spring of 1923 either, and his disputed appearance on at least one of the 1924 Sweatman record sessions is discussed at length later.

Another newcomer who joined Sweatman's band at the same time as Ellington, Greer, and Hardwick was another Washington-based musician, tuba player Rafael (Ralph) Escudero (1898–1970), best known for his long tenure with Fletcher Henderson's Orchestra and later with McKinney's Cotton Pickers. Puerto Rico–born Escudero had been playing with Marie

Lucas's orchestra at the Howard Theater where, like Sonny Greer, he was spotted by Sweatman, who offered him work with his band. Escudero, although resident in Washington since at least 1920, had previously worked in New York from as early as 1912. Given the frequently casual personnel of black bands in New York at that time, not to mention Escudero's prowess as a double bass and tuba player, he would probably have already been known to Sweatman.[13]

Although his appearances on record were becoming less frequent, Sweatman was still a big enough name to be called in to supply the music with his Acme Syncopators for the opening of Connie's Inn, the well-known Harlem cabaret, in July 1923. Located in the basement of the Lafayette Hall Building at 2221 Seventh Avenue, at the corner of 131st Street, Connie's Inn was to gain a reputation for African American entertainment second only to the Cotton Club. However, its opening was not applauded unanimously by Harlem's black community. Owners Connie and George Immerman (actually Connie Bamberger, brother-in-law of Louis Immerman, a well-known Harlem bootlegger) had previously run the venue as a delicatessen, for a while employing the young Thomas "Fats" Waller as the delivery boy. From November 1921 it was run as a speakeasy and nightclub, The Shuffle Inn, its name trading on the success of the Sissle and Blake musical *Shuffle Along*, which had opened a few months earlier and was playing to packed houses on Broadway. The featured entertainer there was pioneer blues recording artist Lucille Hegamin (1894–1970), at twenty-six already a veteran of the entertainment business. The Shuffle Inn was closed down the following year for selling liquor in violation of the Volstead Act.

When it became known that the Immermans and Bamberger were reopening the club, there was an outcry in Harlem's black press. The *New York Age*'s editor, Fred Moore, personally conducted a crusade against white (and by inference, Jewish) bootleggers tainting the streets of Harlem, naming Immerman and Bamberger as chief culprits. In part this outcry was a genuine show of concern by middle-class African Americans over the infiltration of Harlem by white mobsters. But on a more symbolic level, the fact that Connie's Inn, white-owned and with a whites-only admission policy, shared the building with the Lafayette Theater, home of black theater in New York, and itself the target of a successful anti-segregation campaign in 1913, was enough to incense Harlemites.

Despite the furor in the press, the venue opened as Connie's Inn on the evening of July 21, 1923, and Wilbur Sweatman and His Acme Syncopators supplied the music, both for the floor show and for dancing. With an audience capacity of 500, sumptuous decor and a show cast of thirty-one singers and dancers, Connie's Inn was like no other club or cabaret then operating in Harlem. From opening night it actively sought to attract white, well-heeled, downtown revellers through its doors for an evening of exotic "slumming." The cabaret was under the direction of Leonard Harper, a veteran of Harlem cabaret and revue production, who also danced in the show, along with his wife Osceola Blanks.[14] Harper needed a daytime rehearsal pianist to accompany the singers and dancers prior to the opening night, and found the ideal candidate working at Harlem celebrity and club owner Barron Wilkins's nightclub, Club Barron—none other than Duke Ellington![15] Another of Harper's Club Barron finds was singer and dancer Ada "Bricktop" Smith (1894–1984), who later became a legendary nightclub owner in Paris and the friend of such notable personalities of the age as the Prince of Wales, Cole Porter, and F. Scott Fitzgerald. Bricktop recalled that she did not join the cast immediately:

> Connie's Inn had been open for about a month when Connie sent word that he wanted me to work for him. He was putting all his dreams into practice and had Wilbur Sweatman's Rhythm Kings and Leonard Harper to stage the shows. Now he needed a soubrette and I fitted the bill.
> . . . I made quite a debut at Connie's Inn. I came out in a flower number with all the girls as flowers. I danced in at the end as a red rose. I held the petals over my head so you couldn't see my face. I wore little short pants.[16]

Included in Sweatman's Connie's Inn band was Lucius Eugene "Bud" Aiken, doubling cornet and trombone, Wellman Braud (who had worked in England earlier in 1923 with Leonard Harper's *Plantation Days* revue) on string bass and, for a while at least, the legendary tenor saxophonist Coleman Hawkins. Hawkins had recently settled in New York after nearly two years on the road touring from coast to coast with Mamie Smith and her Jazz Hounds. During this time he had made several records in New York with the Jazz Hounds for the General Phonograph Company's OKeh label, both instrumental and as backing accompaniment to Mamie's singing. Hawkins had joined Mamie Smith's Jazz Hounds in Kansas City in the summer of 1921; however, he got tired of touring and left Mamie Smith's troupe while they were playing at the Garden of Joy in Harlem. For a while he gigged around New York and, by July 1923, was working with Sweatman's band at Connie's Inn. It was here, in August 1923, that Hawkins was spotted by Fletcher Henderson (according to a 1936 interview with Henderson), who invited him to join the pickup band he had assembled for lucrative recording work. The rest, as they say, is history. The paths of Sweatman, Henderson, and Hawkins were to cross again at the end of 1924 when, on December 7th, both the Sweatman and Henderson bands were among those featured at the Renaissance Casino for "Bud Allen's Affair," a dance held by composer and publisher Bud Allen.

On completion of the Connie's Inn engagement in early September 1923 Sweatman's group was replaced by Leroy Smith (billed as "The Colored Paul Whiteman") and his Orchestra from Philadelphia, a position he and his band were to hold until February 1926. Sweatman took his band and a girl dancer, probably Ada "Bricktop" Smith, on a tour of the Keith-Albee vaudeville circuit organised by the Pat Casey booking office, commencing September 10, 1923.[17] The *Baltimore Afro-American* reported the band's tour and even gave a personnel for the musicians but, unfortunately, failed to identify the dancer:

> Wilbur Sweatman, the clarinet specialist and conductor who has for some weeks been a feature with his band at the New Connie's Inn in Harlem, is again in Vaudeville. Tim O'Donnell of the Pat Casey office has booked him with ten musicians and a single dancer for the coming season. The act opened on Sept 10. Besides Sweatman there is Leslie Davis, cornet; Aikens [*sic*], with cornet and trombone [presumably Bud Aiken, who played both instruments], Ramon Hernandoz [*sic*, Ramón Hernández], saxophone [*sic*], Percy Green, saxo [*sic*], Cal Jones, trombone, Edwin A. Stevens, piano, Joy Reed, drums, Wilms Broad [*sic*, Wellman Braud], string bass, Romeo Jones, brass bass, doubling other instruments.[18]

Of the personnel quoted in the *Afro-American*, bassist Wellman Braud (1891–1966) is the best-known, mainly for his eight years starting in 1927 with Duke Ellington's Orchestra. Trumpeter/trombonist Lucius Eugene "Bud" Aiken (1897–1927) was, along with his younger brother Gus, an alumnus of the celebrated Jenkins Orphanage Band of Charleston, South Carolina. The Aiken brothers had toured with the band nationally and had even visited England in 1913. Pianist Edwin Stevens had been a member of Charles Elgar's Orchestra in Chicago before coming to New York, where he mainly worked in the music publishing business. Trombonist Calvin Jones had been a fixture on the black New York scene for many years, working with the likes of James Reese Europe, Ford Dabney, and in Eubie Blake's pit orchestra for the hit show of 1921–23, *Shuffle Along*.

One name from the *Afro-American*'s roster deserves greater recognition than that hitherto afforded him: trumpeter Leslie Davis. Like Sweatman, Davis had been a member of P. G. Lowery's sideshow band; in 1915 he and fellow Lowery musician, trombonist Earl Granstaff, teamed up to form a vaudeville act. Their act, which included singing and dancing, also included instrumental jazz and blues numbers, and they would have undoubtedly gone on to even greater fame had not the World War I intervened. Granstaff was drafted and sent to France, where he played trombone with the 807th Pioneer Infantry Band under the direction of bandmaster Will Vodery.[19] Davis is a very likely candidate for the fine trumpet playing on the 1924 Sweatman Gennett and Edison titles, records that frequently have been ascribed to legendary New Orleans cornetist Freddie Keppard.

By January 1924 Sweatman had temporarily quit vaudeville work and was back in New York, working at the newly opened Amber Grill, a whites-only restaurant and cabaret. Under the headline "Sweat Busy," the *Chicago Defender* reported it thus: "Wilbur C. Sweatman, King of Clarinetists, with his Acme Syncopators and five star entertainers, is doing his stuff at the Amber Grill, the newest, biggest and best of all the Ofay cabarets in N.Y.[20] Unfortunately the *Defender*'s report sheds little light on either the venue or the identities of the band and the troupe of dancers. Despite diligent research, I have not been able to come up with any other references to the Amber Grill in New York—daily newspapers, theatrical journals, and city directories are totally devoid of reference to any such venue, and one may have to consider whether this was a piece of theatrical hyperbole. Or it may have been a short-lived venue that closed soon after opening.

Considerably more evidence survives for Sweatman's next engagement. The *New York Telegram and Evening Mail* for March 1, 1924, carried an advertisement for Yates' Restaurant at 147–151 West 43rd Street—"Ten Steps from Broadway"—for the appearance of "Wilbur Sweatman, King of Jazz, Assisted by Ed Lee's Rainbow Orchestra." This eatery, just off Times Square in the heart of New York's theaterland, had apparently booked Sweatman to appear with another band, possibly their regular house band, to entertain diners. They continued to promote Sweatman's appearance there until May 17, 1924, when all references to Sweatman cease. During the Yates engagement Sweatman made his first known broadcast; an item in the *Baltimore Afro-American* noted that he broadcast over WHN on April 26, 1924, from 8:30 to 9:00 p.m.[21] Sweatman made several broadcasts with his band in 1924, another being made over station WFBH on October 1, 1924, at midday and again on October 8 and 29, both at midday. WHN and WFBH were both pioneering New York–based radio stations: WHN first went on air on March 18, 1922, WFBH on July 15, 1924. WHN in particular had a reputation for broadcasting local jazz bands, including several black bands, among them the bands of Fletcher Henderson, Duke Ellington, and Wilbur Sweatman.

The spring of 1924 also saw Sweatman setting up the Wilbur Sweatman Music Publishing Company, taking an office in room 608 of the Gaiety (sometimes spelled Gayety) Theatre building, located at 1545-7 Broadway, near 46th Street, the ground floor of which housed the well-known theater of the same name. Built in 1908 by theater magnates Marcus Klaw and Abe Erlanger, it was never a successful theater despite its central location, and in 1926 became a movie house. In the mid-1930s it became part of the Minsky's burlesque chain before returning to cinema use as the Victoria. The building's key claim to fame was that throughout the 1920s and 1930s it was home to the offices of some of the best-known figures in the world of black music and music publishing. It was demolished in 1980, along with five other theaters, to make way for the Marriott Marquis Hotel.

Sharing the address in 1924 was an impressive array of black songwriters, composers, arrangers, publishers, and bookers, including Clarence Williams, Perry Bradford, Will Vodery, Charles A. Matson, and H. Qualli Clark.[22] The Gaiety offices were a familiar location for songwriters, bandleaders, musicians, singers, record company A & R men, talent scouts, and theatrical agents, who would drop in for the latest songs, order new "patter" material to personalize a song, book bands for gigs and recording sessions, or just catch up on the latest news and gossip. Perry Bradford gives a vivid description of life in the Gaiety Building: "Any time musical shows were casting, they would phone to ask: Send me an act, or an individual for this or that part. The Keith, Loew's and Pat Casey agencies always knew where to fill disappointments or club dates, for all the colored actors made my office their downtown hangout."[23]

Besides song publishing, Sweatman was actively involved in booking both his and other bands, black and white, for engagements of all sorts—private parties, weddings, social engagements, theater and dance hall work, and recording sessions. After years of itinerant touring, living in rooming houses, boarding with black families in strange and unfamiliar towns, and constantly moving from engagement to engagement on a weekly basis, settling down to a desk-bound job must have been a shock to Sweatman's system. Although a member of many black music and theatrical clubs and associations, not to mention Masonic interests and his prestigious membership in the American Society of Composers, Authors, and Publishers alongside Irving Berlin, John Philip Sousa, and George Gershwin, Sweatman was a deeply private man who rarely mixed socially with his peers. Years of dealings with unscrupulous theater managers, duplicitous agents, and more than his share of racial prejudice had hardened his exterior appearance and manner, causing him to present himself, especially to whites, as gruff, unemotional, and plain-speaking. Office life at least gave him the chance to mix with other business-minded black musicians and songwriters, such as Clarence Williams and pianist and booking agent Charles Matson, the former in particular carving a distinguished niche for himself in the white man's world of the recording and music publishing industries.

During the summer of 1924 Sweatman and his band played at a number of popular summer resorts in upstate New York, including residencies at the Colony Inn on the Schenectady road and at summer resorts in the Finger Lakes. Sweatman's replacement at the Colony Inn was another reedman just starting out as a bandleader—Fess Williams.[24] The *Syracuse Herald* noted that "A Novel attraction at the dancing pavilion at Lakeside Park at the foot of Owasco Lake the first three days of last week [July 7–9] was Wilbur Sweatman's Original Colony Inn Band of New York City, in addition to the regular orchestra. Neil Golden, tenor soloist, accompanied the metropolitan players as a specialty."[25] Lakeside Park was a summer amusement resort, with a roller coaster, water chute, merry-go-rounds, and a beautiful dance pavilion—which still stands. In the summer months dances were held in the pavilion every evening, with afternoon dances on Saturday. Many big-name bands played in its heyday in the twenties and thirties.

The figure of music publisher Joe Davis entered Sweatman's life again in the fall of 1924. Davis, forever cajoling record company executives to record Triangle numbers to the extent of providing artists and accompanists (a ploy used with great success by black music publishers Clarence Williams and Perry Bradford), had persuaded the normally conservative Edison company to try and tap into the potentially huge market of black record buyers. Apparently the Edison company failed to consider, or chose to ignore, the fact that their records were made using the "hill and dale" vertical-cut recording groove and therefore unplayable on standard (and much cheaper) gramophones that could only play laterally cut records—the type most black record buyers possessed. Davis organised sessions for blues singers Rosa Henderson, Helen Gross, Ethel Finnie and her husband/accompanist Porter Grainger, Viola McCoy, Josie Miles, Andy Razaf (whose test records were unissued), and almost certainly had a hand in organising Sweatman's Edison recording session, as well as the two sessions for the

Starr Piano Company's Gennett label—all this despite the fact that none of the tunes recorded were published by Triangle.[26]

The first known recording session by Sweatman since his departure from Columbia in 1920 took place at the Gennett studio at 9-11 East 37th Street in New York on August 12, 1924, when two titles were recorded. The first was his own composition and publication, "Battleship Kate," with lyrics by white theater and cinema organist and pianist Ada Rives.[27] This tune was a regular in Sweatman's repertoire on stage and on record for many years, and he recorded versions in 1924, 1929, 1930, and 1935. However, neither this particular version nor its session mate, the popular tune "She Loves Me," found favor with the Gennett executives, and both were rejected for issue. Just over a month later he and the band were back for another attempt at the same two tunes and, although "She Loves Me" was again rejected, the second take recorded of "Battleship Kate" was approved for issue and released on Gennett 5584 in December 1924.

On October 10, 1924, Wilbur Sweatman's Brownies, courtesy of Joe Davis's efforts, found themselves in Edison's Fifth Avenue recording studios. Two titles were recorded that day but inexplicably only one, "Battleship Kate," was issued. According to files that survive at the Edison National Historic Site at West Orange, New Jersey, Sweatman was paid $125, the company's standard rate for one acceptable recording. Test pressings also survive of all three takes of the other title recorded that day, Edgar Dowell's composition "It Makes No Difference Now." By this time most record companies had standardized on issuing just one approved take, but Edison—at least from late 1920 to its demise in October 1929—had, for technical reasons, routinely issued three takes of most recorded titles, take C generally being the first choice (which leads one to suspect that the take designations on Edison recordings do not necessarily follow the actual sequence of recording). Sweatman's solitary Edison issue appears as three takes, which allows comparison between the performances. All three takes are very similar, as might be expected, considering that it is a tight arrangement and that Thomas Edison had a personal distaste for jazz (he is purported to have said, "I play jazz records backwards—they sound better that way"). However, within the confines of the arrangement there are opportunities for variations, especially the fine trumpet solos and Sweatman's bass clarinet solos, clarinet breaks, and the ensemble playing.

As might be expected, sales of most of the Edison output by the blues singers and black jazz bands brought to the company by Joe Davis were abysmal, due to the target audience's inability to reproduce them. The Sweatman recording of "Battleship Kate" fared somewhat better, his name being well known to white record buyers through his years in vaudeville. Sales were also helped in no small part by its coupling with a recording by the Georgia Melodians, a white jazz group that had built up a popular following via their regular Edison Diamond Disc releases and a residency at the popular Cinderella Ballroom in New York, from where they also broadcast. Issued on Edison Record 51438 in November 1924, "Battleship Kate" sold reasonably well before being withdrawn from catalog in May 1926.

Controversy on two counts surrounds Sweatman's 1924 sessions. There are persistent rumors that Freddie Keppard is present on the Gennett and Edison sessions, and that Duke Ellington also played on these sides. Sweatman himself was adamant regarding Keppard's presence on these sessions and equally emphatic in his denial of Ellington having ever recorded with him. Keppard certainly did work for Sweatman at the Brighton Beach Hotel at Coney Island in 1919, but he is most definitely not on any of the Columbia recordings made at that time. By 1924 Keppard was a regular sideman with Charles L. "Doc" Cooke's Dreamland Orchestra in Chicago, which makes his appearance with Sweatman unlikely to say the least. However, the strongest evidence for his not being on these sessions is the records themselves; the trumpet solos simply are not in Keppard's style, either tonally or stylistically. The most likely candidates are either the enigmatic Leslie Davis or Eugene "Bud" Aiken (the latter best known as a trombonist but who also doubled on trumpet), both of whom are thought to have been working with Sweatman at about this time. This is backed up by the personnel shown in the discography for the Edison session which (with minor amendments) appeared in the *Pittsburgh Courier* of September 15, 1923.

The rumors concerning Ellington's presence on some of Sweatman's records have circulated for years. Ellington had already been associated with Sweatman and in fact he, along with Otto Hardwick, Sonny Greer, trombonist John Anderson, banjoist Maceo Jefferson, and bassist Ralph Escudero worked for an undetermined period in the spring of 1923 as Sweatman's supporting group in vaudeville, including a weeklong engagement at the Lafayette Theater in Harlem March 5–11. Ellington's connection with Sweatman at an even earlier date is hinted at by banjoist Ike Hatch, who in an interview in a British magazine recalled "I particularly remember Wilbur Sweatman, for I used to work in his Sunday concerts at the Eltinge Theater. Dan Paris [*sic*] was on piano and organ then; Ellington took his place a little later."[28] Sweatman was a band contractor, so it is not beyond the realm of possibility that Ellington obtained some bookings through Sweatman's offices and was occasionally drafted into Sweatman's own bands prior to the March 1923 engagement. Conversely, Hatch could have been generalizing and simply referring to the fact that Ellington worked with Sweatman after the period Hatch was working with him. It can be categorically stated that there is no evidence whatsoever of Ellington being present on any of the Columbia records. The possibility of Ellington working for and even recording with Sweatman in the summer of 1924, however, cannot be discounted, as his activities (some of the best-documented of any jazz musician of any period) from mid-July to early September 1924 are completely untraced. Despite the dozens of books and the volume of research conducted on Ellington and his career, virtually nothing is known of his activity at this time.[29]

Ellington had been working as pianist in Elmer Snowden's band, the Washingtonians, and they had been employed as the house band at the Hollywood Café (sometimes referred to in contemporary press reports as the Hollywood Restaurant or Hollywood Cabaret) at 203 West 49th Street, near Broadway, since September 1, 1923. As well as providing dance music, they accompanied the cabaret, produced by Leonard Harper, which attracted complimentary reviews in the theatrical press and New York newspapers. On January 30, 1924, Federal agents made an incognito visit to the club where they were served alcohol. A subsequent raid by Federal agents on February 24th confirmed that alcohol was being served. At about the same time Elmer Snowden was ousted from his position as leader of the Washingtonians and Ellington assumed leadership. A fire (a regular occurrence at the Hollywood Café) on April 4 closed the club for a month, during which period the Washingtonians made a short tour of New England. The Hollywood reopened on May 1, but with James P. Johnson's band providing the music.

Ellington's movements, along with those of the Washingtonians, are untraced from the end of April to June 10, when they reopened at the Hollywood, replacing Johnson's band. References in the New York press to the Hollywood cease between July 13 and September 6, when the Hollywood's new show, *Creole Follies Revue*, opened with Ellington and the Washingtonians furnishing the music. Ellington and the Washingtonians are thought to have secured a short engagement in Salem Willows, Massachusetts, but nothing definite is known of either Ellington or the band's activities in this period. Considering that Ellington had already worked for Sweatman and that he knew that Sweatman was working as a band contractor, it is not inconceivable that he approached Sweatman for work, or vice versa.

The strongest evidence for Ellington's presence with Sweatman on record comes from an article by Rainer Lotz on the white banjoist Mike Danzi, which appeared in *Storyville* magazine and a subsequent book, *Michael*

Danzi: American Musician in Germany, 1924–1939, based on his interviews with the veteran banjoist.[30] The magazine article states that "Danzi met Wilbur Sweatman who was then also a booking agent booking both white and coloured bands. Sweatman heard Danzi and asked him to do some night club dates with him and also a recording date on which they did 'Battleship Kate.' Danzi was the only white musician on this date and does not remember the names of any of the other musicians except the pianist—Duke Ellington."[31] Danzi's autobiography adds further detail: "During the summer of 1924 . . . I did a recording date with Wilbur Sweatman, the famous clarinetist from California. We recorded 'Battleship Kate,' and our pianist was Duke Ellington. The recording session was from ten until one."[32]

In his conversations with Rainer Lotz, Danzi, apparently recalled the session in detail, stating "If you hear a banjo break on the 16th and 17th bar alone, then that is the record I played on."[33] Unfortunately for jazz history, the issued Gennett version of "Battleship Kate" does not have any banjo breaks. however, that does not rule out Danzi and Ellington's presence on the Gennett session of August 12, the results of which were unissued. According to Rainer Lotz, Danzi worked sporadically with Sweatman from June to September 1924, the final date being a wedding gig in the Bronx on November 11, 1924, immediately prior to Danzi sailing for Germany with Alex Hyde's Orchestra.

Another possible candidate for the pianist with Sweatman's band at this time is Claude Hopkins (1903–1984), who in the thirties and forties led a highly individual-sounding band of great promise that never achieved the success or acclaim of Duke Ellington's or Count Basie's orchestras. A child prodigy and a thoroughly schooled musician, Hopkins gained a degree in music from Howard University in Washington, where both his parents were on the faculty. He subsequently studied for a year at Washington Conservatory before forming his own band in 1924 for a summer engagement at Atlantic City, after which he joined Wilbur Sweatman's Orchestra. Just how long the Atlantic City engagement lasted is uncertain, but it may just be possible that Hopkins was with Sweatman for at least some of the recording sessions in the fall of 1924.

The lure of vaudeville took hold of Sweatman once again and, after being quoted in the black press to the effect that he was determined to re-enter vaudeville with a band, he embarked in March 1925 on an extensive vaudeville tour on the Keith-Albee and Orpheum circuits, both in the United States and Canada. It was a gruelling schedule that would keep Sweatman, now in his mid-forties, on the road for the best part of three years.[34] Working with Sweatman was an accompanying quartet including pianist Claude Hopkins and a talented blues singer and dancer, Zaidee Jackson.[35]

Hopkins left Sweatman in the fall of 1925 to sail to France with an all-black show that was to make history. White socialite Caroline Dudley had long appreciated and admired black stage performers and, when her diplomat husband was posted to the American embassy in 1925, she thought it a great idea to put together an all-black cast musical show to take to Paris, too. Contracts had been drawn up, but no female star found; a chance visit to New York's Plantation Club brought to her attention a young comedienne and dancer on the end of the chorus line—Josephine Baker. The *La Revue Negre* company, with a band led by Claude Hopkins and that included Sidney Bechet and trombonist Earl Granstaff, sailed on September 15, 1925, aboard the S.S. *Berengaria* for France and the history books.

Hopkins's replacement with Sweatman's band was pianist Walter Hall, about whom little is known. The following week Sweatman and his band were in Canada, playing at the Imperial Theatre, Montreal.[36] A revue of Sweatman's act in the *Chicago Defender* in November 1925 provides insight into the jazz and blues–oriented nature of the act and, unusually, identifies the personnel.

> Wilbur Sweatman, a former Chicago boy has a hot five-piece band combination, with Miss Zadie Jackson [*sic*], a singing and dancing soubrette out in the front. They are working the Keith Houses with unusual success. The personnel is as follows: Wilbur Sweatman, clarinets, featured by playing four [!—MB] at one time, Percy Arnold, drums, sax and dancing, Walter Hall, piano and drums, Harry Batcheldor, piano, singing and banjo and Bobby Everleigh, sax and dancing. This is a red hot combination. I might add they use an organ along with two pianos.
>
> Everybody doubles. It's A Novelty.[37]

Multi-instrumentalist and dancer Robert Langley "The Jelly Roll Kid" Everleigh's career, like Sweatman's, began with tent shows. Born on September 24, 1899, Everleigh was working with travelling shows as a fifteen-year-old: in 1914 he was doubling as singer, dancer, and clarinetist with the Rabbit Foot Minstrels, and in 1917 joined the *Silas Green From New Orleans* troupe, again doubling band and comic vocalist.[38] By the early 1920s he was working primarily in the Canadian province of Alberta, commuting on a regular basis between Edmonton and Calgary. After leaving Sweatman, probably in early 1926, Everleigh settled in Montreal where he continued to work in music.[39]

Starting in February or March 1925, Sweatman spent nearly three years in vaudeville, but now the itineraries were limited to East Coast states, with the occasional foray into Canada. A flavor of Sweatman's act and the versatility of his troupe of musicians and dancers can be gauged from an August 1926 review in *Variety* of their appearance at New York's American Theater. The American, in common with many other vaudeville houses, was feeling the pressure of competition from the powerful cinema chains and fought back by presenting the latest feature films together with a vaudeville show. The review is remarkable for the depth of description of Sweatman's act, though the writer's inability to tell the difference between a clarinet and a saxophone gives rise to doubts as to the extent of his musical knowledge.

Wilbur Sweatman and Co. (8) Band and Dancers

19 Mins.; Full Stage (Special) American (V-P)

Wilbur Sweatman is the saxophonist artist. He formerly did a sax act with a company of two and of late has been popular on phonograph records.

Mr. Sweatman is an excellent exponent of the sax wielding the instrument beautifully in show time numbers and almost hotter than hot in the fast ones.

In the present turn, Sweatman has surrounded himself with a fine company. It holds a six-piece band, including Sweatman, who leads with his sax, two dancers man & girl. The bandsmen are versatile. The pianist sings while a saxophonist plays the piano and the drummer dances while the banjoist plays the drums. The banjo player's accompaniment during a vocal number stands out.

The girl, well appearing does a hit Charleston. While her later attempts at stepping are not above the ordinary, her work in the one number stamps her as a capable specialist. The winging of the male dancer is good. A trio dance with the girl and the man dancers and the banjoist (or it maybe the celloist [*sic*]) had them yelling on a hot evening when it rose out of its slow tempo into one of speed.

Sweatman is a good showman. His little jazzy touches are helpful. He has assembled a turn that is slated from appearances for the big time. There he should sail easily. As a picture house prospect Sweatman has few vaudeville production turn competitors.[40]

One multi-instrumentalist who worked for Sweatman in 1926, and who may well have been one of the musicians mentioned in the *Variety* review, was Jimmie Lunceford, later to lead one of the best-known and most polished bands of the Swing Era. Lunceford had graduated in sociology from Fisk University in the spring of 1926 and came east for a year of postgraduate studies at New York City College. During college vacations he found work with a number of black New York bandleaders, including Elmer Snowden, Deacon Johnson, and Wilbur Sweatman.[41]

In 1926 Sweatman got to record again, this time for the dime-store label Grey Gull with piano and banjo accompaniment, and again in 1929 for the same company. These Grey Gull sides, issued under a bewildering variety of pseudonyms on dozens of dime-store labels, are of particular interest, as they give us the first opportunity (apart from the poorly recorded 1916 Emerson of "Down Home Rag") of hearing Sweatman's clarinet playing in detail, free from other front-line instruments. The 1926 sides, despite being acoustically recorded, are the best of Sweatman's output for Grey Gull—his tone is quite broad, more so than on the Columbias, with a fast vibrato; and he seems particularly at ease with the popular song "Poor Papa," leading one to suspect that he used the number in his vaudeville routine at the time. In comparison, the 1929 sides are rather disappointing, not helped by the presence of a pedestrian trombonist (not John Reeves as listed in most discographies—he was shot dead by his wife in 1922) who tends to get in Sweatman's way. Also, despite these sides being electrically recorded (albeit primitively), the musicians sound distant and poorly balanced, favoring the trombonist. "Battleship Kate," taken at a much slower tempo than on the other Sweatman recordings, at least has the added interest of a female blues singer, probably Hazel Vanverlayer, who was vocalist with Sweatman's group in 1928 and who sings the chorus and bridge. Best of the 1929 Grey Gull recordings is "Jim Town Blues," not the well-known 1924 Charlie Davis composition but an original Sweatman composition of unusual construction.

In the mid-twenties, vaudeville work was still the major money earner for Sweatman, despite or even because of the rapid changes in musical taste that were then occurring. Novelty was one of the main things that attracted audiences to vaudeville, and Sweatman's ragtime and jazz clarinet style, a novelty in itself in 1911, was now commonplace—records, radio, and cabarets featuring jazz bands good and bad had enlightened the man in the street to jazz music. Sweatman in turn had to move with the times, and increasingly his vaudeville act changed to pander to public taste; a singer and dancer was now an essential part of the act and, for his 1927 tour, which commenced in April 1927 at Woonsocket, Rhode Island, Sweatman featured Gladys Ferguson in that capacity.

Tom Whaley, pianist and longtime orchestrator for Duke Ellington, recalled in Stanley Dance's book *The World of Duke Ellington* that he left his
hometown of Boston to work with Sweatman: "Wilbur Sweatman, the guy
that played three clarinets at once, came to Boston, and he was looking for
a piano player. I travelled all over New England with him, and ended up in
New York."[42]

It may well have been this 1927 New England tour during which Whaley
joined Sweatman's band as pianist; unfortunately, Whaley's chronology is
suspect (he recalled Louis Armstrong with Fletcher Henderson in 1922, two
years before Armstrong joined the band). Bearing in mind that Sweatman
frequently toured New England, it is not possible to give a precise date for
Whaley's sojourn with Sweatman. What is certain is that by the middle
of May 1927 Sweatman and his "Creole Revue" were back in New York
City; they were slated to appear at a midnight benefit on May 10, 1927, at
Harlem's Lafayette Theater to help victims of the terrible Mississippi River
floods, and by the end of the month were working downtown at the prestigious Hippodrome Theater.[43]

The personnel of Sweatman's groups at this time are extremely difficult
to identify—his work as a booking manager brought him into contact with
many musicians on a day-to-day basis, many of whom would have been
reluctant to spend weeks on the road touring vaudeville houses, preferring the relative stability of a nightclub or cabaret residency. As a result,
Sweatman's groups tended to change personnel regularly, and only on rare
occasions did names come to light in the black press. One such mention is
in the *Chicago Defender* of February 25, 1928, which reports that drummer
Eddie Roberts left Sweatman's band in New York.

One rather surprising reference to Sweatman's vaudeville work at this
time is an advertisement for the New Lyric Theater at Broadway and
Newton Avenue in Camden, New Jersey, which by 1928, in common with
most vaudeville houses, was presenting a combined bill of live acts and a
feature film plus newsreels. A typical evening bill would start at 7:00 p.m.
with the feature film plus comedy shorts, followed at about 8:30 by the
vaudeville presentation, which could range from two to as many as five acts.
This would last for about an hour or just over, when the main feature film
and shorts would be repeated. The bill for the week of January 27, 1928, featured the film *Becky*, starring Sally O'Neill and Owen Moore, and listed as
"Extra Stage Attraction" was "Wilbur Sweatman and His Victor Recording
Orchestra." This was two years before he recorded for Victor (if we dis-
count the 1917 test recording of "Boogie Rag"), so one wonders whether this
was a case of theatrical hyperbole on the part of either Sweatman or the

theater management, considering that they were playing in Victor's hometown. Certainly it is the only known occasion when this billing was used, although of course there may be others in newspapers I have not been able to check.

Another unusual billing for Sweatman's act at this time was noted in the Kingston (New York) *Daily Freeman*, when they were appearing on a combined cinema/vaudeville bill at the Broadway. It notes the appearance of Wilbur Sweatman And His Band and adds that they are "Those Real 'Hot' Radio Favorites" and that the act comprised eleven performers.[44]

In August 1928 Sweatman and his band were touring the East Coast states when his act was reviewed during their stay in Syracuse, New York:

> Charlie Murray is booked as the lead in "The Big Noise" feature picture at the Empire this week but Wilbur Sweatman is really the 'big noise' at this popular playhouse. Wilbur, a gentleman of color, plays while directing his orchestra, and he sure knows how. During one number he astounds the audience by playing three piccolos [!] at the same time. And his opening solo deserved all the applause he received, and more. The orchestra, two pianos, a drummer, the black boy who played the bass horn and the conductor—made up in volume what they lacked in numbers. There were four colored dancers with the orchestra. The man could dance extraordinarily well, but the three girls only shuffled, and did not display extraordinary grace in that. What they did possess was a whole lot of "It" and that went over big with at least some of the audience.
>
> However these darkies from the Cotton Club, New York, gave a fairly good entertainment and were heartily applauded.[45]

Racist language aside, this report raises an interesting question: was Sweatman trading on the fame of the Cotton Club, or did his act indeed include dancers from the celebrated Harlem nightclub? Or did he himself make an appearance at the Cotton Club? Newspaper advertisements for that week all mention the fact that the act was "Direct From Cotton Club, New York City" which may, of course, just be typical theatrical hyperbole but, in the absence of evidence to prove or disprove the accuracy of the billing, it is impossible to be certain.

Being an astute businessman as well as a musician, Sweatman was never one to let an opportunity to make a few dollars from an ad hoc gig get away from him. During the same week as his engagement at the Empire Theater, the *Syracuse Herald* gave a celebration dinner in honor of local sporting hero Ray Barbuti, winner of two gold medals in the 1928 Amsterdam Olympics.

Asked if his orchestra would play for the dinner, Sweatman jumped at the chance. The dinner was held at the Onondaga Hotel on August 27, and was attended by many sporting personalities and civic leaders.

There is obviously a great deal of research still to be done via the black papers and other firsthand sources, to ascertain who played with Sweatman at this time. One important piece in this jigsaw puzzle is a photograph of Wilbur Sweatman's Orchestra, dated 1929, and reproduced in this book. Identification of those present was verified independently by William 'Cozy' Cole, Eddie Gibbs, and Sweatman himself, and it is interesting not only for the presence of a number of well-known jazz musicians, most notably Cole, Gibbs, and Teddy Bunn, but also for the fact that it shows Sweatman's "company," including the dancers and vocalist. The full personnel of the company was:

Edward "Wash" Washington—1st trumpet
Charles "Bubia" Bowyer or Bowier—hot trumpet
Henry "Greenie" Green—trombone
Wilbur Sweatman—clarinet and bass clarinet
Henry Doarch or Leroy "Roy" Dortch—piano and trumpet
Ida Roberts—piano
Eddie Gibbs—banjo and guitar
Theodore Leroy "Teddy" Bunn—guitar
Emmanuel Cassamore—tuba and trombone[46]
William Randolph "Cozy" Cole—drums
Hazel Vanverlayer—vocalist
Revella Jentes—dancer
Rudolph Tumes or Toombs—dancer
Inez Seeley or Alice Curtis—dancer

The variations in name or spelling are based on the identifications provided by Sweatman and Gibbs.

For the young and inexperienced drummer Cozy Cole, on his first professional engagement, working with Sweatman was not the most pleasant experience—he was sacked! He recalled: "Sweatman fired the devil out of me because I couldn't play nothin'—I had a beat but I couldn't read!"[47] In a 1944 interview with the New York Times, when he was the featured drummer in the show Carmen Jones, Cole recalled that his career with Sweatman was cut short after two weeks because he "was nervous and couldn't read fast enough. Sweatman fired me because I got all out of time and mixed up the chorus girls."[48]

Sweatman had for many years lived a nomadic lifestyle, touring the country in vaudeville and playing usually short residencies such as the ill-fated Lafayette engagement in 1914, was used to the ups and downs of the music profession, and knew how to prepare for lean times. Therefore it comes as no surprise to discover that, according to the 1920 Federal census, taken on January 7, he and Nettie had two lodgers living with them at their West 143rd St. apartment. Interestingly one, Henry Green, was from Nettie's home state of Pennsylvania, and may have been either a relative or a family friend. The strain of the years of having a husband continually on the road or, even if performing in the New York area, returning home late at night or early in the morning, not to mention jealousies over real or imagined dalliances with female performers, eventually took its toll on Nettie and the Sweatmans' marriage. In September 1927 Wilbur's daughter Barbara Doris Sweatman was born, but Nettie Sweatman was not the mother of the child. Undoubtedly this was the catalyst for Wilbur and Nettie's separation, and by 1928 he was lodging at one of the numerous Harlem boarding houses operated by Scott Joplin's widow, Lottie, initially at 163 West 131st Street.

There is little doubt that Sweatman was acquainted with Scott Joplin (his notes for an autobiography he was working on before his death, ninety-odd pages in length and shown to Len Kunstadt in the late 1950s, make mention of Sweatman's friendship with Joplin), both moving in similar musical circles. Lottie Joplin had for several years subsidized her husband's meager income from his compositions by running a number of boarding houses in Harlem, some of them having rooms rentable by the hour for sexual liaisons. The West 131st Street address had been the Joplin family home, and it was to this address that many of the big names in African American entertainment made their way when staying in New York.

By the late 1920s Sweatman had moved to another of Lottie Joplin's boarding houses, at 246 West 138th Street, a fact confirmed both by his entry in the 1929 American Federation of Musicians Local #802 Directory and by the 1930 Federal census taken on April 23. According to the census, Sweatman was sharing the lodging with fourteen others, including fellow musicians Johnny Dunn, drummer Leroy Maxey of the well-known band the Missourians (shown as Massey), and West Indian–born pianist and composer Donald Heywood. Practically all of the lodgers were involved in the entertainment business, with descriptions such as "actor," "actress," "drummer," "songwriter," and "musician." On another occasion Sweatman shared the house with two of the most outspoken personalities in the history of early jazz, Perry Bradford and Jelly Roll Morton. Jelly, as any enthusiast of the Golden Age of Jazz knows, was an ardent proponent of the argument that jazz was "invented" in New Orleans, while Sweatman and Bradford were equally vociferous in the opinion that there were no jazz bands in New Orleans in the early years of the twentieth century. Sweatman recalled to researcher Len Kunstadt that he had played there with Mahara's Minstrels in 1902 and recalled only hearing one band, and not a good one at that.[49] According to his autobiography, *Born with the Blues*, Perry Bradford visited New Orleans with Allen's New Orleans Minstrels in 1908 without hearing anything remotely like jazz.[50] Morton, like most black New Orleans musicians, was immensely proud of his home town's musical heritage and Sweatman and Bradford both took delight in denigrating New Orleans's claim to be the birthplace of jazz and many fierce arguments took place between these three equally stubborn, strongwilled, highly opinionated personalities.[51]

Around this time Sweatman discovered the secret of Lottie Joplin's basement: hundreds of manuscripts written by her late husband, deposited there after Scott Joplin's death in 1917. Sweatman, astute in the world of music publishing, would no doubt have realized the potential that lay therein, and was probably instrumental in ensuring that Lottie renewed the copyright of "Maple Leaf Rag" in 1927 and other compositions as and when they came up for renewal, including Joplin's opera *Treemonisha* in 1938 and 1940.[52] One thing is certain—Lottie increasingly trusted and relied upon Sweatman's business acumen and knowledge of the music publishing industry, as far as her late husband's compositions were concerned. This reliance and trust would eventually be formalized by her appointing Sweatman as a trustee of the Lottie Joplin Thomas Trust, set up to protect her late husband's copyrights.

The summer of 1929 saw Sweatman working with his company of musicians, singers, and dancers, which he had assembled for Addison Carey's "Hawaiian Nights Revue" at the Lafayette Theater in Harlem. In those days most theaters closed for the summer, as air conditioning was still a novelty; however, the Lafayette had already installed air conditioning equipment, rightly billing itself as "Harlem's Coolest Theater."

In 1930, with the assistance of his friend Harrison Smith, the booking agent and onetime manager of Jelly Roll Morton and Duke Ellington, Sweatman obtained a booking at Victor's New York studios to record four sides. At this time Smith was in partnership with Morton, running a famously unsuccessful music publishing company, and had contacts within Victor through Morton's four-year connection with the record company. Morton and Smith's acrimonious and quite bizarre falling out is well told in Alan Lomax's biography of Morton, *Mister Jelly Roll*, albeit with Smith being referred to as "the West Indian" in order to stave off possible libel action.[53]

These Sweatman records are extremely rare—Victor 23254 sold only 604 copies—but they rank among his best. The accompanists on these sides are generally shown in discographies as George Rickson, piano, and Eddie Gibbs, banjo. However, in an interview with the French record collector and researcher Bertrand Demeusey, pianist Benton Heath (1901–1982) revealed that he was the pianist on the Victor session and that the banjoist and guitarist was Lester Miller.[54] Heath is a truly fine player who plays in a strong rhythmic stride style, with interesting treble figures and a solid bass. The equally proficient banjoist and guitarist Lester Miller takes a particularly fine banjo solo on "Battleship Kate," and on the three other sides his playing is equally flawless and noteworthy. Sweatman plays his heart out, particularly on the up-tempo numbers, a far cry from the 1929 sides. He does not sound as comfortable on the two slow tempo numbers; they seem to be a deliberate attempt to cash in on the success of the popular white "gaspipe" clarinet soloist, Boyd Senter, then also recording for Victor, and as such have more than their fair share of novelty effects. "Breakdown Blues," despite the title, is an up-tempo number and in fact a re-working of Sweatman's 1914 composition "Old Folks Rag," the second strain being note-for-note faithful to the original.

These 1930 Victor sides were beautifully recorded and afford us the first real opportunity of hearing all the nuances of Sweatman's playing, a style rooted in the very beginnings of ragtime and jazz. Had Sweatman been born in New Orleans, these records would have been lauded as prime documentary evidence of turn-of-the century style playing à la Bunk Johnson. As it is, they had to wait until 2005 to be reissued, along with all of Sweatman's known recordings, on CD (Jazz Oracle BDW 8046).

By the late 1920s vaudeville, for many years America's most popular and accessible live entertainment, was in terminal decline. Technological advances made commercial radio the dominant power in entertainment from the mid-1920s onward. Whereas with the Victrola one needed to continually purchase records to keep up with the latest hits, entertainment was freely accessible to radio owners at the push of a button. Vaudeville contributed to its own decline through the ever-increasing salary demands of the major stars in a time of recession and plummeting box office takings. For example, in the 1910s, a week's bill at the mecca of vaudeville, New York's Palace Theater, cost $10,000 to $12,000 to produce, with a top seat price of $2, the Palace making an annual profit of $500,000 plus. By 1931, stars of the magnitude of Eddie Cantor were demanding $7,500 a week for a nine-week run.

The final death knell for vaudeville came with the introduction of sound film in 1927, making an already massively popular entertainment even more popular. Vaudeville theaters closed or adapted to showing films, and once-powerful theater chains such as the Keith-Albee and Orpheum circuits—which once showed one-reel films to amuse audiences and, after the novelty wore off, to clear them out of the theater in readiness for the next show—were swallowed up by radio and film companies anxious to lay their hands on prime-location theaters ripe for conversion. Even the Palace succumbed to the might of the cinema; on July 9, 1932, the last straight vaudeville bill played the Palace, thereafter switching to "two-a-day" vaudeville plus feature films until January 7, 1933. From February 11 to April 2, 1933, in an obviously experimental (or desperate) move, the Palace switched to a straight movie policy, but then moved to playing movies and vaudeville as a continuous show. The Palace finally moved to an all-movie policy from September 1935 until May 1949, when the combination of big-name stars such as Judy Garland and Jimmy Durante with the latest feature films heralded the return of live performers to the Palace stage.

Despite the dramatic downturn in business, Sweatman was still in demand, working the 1930 vaudeville season with his troupe over the Keith-Albee-Orpheum circuit (they had merged in 1927 and were subsequently brought under the control of the Radio Corporation of America in 1928).[55] In 1931 he undertook a tour of the Keith-Albee-Orpheum circuit with a new group of singers and dancers. The combination of the Depression and the conversion of cinemas to showing sound films hit theater and cinema musicians particularly hard. During the era of silent films, many larger movie houses had employed large orchestras to accompany the films that were as much a part of the entertainment as the films. However, the arrival of sound film—where the music was usually an integral part of the film, either as a feature, as in a musical, or background, or the mainstay of the short fifteen-minute "variety" feature—coincided with the Wall Street crash.

Cinema musicians were among the first victims of the Depression, with many having to take work out of their music profession—if it could be found. Popular Chicago bandleader and pianist Sammy Stewart lost his long-held job at the Metropolitan Theater, one of Chicago's biggest and most popular cinemas catering to black audiences, and he brought his band to New York to try their luck. They managed to secure an engagement at Harlem's Savoy Ballroom for two months, commencing on February 22, 1930, and then played at the Arcadia Ballroom for an extended engagement which lasted into 1931.[56] At the end of the Arcadia engagement the band broke up, and Stewart and several of his musicians. including banjoist Ikey Robinson and drummer Sid Catlett, joined Sweatman for his forthcoming vaudeville tour. Sweatman also engaged singer and dancer Tressie Mitchell (who with partner Dave Stratton had a very successful vaudeville act, Dave and Tressie, in the early to mid-1920s that regularly used top-flight jazz musicians in their backing group), who was later to become Ikey Robinson's wife. Robinson recalled:

> After I'd been at the Arcadia with Sammy Stewart, the band broke up. Musicians had left and it was difficult to get work. I joined the Wilbur Sweatman shows, playing the theater circuit. . . . I met Tressie in 1931, she was with Wilbur as well. I was the singer with the band. He had Sammy Stewart on piano, Sid Catlett on drums, and me on guitar as well as singing, and Wilbur played two clarinets at the same time. Tressie was the star of the show.[57]

The first appearance of Sweatman and his new act that has been traced was at the Royal Theater in New York at the beginning of June.[58] The tour probably lasted at least through mid-August, when the act, billed as "Wilbur Sweatman and Pals, Famous Syncopators, direct from big time vaudeville" appeared at the State Theatre, in Middletown, New York, for an engagement commencing Thursday August 13, 1931.[59] Ikey Robinson also recalled them playing Reading, Pennsylvania, where the mayor threw a party for them.[60]

In the summer of 1931 Sweatman and the celebrated comedian Flournoy Miller (who, along with partner Aubrey Lyles and Noble Sissle and Eubie Blake, had brought black theater back to Broadway in 1921 with their show *Shuffle Along*) paid a nostalgic visit to their onetime employer, Perry G. Lowery. Although in his mid-sixties, Lowery was still leading a sideshow band working the summer circus routes, as he continued to do until his death in 1942. The 1931 season—by all accounts a short and unprofitable one—saw his band as a sideshow feature with the Ringling Brothers and Barnum & Bailey's circus. Sweatman and Miller caught up with him in Pennsylvania. Much had happened to all three men since 1902, and one can imagine the reminiscences bandied about over a few drinks.[61]

Sweatman, who since 1910 had earned the bulk of his income from coast-to-coast vaudeville appearances, was one of the many victims of the decline of vaudeville. Opportunities in the thriving worlds of radio and cinema were practically nonexistent for a middle-aged black clarinetist who, although he pioneered and popularized jazz in the 1910s, was now hopelessly outclassed by smart, technically accomplished young musicians anxious to make their way in the fiercely competitive world of the professional dance band. Finding relatively few openings for himself as clarinetist or bandleader, Sweatman fell back on band booking and music publishing as his prime sources of income. More than thirty years in the music business had given Sweatman the contacts and credentials to operate in both these areas with a reasonable degree of success, and he continued working in these fields for the rest of his life.

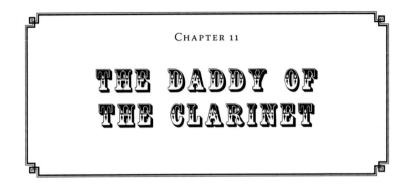

CHAPTER 11

THE DADDY OF THE CLARINET

THE ALMOST COMPLETE COLLAPSE OF TWO-A-DAY VAUDEVILLE, brought about by the domination of entertainment by radio and talking films, coupled with the onset of the Great Depression, saw many hundreds of long-established performers looking for work. Many had known no other life than the stage, and for them it meant taking whatever work they could find—if any. Sweatman, now in his fifties, had not only lost his main income, but his wife and home as well. It was a tough time for him but, unlike many of his contemporaries, at least he had some income from his music-publishing and band-booking businesses. While these desk-based activities consumed most of Sweatman's time in the 1930s, he still led pickup bands whenever the opportunity for such work arose.

In the summer of 1932 he was contracted to provide bands and entertainers for the Hudson River Night Line whose pleasure boats, on summer evenings, plied the Hudson between New York City, Troy, and Albany. For a one-way fare of $2 or $3 round-trip one could board at 6.00 p.m. at Pier 52, near 14th Street, have an evening meal, watch a feature film and the latest newsreels, enjoy a cabaret, and dance to the band. These "night boats" to Albany were a popular attraction with tourists and locals alike, especially with courting couples, and were even immortalized in film and song. Jerome Kern's romantic musical comedy of 1920, *Good Night Boat*, and Joe Young, Sam M. Lewis, and Jean Schwartz's 1918 song for Al Jolson, "Why Do They All Take the Night Boat to Albany?" both celebrate night boat excursions, as does the 1928 film *The Albany Night Boat* starring Olive Borden. Sweatman's involvement with the night boat excursions was first noted in an advertisement for the Hudson River Night

Line in the *New York Times* in July 1932, which mentioned "6 Acts of Refined Entertainment" plus "Wilbur Sweatman and His Famous 10 Piece Orchestra" as a special feature every Friday night on the S.S. *Berkshire*.[1] The *Baltimore Afro-American* picked up on the cruises, and the edition of August 20 reported that Wilbur Sweatman's Orchestra was being featured on the *Berkshire*. The following year he was still active in this field; a *New York Times* advertisement, rather grander and more prominent than that of the previous year, announced that their cruising season commenced on Friday, May 12, with the "Magnificent Steamers 'Trojan' and 'Rensselaer' . . . Featuring WILBUR SWEATMAN, R.K.O. Artist with his Band of Unique Entertainers."[2]

A photograph has recently been discovered of Sweatman and his band from this period, taken by Harlem-based photographer De L'aigle in 1933. It shows "Wilbur Sweatman's Orchestra and His Famous Sepia Entertainers" and, judging from the bulkhead step in the floor, was taken aboard one of the Hudson River steamers. Sweatman, dressed from head to toe in white, and with an uncharacteristic hint of a smile on his face, is seated, surrounded by the members of his band, all of whom are smartly attired in striped blazers and bow ties. Considerably older than the rest of the sidemen is a bespectacled figure, probably the band's pianist, seated opposite Sweatman. Presumably the "Famous Sepia Entertainers" were a troupe of singers and dancers Sweatman employed, and it is a shame that they do not appear as well. Unfortunately, it has not been possible to identify any of the musicians shown in this photograph.

These cruises were not without incident; the *New York Age* of August 19, 1933, noted that Sweatman had been brought before an AFM Local #802 tribunal for allegedly unfairly dismissing his bass player, one Drayton by name. This was in all probability James E. Drayton, listed in the 1929 AFM Local #802 Directory as a bassist, living at 111 West 143rd Street in Harlem. In October the *New York Age* noted that "Ginger," the drummer with Wilbur Sweatman on the steamer *Rensselaer*, was hurt in a collision, while sleeping in his berth.[3]

Despite his absence from record catalogues and vaudeville theaters, Sweatman was still a sufficiently big 'name' to find work in the depth of the Great Depression; his contract to provide music and entertainment on the Hudson River night boats was not renewed after the 1933 season, but in the late spring of 1934 he was booked to appear at the opening on Saturday, May 26, of the Anchor Inn on the boardwalk at Long Beach, Long Island. A prominent advertisement in the *Brooklyn Daily Eagle* of May 25, 1934, stated that the Anchor Inn (a seafood restaurant with an evening cabaret), was offering a "Maine Lobster Dinner Dance and Entertainment" for $1.50, and diners could listen and dance to Wilbur Sweatman and His Harlem Sepia Syncopators.

Wilbur Sweatman made his last commercially released recordings in March 1935, when he recorded four sides for Vocalion with what was probably a band comprised of men on his regular booking roster at that time. The band is thought to have consisted, for the most part, of sidemen whose connections with Sweatman, in some cases, went back to the second decade of this century, making them important historical documents that have only recently been reissued. Trumpeter Russell Smith, trombonist Calvin Jones, tuba player Ogese McKay, and drummer Zeno Lawrence had all appeared on Sweatman's Columbia sides, and time, apparently, had not impaired their talents. They play particularly well on "Florida Blues" and "Battleship Kate" and McKay's tuba is impressive on "Whatcha Gonna Do," driving the band forward behind Gerald "Corky" Williams's vocal. Guitarist Eddie Gibbs's presence is confirmed aurally by comparison with his slightly later work with Eddie South, and his solid, steady 4/4 rhythm gives the recordings a modern dimension.[4]

The 1935 Vocalion sides are all high-spirited small-group jazz, akin in style to the Clarence Williams Vocalions of the same period. Two of these four sides, "Whatcha Gonna Do" and "Hooking Cow Blues," were released in Europe on the French Brunswick label (curiously, all known copies have their labels reversed). This issue is highly prized by Sweatman completists because, although the American pressings are good quality, the French Brunswicks are pressed on the highest quality material with a very high shellac content, giving superb reproduction, free from surface noise, crackle, and distortion.

Sweatman's Vocalion records sold reasonably well, and it was probably on the back of their success that he formed a band to play summer engagements in 1936. Details of his performing activity at this date are sketchy, but an advertisement in the *Poughkeepsie Star-Enterprise* of June 19, 1936, notes that Wilbur Sweatman's Swing Band "Brunswick, Columbia, Emerson Recording Artists" were playing a 3-night engagement at the Golden Rule Inn, on June 20-22. The Golden Rule Inn was a roadhouse providing cabaret-style entertainment and was located on Route 9W, 5 miles south of Kingston, in the Hudson Valley. Subsequent advertisements in the Eagle-News confirmed that Sweatman's engagement The Golden Rule Inn continued throughout the rest of June and into early July, as part of a floorshow that also included Ziegfeld Follies and Earl Carroll's Vanities dancing star Helen Wehrle.

An unexpected boost to Sweatman's finances in the mid- to late 1930s came by way of the sudden popularity of his old warhorse "Down Home Rag." Its repetitive stanzas and thematic construction made it an ideal "flag-waver" piece for the new swing bands, starting with a hard-driving version by Benny Goodman's Music Hall Orchestra, recorded for Columbia in January 1935. In June of the same year Decca recorded a version by Chick Webb's Orchestra, and soon competing versions aimed at both black and white record buyers were on the market, by such bands as Tommy Dorsey (Victor), Don Redman (Bluebird), Larry Clinton (Victor), Henry Busse (Decca), and Willie Farmer (Bluebird). "Down Home Rag" had long been a favorite of country music groups and, to capitalize on the tune's popularity, recorded versions were issued by the Happy Hollow Hoodlums (1935), the Hoosier Hot Shots (1938), and even as part of a medley by the Plehal Brothers, a polka band. Over in England, Harry Roy, the veteran clarinetist and bandleader who had made something of a specialty of recording long-forgotten rags, made his own version for Parlophone in 1937. All this new exposure of "Down Home Rag" prompted music publishers Shapiro, Bernstein & Company, who had purchased the Will Rossiter catalog, to set the tune to new, more up-to-date, lyrics by Lew Brown and republish it in 1939, adding a welcome boost to Sweatman's income. The cover of the new Shapiro, Bernstein sheet music boasts THE FAMOUS DOWN HOME RAG (DEETEN DAT-TEN DOOTEN) with a feature cover photo of film star Judy Canova and her siblings Ann and Zeke. To cash in on the success of the various swing band recordings, Shapiro, Bernstein also published an orchestral version, penned by the prolific big band arranger Larry Clinton. In 1946 "Down Home Rag" was even published by the Alfred Music Company, a leading educational and tutorial music publisher, in an edition for piano-accordionists, arranged by the celebrated accordionist Anthony Galla-Rini.[5]

The late 1930s and early 1940s saw Sweatman working almost exclusively at his booking agency and music publishing businesses, but he was still playing with a small group in and around New York during the 1940s. These jobs included a residency at Paddell's Club with his trio and a number of appearances at gala concerts held in 1943 and 1944 at the Alexander Hamilton High School in Brooklyn, where he was billed as "The Daddy of the Clarinet." One such concert took place on Sunday May 2, 1943, when he shared the bill with two old friends from the days of circus sideshow bands and minstrel shows. One was his employer over forty years earlier, W. C. Handy, and the other was trombonist Fred Simpson, who was directing the Monarch Symphonic Band at that time but who, back in 1902, was a sideman alongside Sweatman in P. G. Lowery's band. Curiously, an advertisement in the *New York Age* for the concert claims that Sweatman had recorded for Brunswick, as well as Columbia and Victor. Presumably this is a reference to the 1935 sides issued by Brunswick's subsidiary Vocalion.[6]

It appears that in the late 1930s Sweatman remarried or was living with a common-law wife. When he registered for the draft on April 26, 1942 (the so-called "old man's draft," as it included all males born after 1875), he was living at 371 West 120th Street in Harlem (where he lived for the rest of his life) with one Dorothy Sweatman. Presumably Dorothy Sweatman was his common-law wife, as there is no known record of him remarrying, and his daughter, Barbara, was apparently born out of wedlock. His draft card confirms that he was still musically active, the registrar noting: "Is his own employer. He has an orchestra which he leads." It also records that he was aged 60, that he was 5'5" in height and weighed 175 pounds.

For Sweatman, now in his sixties, the years of touring that had started in the 1890s were taking their toll, and it was time to lead a more sedate life behind the desk of his music publishing and band management business. However, he did make one final appearance on record in 1950, a private session made by an unknown record company that featured vocalist Delphine Carmichael. The pianist on this session was his old friend and sideman from the late teens and early twenties, Bill Hegamin, onetime husband of pioneering blues singer Lucille Hegamin. Despite exhaustive searches among record collectors and archives, the results of this session are not known to survive; two photographs taken at the session, one with Delphine Carmichael at the microphone and Sweatman playing the bass clarinet, and one without Carmichael with Sweatman playing a B-flat clarinet, are the only proof that it ever took place.[7]

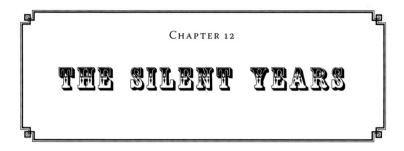

CHAPTER 12

THE SILENT YEARS

IN THE 1940S AND 1950S a worldwide awakening of interest in early jazz occurred, with many old players being dragged out of retirement to record (including several who should not have bothered), and a mini-industry grew up among writers anxious to tell the story of the birth of jazz "as it was"—which for the most part meant the story of New Orleans musicians. A few brave souls, such as Sam Charters and Len Kunstadt with their fine book *Jazz: A History of the New York Scene*, attempted to show that the development of jazz also took place outside of Louisiana and stressed the importance of pioneers such as James Reese Europe and Ford Dabney; but, on the whole, such efforts were cries in the wilderness.[1] A few oldtime performers went into print to set the record straight, and one, Perry Bradford, wrote a bitter and vitriolic but highly entertaining, passionate, and occasionally informative book, *Born with the Blues*.

Throughout this period Sweatman maintained a stony silence. The reasons for this were accurately assessed by Kunstadt and Bob Colton in a 1959 *Record Research* magazine feature on Sweatman:

> Many may ask why Sweatman has been so reticent, why he has not inundated countless tomes and magazines with his reminiscences of his more-than-sixty years in the music game. Wilbur is really too proud to give a direct answer, but we can read between the lines: he feels that he has been woefully neglected by our jazz authors, and also he has a low opinion of the "folk-lorist" treatment of the history of jazz.[2]

It is history's loss that not only Wilbur Sweatman but hundreds of other musicians (some of whom were still performing), who were active in the earliest days of the development of jazz, were ignored by writers and record producers. Reasons for their neglect were twofold: one, they did not adapt to subsequent trends in jazz development, which stressed the blues content of jazz; and two, they did not fit into the mantra-like view—still widely held—that only black New Orleans musicians were the "true" originators of jazz. Even a musician of the stature of pianist Eubie Blake found the 1950s a tough time, only making rare appearances in the recording studios and spending much of his time in studying music theory. For the majority of jazz fans and record producers, Blake was merely a name from a long-distant past—to the extent that a late-1940s reissue (on John Steiner's resurrected Paramount label) of a blank-label Emerson test pressing of his 1921 masterpiece "Sounds of Africa" was credited as being performed by "Unknown Rag Pianist"!

Probably as a response to the neglect shown by jazz writers toward his pioneering role in the development of ragtime and jazz, Sweatman started to write his autobiography using the vast quantity of material he had amassed over the years and aided by a razor-sharp memory of events and personalities he had known. Len Kunstadt was fortunate enough to be shown the ninety-odd pages of Sweatman's draft that had been dictated to his secretary, and he enthused in the pages of *Record Research* about Sweatman's reminiscences of Scott Joplin, Tony Jackson, Mike Bernard, Jelly Roll Morton, Freddie Keppard, and many, many more. Tucked away in his bedroom, in World War I army kit bags, Sweatman had kept checks paid to musicians, booking details, accounts records, and other important documents. However, after his death all of this material, including the autobiography and unpublished compositions by both Sweatman and Scott Joplin, was scrapped by his daughter, Barbara, who was unaware of their historical importance and value. Thus subsequent generations of jazz and ragtime enthusiasts and researchers have been robbed of what would have been an important firsthand account of a life spanning the most fertile period of African American music history.

A car accident in the mid-1950s curtailed Sweatman's playing career (as well as forcing him to stop smoking and drinking, according to Harrison Smith), but he continued his music publishing business and the handling of musicians' estates from his office at 1674 Broadway. He and his arranger, the oldtime vaudevillian and multi-instrumentalist Sidney Easton, who had worked with W. C. Handy's Band as early as 1914, whiled away the time catching up on the gossip from old friends and acquaintances from the days when he was the "Original and Much-Imitated Ragtime Clarinetist" and "Originator of the Jazz Clarinet."[3]

Examination of Library of Congress copyright records shows that Sweatman was not only active both as a composer and publisher of his own works, but also considered work by other writers for publication. One unpublished item from 1960 is a composition by the unlikely sounding title "Tweets Says (I've Got Nine Lives, Have You?)," written by his old friends Noble Sissle and Eubie Blake in collaboration with Roslyn Stock. Virtually all of the material from this period has sunk without trace, and it is interesting to speculate who actually bought any of Sweatman's music publications at the time; certainly the impression one is left with is of an outmoded old man desperate to keep in touch with the business he knew and loved and which had been his lifeblood for over sixty years. Several of the song titles known to have been published by Wilbur Sweatman Music Publishing in the 1950s demonstrate his desire to appear hip to the latest musical styles, with such titles as "Battleship Kate (Cha-Cha)" and "Baby, That'll Get It" (a reworking of "Get It Now"). As late as 1959 he was regularly advertising his publishing company's catalog in *Billboard*, using the optimistic heading "Great Tunes Will Make Great Records!" and listing the titles with snappy descriptions such as "Fine Fine Fine—the chick clicked." By maintaining an office, regardless of the success or otherwise of his publishing and musical executorship businesses, Sweatman was able to keep in touch with his old show business cronies, as well as to tenuously hang on to the last vestiges of a public profile within the music business.

In March 1953 Scott Joplin's widow formed the Lottie Joplin Thomas Trust to protect the copyright of her late husband's published compositions and, by virtue of both his intimate knowledge of the music publishing industry and their long-term friendship, made Sweatman a trustee. Lottie Joplin Thomas died on March 14, 1954, and, two weeks later Sweatman applied to the New York County Surrogate's Court for executorship of her estate. This was duly granted and, shortly thereafter he removed all of Scott Joplin's sheet music and manuscripts from Lottie's West 131st Street address to his office, where he also kept most of his unpublished material, along with scrapbooks and memorabilia of his long career.

Under his powers of executor and administrator, Sweatman, via his attorney Robert Rosborne, applied to the Surrogate's Court of the County of New York on June 2, 1954 (a document clearly signed Wilbur) for the exemption of Lottie Joplin Thomas's estate from tax. In the application he outlined the gross value of the estate at $6950.76, which, after funeral expenses, administration, legal fees, and debts, left a net estate value of $3752.96, shared equally between her brother, John D. Stokes, her two sisters, Cora D. Jackson and Anna M. Stokes, and the daughter of a predeceased brother,

Mary L. Warmley. The estate was duly declared tax-exempt on June 22, 1954, by the court. Sweatman was to maintain executorship of the Lottie Joplin estate and trusteeship of the Lottie Joplin Thomas Trust for the rest of his life, ensuring that Scott Joplin's copyrights and royalties were professionally handled. Curiously, on August 14, 1959, Sweatman reassigned the copyright of Joplin's opera *Treemonisha* to Wilbur Sweatman Music, a highly unusual move (and one that apparently went unrecorded in the files of the Lottie Joplin Thomas Trust) at the time, considering it was years before the revival of interest in ragtime, and when the likelihood of its performances was virtually nonexistent.

Having been granted executorship of Lottie Joplin's estate, Sweatman now legally had in his possession Scott Joplin's sheet music and unpublished manuscripts safely stored in his office. There they joined the heaps of his own unpublished material, boxes of cashed checks, receipts, photographs, scrapbooks, and other memorabilia.

In 1961 Wilbur was admitted to hospital for a minor operation; shortly afterwards, he suffered a heart attack and died at the Flower-Fifth Avenue Hospital in New York City on Thursday, March 9, leaving a daughter, Barbara. The *New York Times* reported his death in a somewhat factually inaccurate obituary, but perceptively noted that "Mr. Sweatman's place in the world of music has been based partly on the fact that his original all-Negro orchestra, which he organised in Minneapolis in 1902, became a rung through which many Negro artists found their way up the ladder."[4] The same edition carried in its "Deaths" columns a short tribute mourning "with deep sorrow the death of our beloved member and colleague, Wilbur C. Sweatman" from the American Society of Composers, Authors and Publishers.[5]

Len Kunstadt and Bob Colton, editors of *Record Research* magazine, had befriended Sweatman a few years earlier and often turned to him for his help and advice on the bands and musicians of the Golden Age of jazz. Their touching tribute to him in the July issue is worth quoting in full.

On Thursday, March 9th, WILBUR SWEATMAN, our dear friend and great advisor in things historical, passed on. After coming through a minor operation he incurred a fatal heart attack. Friday and Saturday New York Times carried his obituary. On Saturday morning Sweatman lay in state at Weaver's Funeral Home on w. 131 St. in N.Y.C. Sweatman, a small man, even appeared smaller. The grayness which was so much a part of Wilbur's countenance, was ashen gray now. Yet his face with its prominent nose and tightened lips were nearly alive. Mr Sweatman, in

life, was a gruff speaking individual, a chap who fought hard for his lau-
rels, and the hard knocks apparently built that wall of gruffness around
his very sensitive, warm inner self.

On Monday, March 13, 8pm at Prince Hall Temple, W. 155 Street,
Masonic services were held for Sweatman, a 32nd degree mason. The
entire hall was filled with his family and friends. Such royalty as Mr. And
Mrs. Eubie Blake, Luckey Roberts, Mrs. W.C. Handy, Sidney Easton, Fess
Williams, Wellman Braud, Gene Sedric, Cliff Jackson and innumerable
others came to pay their last respects. The audience sang among others,
"Nearer My God To Thee," "Swing Low Sweet Chariot." Many fine voices
were heard. The tribute was complete.[6]

Soon after his funeral a bizarre twist in the Sweatman saga occurred.
Shortly before he died he was visited at the Flower-Fifth Avenue Hospital
by his daughter Barbara, and he turned over to her the keys to his apartment and office for safekeeping. After his death, Barbara took possession of
the apartment and proceeded to try and sort out the contents. The apartment contained everything that Sweatman had considered important in
his life: his three clarinets, photographs, tape recordings (what did they
contain?), scrap books, and enormous quantities of sheet music and music
manuscripts. Barbara cleared the apartment of anything she considered
valuable, and placed it in storage with a friend, throwing much material
away and selling and giving away other articles. In June she moved into the
apartment herself, retrieving the stored articles and moving them back in
to the apartment.[7]

Despite Sweatman's years of experience in the business side of show
business and his own extensive personal involvement in the estates of dead
black composers and performers, most notably that of Scott Joplin, it transpired that Wilbur Sweatman had died without making either a will or any
other arrangements for the handling of his business or publishing interests.
In April 1961, one month after Sweatman's death, his sister Eva, still living
in Kansas City, challenged Barbara Sweatman's possession of the estate on
the premise that her brother had no legitimate children. Eva Sweatman appointed Harry G. Bragg, a noted black lawyer with experience in handling
the estates of prominent black performers, to appear in court in an effort to
be appointed executor of the estate of Wilbur Sweatman. At the court hearing it was accepted that Barbara Doris Sweatman was Wilbur Sweatman's
daughter but, as she was born out of wedlock, she had no claim or rights
to the estate. Bragg was appointed administrator of the estate, and Barbara
Sweatman was ordered to hand over all of the estate's property to Bragg.

Barbara refused to comply with the court order, and it took the threat of arrest and a further court hearing on September 22, 1961, for her to turn the property over to Bragg. After the hearing Barbara Sweatman handed over the property in the apartment to Bragg, but whether what she handed over was merely the contents of Wilbur Sweatman's apartment or the combined effects from both his apartment and office is not known. The autobiography that Wilbur had kept at the office (that he had shown to Len Kunstadt and Bob Colton) was not among the items handed over, as far as is known. Although she knew that her father had been working on an autobiography, Barbara claimed that she had never seen it.[8]

In 1962 Eva Sweatman discharged Harry Bragg as executor of the Wilbur Sweatman estate and took charge of it herself, including the collection of royalties. Eva died on July 21, 1964, leaving the bulk of her estate to one Robert L. Sweeney of Kansas City and, pointedly, the sum of $1 to Barbara Sweatman, who she described in her will "is said to be the daughter of my brother Wilbur Sweatman, deceased, and was born out of wedlock."[9] Efforts by Edward Berlin, Scott Joplin's biographer, as well as by this author, to trace both Barbara Sweatman and Robert L. Sweeney have proved fruitless, so it is unlikely that Sweatman's autobiography, scrapbooks, and memorabilia, or Scott Joplin's unpublished manuscripts are ever likely to be found.

It is particularly sad that documents that would help researchers and jazz enthusiasts alike to understand the formative years of ragtime and jazz—the archives of two remarkable men's lifetimes devoted to music writing and music making—ended up being the subject of legal wrangles between parties only interested in the worth of published items likely to accrue royalties. Equally ironic is the likelihood that items then considered worthless by the respective parties involved—unpublished Joplin and Sweatman compositions, together with Sweatman's scrapbooks and autobiography—are now historically priceless. One can only hope that there is someone still sitting—unwittingly or otherwise—on this historical goldmine.

Sweatman and his music faded into obscurity after his death, and even the revival of interest in ragtime in the 1970s did nothing to resurrect interest in either him or his music, concentrated as it was on the so-called "classical" rag composers such as Joplin, Joseph Lamb, James Scott, and Louis Chauvin. However, a worldwide awakening of interest in early African American music in general in the last few years has started to question the received opinion of Sweatman and other pioneering black musicians and bandleaders working in the field of popular music, such as James Reese Europe, Will Marion Cook, and Perry Lowery. Diligent research by dedicated authors has shown that these men, and others like them, played a hugely significant role in the course of musical development throughout the twentieth century, reaching far beyond their own lifespan. Sweatman's place in the pantheon of such exalted names is both apposite and well-deserved; his compositions are still regularly performed, and his legacy, as both performer and nurturer of young talent, can now be fully appreciated.

Appendix 1

THE FOLLOWING LISTING is an attempt to chronicle all known compositions by Wilbur Sweatman. This has been no easy task; in the course of a long career he probably wrote hundreds of compositions—particularly in his Chicago years as musical director of the Grand and Monogram theaters, where part of his role would have been to compose pieces for short musical productions ("tab shows"), individual acts, and specialties. Much of this material was of a throwaway nature, intended for a few performances, and consequently unpublished. The titles of some of these compositions, however, were mentioned in contemporary newspaper reports, and those that the author knows of have been included in the list.

By the time he was recording regularly, Sweatman copyrighted several of his recorded compositions, even though they were never published. By assigning a composition to a music publisher, in the knowledge that it may never appear as a printed score, Sweatman was ensuring that royalties from record sales (and later, broadcast performances) of the record were collected, the publisher acting as agent.

I am deeply indebted to Wayne Shirley of the Library of Congress, Music Division, for his help in making the following list as authoritative as is possible.

"Two Hundred Miles an Hour" (with Dave Peyton). 1909. No copyright entry at Library of Congress (unpublished).

"I Ain't Goin' Back to Kansas City No More." 1909. No copyright entry at Library of Congress (unpublished).

"Cross the Way." 1911. No copyright entry at Library of Congress (unpublished).

"Down Home Rag" (Instrumental). Copyright September 18th 1911. Published by Will Rossiter, Chicago.

"Down Home Rag" (Vocal version) (Lyrics by Roger Lewis). Copyright 1913. Published by Will Rossiter, Chicago.

"Down Home Rag" (Orchestral arrangement). Copyright 1922. Published by Melrose Bros., Chicago. Arranged by Elmer Schoebel.

"Down Home Rag" (Vocal version) (Lyrics by Lew Brown). Copyright 1939. Published by Shapiro, Bernstein & Co.

"Old Folks Rag." Copyright 1914. Published by Jos. W. Stern & Co., New York.

"Virginia Diggins" (Orchestral arrangement). Published by Will Rossiter, Chicago, 1915. Arranged by F. Henri Klickmann.

"Virginia Diggins (Skeet, Scat, Scutten)" (Piano arrangement). Copyright 1941. Published by Will Rossiter, Chicago.

"Boogie Rag." Arranged by Milton Ager. Copyright 1916. Published by Shapiro, Bernstein & Co., New York.

"Boogie Rag" (For piano). Copyright 1917. Published by Shapiro, Bernstein & Co., New York.

"That's Got 'Em Rag" (Instrumental). Copyright 1919. Published by Triangle Music Co.

"That's Got 'Em Rag" (Lyrics by Joe Davis). Copyright 1919. Published by Triangle Music Co.

"Battleship Kate" (Lyrics by Ada Rives). Copyright 1924 by Wilbur Sweatman. Published by Wilbur Sweatman, 1547 Broadway, New York. Stock arrangement published 1931 by Alfred Music.

"Sweat Blues" (also recorded on Grey Gull as "Lead Pipe Blues"). Copyright 1930, Southern Music (unpublished).

"Jim Town Blues" (not "Jimtown Blues," the Charlie Davis composition). No copyright entry at Library of Congress (unpublished).

"Breakdown Blues." Copyright 1930, Southern Music (unpublished). (NB: This is a reworking of "Old Folks Rag")

"Got 'Em Blues." Copyright 1931 by Southern Music (unpublished).

"Sweat Mania." Copyright 1936 by Wilbur Sweatman (unpublished). Stock arrangement published 1959 by Wilbur Sweatman, 371 W. 120th Street, New York.

"Sissie and Bob." Copyright 1938 by Wilbur Sweatman, 371 W. 120th St., New York (unpublished).

"I Close My Eyes" (Lyrics by R. Leatman). Copyright 1957 by Wilbur Sweatman Music (unpublished).

"Please, Lord, Bless My One and Only Love" (Lyrics by R. Leatman). Copyright 1957. Published by Wilbur Sweatman Music.

"Why Did You Leave Me?" (Lyrics by R. Leatman). Copyright 1957 by Wilbur Sweatman Music (unpublished).

"Baby, That'll Get It (Get With It Now)" (Lyrics by Steve Stevens). Copyright 1958. Published by Wilbur Sweatman Music.

"Don't Stop Loving Me Now" (Music and Lyrics by Wilbur Sweatman). Copyright 1958 (unpublished) and 1959 (published). Published by Wilbur Sweatman Music.

"Down Missouri Way" (Lyrics by Steve Stevens). Copyright 1959. Published by Wilbur Sweatman Music.

"Fine, Fine, Fine" (Lyrics by Steve Stevens). Copyright 1959. Published by Wilbur Sweatman Music.

"Honolulu Cha-Cha" (Music and lyrics by Wilbur Sweatman). Copyright 1959 by Wilbur Sweatman Music (unpublished).

"If the World Is Round (It's Crooked Just the Same)" (Lyrics by Joe Simms and Steve Stevens). Notice of Use only deposited with Library of Congress, 1959 (unpublished).

Wilbur Sweatman Music also copyrighted at least one song not by Sweatman:

"Tweets Says (I've Got Nine Lives, Do You?)." By Noble Sissle, Roslyn Stock, and Eubie Blake. Copyright 1960 (unpublished).

Appendix 2

I AM INDEBTED TO ERIN FOLEY, Archivist of the Circus World Museum Library, Baraboo, Wisconsin, for her assistance and kind permission to reproduce the following table of the 1902 tour route of the Forepaugh and Sells Brothers Circus, which featured Wilbur Sweatman as assistant orchestra leader of P. G. Lowery's sideshow band.

Day of month	Day of Week	City	State	Country
April 2	Wednesday	New York	New York	USA
April 3	Thursday	New York	New York	USA
April 4	Friday	New York	New York	USA
April 5	Saturday	New York	New York	USA
April 6	Sunday	New York	New York	USA
April 7	Monday	New York	New York	USA
April 8	Tuesday	New York	New York	USA
April 9	Wednesday	New York	New York	USA
April 10	Thursday	New York	New York	USA
April 11	Friday	New York	New York	USA
April 12	Saturday	New York	New York	USA
April 13	Sunday	New York	New York	USA
April 14	Monday	New York	New York	USA
April 15	Tuesday	New York	New York	USA
April 16	Wednesday	New York	New York	USA
April 17	Thursday	New York	New York	USA
April 18	Friday	New York	New York	USA
April 19	Saturday	New York	New York	USA

April 20	Sunday			USA
April 21	Monday	Philadelphia	Pennsylvania	USA
April 22	Tuesday	Philadelphia	Pennsylvania	USA
April 23	Wednesday	Philadelphia	Pennsylvania	USA
April 24	Thursday	Philadelphia	Pennsylvania	USA
April 25	Friday	Philadelphia	Pennsylvania	USA
April 26	Saturday	Philadelphia	Pennsylvania	USA
April 27	Sunday			USA
April 28	Monday	Baltimore	Maryland	USA
April 29	Tuesday	Baltimore	Maryland	USA
April 30	Wednesday	Washington	D.C.	USA
May 1	Thursday	Washington	D.C.	USA
May 2	Friday	Hagerstown	Maryland	USA
May 3	Saturday	Cumberland	Maryland	USA
May 4	Sunday			USA
May 5	Monday	Clarksburg	West Virginia	USA
May 6	Tuesday	Fairmont	West Virginia	USA
May 7	Wednesday	Connellsville	Pennsylvania	USA
May 8	Thursday	Washington	Pennsylvania	USA
May 9	Friday	Pittsburgh	Pennsylvania	USA
May 10	Saturday	Pittsburgh	Pennsylvania	USA
May 11	Sunday			USA
May 12	Monday	Johnstown	Pennsylvania	USA
May 13	Tuesday	Altoona	Pennsylvania	USA
May 14	Wednesday	Lewistown	Pennsylvania	USA
May 15	Thursday	York	Pennsylvania	USA
May 16	Friday	Reading	Pennsylvania	USA
May 17	Saturday	Pottsville	Pennsylvania	USA
May 18	Sunday			USA
May 19	Monday	Wilkes-Barre	Pennsylvania	USA
May 20	Tuesday	Scranton	Pennsylvania	USA
May 21	Wednesday	Allentown	Pennsylvania	USA
May 22	Thursday	Easton	New Jersey	USA
May 23	Friday	Elizabeth	New Jersey	USA
May 24	Saturday	Jersey City	New Jersey	USA
May 25	Sunday			USA
May 26	Monday	Brooklyn	New York	USA
May 27	Tuesday	Brooklyn	New York	USA

May 28	Wednesday	Brooklyn	New York	USA
May 29	Thursday	Brooklyn	New York	USA
May 30	Friday	Brooklyn	New York	USA
May 31	Saturday	Brooklyn	New York	USA
June 1	Sunday			USA
June 2	Monday	Paterson	New Jersey	USA
June 3	Tuesday	Newburgh	New York	USA
June 4	Wednesday	Kingston	New York	USA
June 5	Thursday	Schenectady	New York	USA
June 6	Friday	Gloversville	New York	USA
June 7	Saturday	Utica	New York	USA
June 8	Sunday			USA
June 9	Monday	Poughkeepsie	New York	USA
June 10	Tuesday	Danbury	Connecticut	USA
June 11	Wednesday	Ansonia	Connecticut	USA
June 12	Thursday	Meriden	Connecticut	USA
June 13	Friday	Holyoke	Massachusetts	USA
June 14	Saturday	Greenfield	Massachusetts	USA
June 15	Sunday			USA
June 16	Monday	Gardner	Massachusetts	USA
June 17	Tuesday	Lowell	Massachusetts	USA
June 18	Wednesday	Lawrence	Massachusetts	USA
June 19	Thursday	Concord	New Hampshire	USA
June 20	Friday	Manchester	New Hampshire	USA
June 21	Saturday	Haverhill	Massachusetts	USA
June 22	Sunday			USA
June 23	Monday	Portsmouth	New Hampshire	USA
June 24	Tuesday	Biddeford	Maine	USA
June 25	Wednesday	Portland	Maine	USA
June 26	Thursday	Lewiston	Maine	USA
June 27	Friday	Berlin	New Hampshire	USA
June 28	Saturday	Sherbrooke	Quebec	Canada
June 29	Sunday			
June 30	Monday	Montreal	Quebec	Canada

July 1	Tuesday	Montreal	Quebec	Canada
July 2	Wednesday	Valleyfield	Quebec	Canada
July 3	Thursday	Ottawa	Ontario	Canada
July 4	Friday	Cornwall	Ontario	Canada
July 5	Saturday	Kingston	Ontario	Canada
July 6	Sunday			Canada
July 7	Monday	Belleville	Ontario	Canada
July 8	Tuesday	Peterborough	Ontario	Canada
July 9	Wednesday	Barrie	Ontario	Canada
July 10	Thursday	Toronto	Ontario	Canada
July 11	Friday	Hamilton	Ontario	Canada
July 12	Saturday	Brantford	Ontario	Canada
July 13	Sunday			
July 14	Monday	Guelph	Ontario	Canada
July 15	Tuesday	Stratford	Ontario	Canada
July 16	Wednesday	Woodstock	Ontario	Canada
July 17	Thursday	London	Ontario	Canada
July 18	Friday	St. Thomas	Ontario	Canada
July 19	Saturday	Chatham	Ontario	Canada
July 20	Sunday			
July 21	Monday	Buffalo	New York	USA
July 22	Tuesday	Rochester	New York	USA
July 23	Wednesday	Geneva	New York	USA
July 24	Thursday	Auburn	New York	USA
July 25	Friday	Cortland	New York	USA
July 26	Saturday	Binghamton	New York	USA
July 27	Sunday			USA
July 28	Monday	Ithaca	New York	USA
July 29	Tuesday	Elmira	New York	USA
July 30	Wednesday	Williamsport	Pennsylvania	USA
July 31	Thursday	Lock Haven	Pennsylvania	USA
August 1	Friday	Du Bois	Pennsylvania	USA
August 2	Saturday	Butler	Pennsylvania	USA
August 3	Sunday			USA
August 4	Monday	Wheeling	West Virginia	USA
August 5	Tuesday	Zanesville	Ohio	USA
August 6	Wednesday	Mansfield	Ohio	USA
August 7	Thursday	Lima	Ohio	USA

August 8	Friday	Springfield	Ohio	USA
August 9	Saturday	Columbus	Ohio	USA
August 10	Sunday			USA
August 11	Monday	Piqua	Ohio	USA
August 12	Tuesday	Richmond	Indiana	USA
August 13	Wednesday	Indianapolis	Indiana	USA
August 14	Thursday	Anderson	Indiana	USA
August 15	Friday	Marion	Indiana	USA
August 16	Saturday	Logansport	Indiana	USA
August 17	Sunday			USA
August 18	Monday	Springfield	Illinois	USA
August 19	Tuesday	Jacksonville	Illinois	USA
August 20	Wednesday	Quincy	Illinois	USA
August 21	Thursday	Keokuk	Iowa	USA
August 22	Friday	Burlington	Iowa	USA
August 23	Saturday	Galesburg	Illinois	USA
August 24	Sunday			USA
August 25	Monday	Kewanee	Illinois	USA
August 26	Tuesday	Sterling	Illinois	USA
August 27	Wednesday	Aurora	Illinois	USA
August 28	Thursday	Elgin	Illinois	USA
August 29	Friday	Racine	Wisconsin	USA
August 30	Saturday	Waukesha	Wisconsin	USA
August 31	Sunday			USA
September 1	Monday	Marinette	Wisconsin	USA
September 2	Tuesday	Green Bay	Wisconsin	USA
September 3	Wednesday	Oshkosh	Wisconsin	USA
September 4	Thursday	Janesville	Wisconsin	USA
September 5	Friday	Freeport	Illinois	USA
September 6	Saturday	Rock Island	Illinois	USA
September 7	Sunday			USA
September 8	Monday	Peoria	Illinois	USA
September 9	Tuesday	Lincoln	Illinois	USA
September 10	Wednesday	Pontiac	Illinois	USA
September 11	Thursday	Bloomington	Illinois	USA
September 12	Friday	Danville	Illinois	USA
September 13	Saturday	Lafayette	Indiana	USA
September 14	Sunday			USA

September 15	Monday	Huntington	Indiana	USA
September 16	Tuesday	Defiance	Ohio	USA
September 17	Wednesday	Toledo	Ohio	USA
September 18	Thursday	Findlay	Ohio	USA
September 19	Friday	Bellefontaine	Ohio	USA
September 20	Saturday	Dayton	Ohio	USA
September 21	Sunday			USA
September 22	Monday	Chillicothe	Ohio	USA
September 23	Tuesday	Athens	Ohio	USA
September 24	Wednesday	Charleston	West Virginia	USA
September 25	Thursday	Huntington	West Virginia	USA
September 26	Friday	Mt. Sterling	Kentucky	USA
September 27	Saturday	Lexington	Kentucky	USA
September 28	Sunday			USA
September 29	Monday	Chattanooga	Tennessee	USA
September 30	Tuesday	Tullahoma	Tennessee	USA
October 1	Wednesday	Nashville	Tennessee	USA
October 2	Thursday	Paris	Tennessee	USA
October 3	Friday	Jackson	Tennessee	USA
October 4	Saturday	Memphis	Tennessee	USA
October 5	Sunday			USA
October 6	Monday	Tupelo	Mississippi	USA
October 7	Tuesday	Birmingham	Alabama	USA
October 8	Wednesday	Anniston	Alabama	USA
October 9	Thursday	Rome	Georgia	USA
October 10	Friday	Atlanta	Georgia	USA
October 11	Saturday	Athens	Georgia	USA
October 12	Sunday			USA
October 13	Monday	Augusta	Georgia	USA
October 14	Tuesday	Anderson	South Carolina	USA
October 15	Wednesday	Greenwood	South Carolina	USA
October 16	Thursday	Greenville	South Carolina	USA
October 17	Friday	Spartanburg	South Carolina	USA
October 18	Saturday	Charlotte	North Carolina	USA
October 19	Sunday			USA
October 20	Monday	Wilmington	North Carolina	USA
October 21	Tuesday	Florence	South Carolina	USA
October 22	Wednesday	Columbia	South Carolina	USA

October 23	Thursday	Sumter	South Carolina	USA
October 24	Friday	Charleston	South Carolina	USA
October 25	Saturday	Savannah	Georgia	USA
October 26	Sunday			USA
October 27	Monday	Jacksonville	Florida	USA
October 28	Tuesday	Waycross	Georgia	USA
October 29	Wednesday	Valdosta	Georgia	USA
October 30	Thursday	Thomasville	Georgia	USA
October 31	Friday	Albany	Georgia	USA
November 1	Saturday	Americus	Georgia	USA
November 2	Sunday			USA
November 3	Monday	Macon	Georgia	USA
November 4	Tuesday	Columbus	Georgia	USA
November 5	Wednesday	Montgomery	Alabama	USA
November 6	Thursday	Selma	Alabama	USA
November 7	Friday	Meridian	Mississippi	USA
November 8	Saturday	West Point	Mississippi	USA
November 9	Sunday			USA
November 10	Monday	Kosciusko	Mississippi	USA
November 11	Tuesday	Greenwood	Mississippi	USA
November 12	Wednesday	Greenville	Mississippi	USA
November 13	Thursday	Vicksburg	Mississippi	USA
November 14	Friday	Port Gibson	Mississippi	USA
November 15	Saturday	Baton Rouge	Louisiana	USA
November 16	Sunday	New Orleans	Louisiana	USA
November 17	Monday	New Orleans	Louisiana	USA
November 18	Tuesday	New Orleans	Louisiana	USA
November 19	Wednesday	New Orleans	Louisiana	USA
November 20	Thursday	SEASON ENDS		

Appendix 3

THE SPEEDS AND PITCHES OF WILBUR SWEATMAN'S RECORDINGS

by Ron Geesin

I HAVE ALWAYS BEEN FOND OF THE WILD RANTINGS leaping out of the Sweatman Columbia grooves. One reason is that the roaring, wailings, and thrashings healthily oppose any idea of "straight" or "classical" postures, even judged by jazz standards and, in any case, appeal to my sense of humor.

But I have also felt that Columbia exaggerated the band's ravings by intentionally recording it at slower-than-normal speed, so that it would appear faster and wilder when played back at 78–80 rpm. However, after years of spasmodic study, I have concluded that my perception of the creative use of actual recording methods in the late 1910s has been over-sensitized by my own compositional development and use of such studio techniques at the present time (the beginning of the twenty-first century). So I was wrong. (Not necessarily. Victor, Columbia's main rival, deliberately recorded Caruso and other singers at a slower speed, so that on playback at 78 r.p.m., the voice took on a brighter edge and gave the impression of the singer possessing a greater range and brilliance.—MB)

Yes, there is a certain amount of speed fluctuation, but I do not think it was intentional. Recording technology was still in its early stages of development; falling weight–driven cutting lathes may have been heavily greased, or incorrectly set, or not warmed up on a cold day. The band simply played fast—as if on some kind of stimulant—and the solo front-line instruments are all played with an unusually fast vibrato. The wildest period is from matrix 77856 to 78192. Although the trombone and tuba sound richer when slowed down by up to one tone in pitch, the trumpet attack becomes too slow. The more one listens, the more confused one can become.

Based on the fact that the standard of pitch in America at that time was the same as in the present day—A above middle C as 440 vibrations per second (Hertz or Hz)—it is possible to pitch records of ensembles that contain a piano fairly accurately. Brass and woodwind instruments can drift a quarter-tone or so either side of center, depending on the temperature and the players' adjustments to the length of tube or pipe. Furthermore, human input—the manner of blowing an instrument, whether calculated or not, can take the pitch further off either side of center. An electronic keyboard capable of being set at A=440, and of generating a fairly pure tone with minimum overtones, is the best pitch reference, and a variable-speed turntable is essential.

I made recordings of all of Sweatman's Columbia sides, repitching as I went, noting all the main keys in each piece and, when I doubted which key (say, whether B♭ or A♭), I recorded both in sequence. Then I was able to go through the whole tape and decide about the keys. I then visited Mark Berresford and not only double-checked the speeds with him, but also subjected the rest of Sweatman's recorded output to the same process. You will see from the discography that the band favored the easiest keys for front-line brass and woodwind instruments: F, B♭, and E♭ (and their relative minors).

Unless one owns some kind of sophisticated digital clock arrangement, it is impossible to set the exact speed in revolutions per minute. Besides this, many early recordings rise in pitch toward the end of the record, sometimes as much as a semitone, due to either a rise in pitch by the musicians as outlined above, or a slowing down of the cutting lathe, or a combination of both factors. This can be corrected manually (with difficulty) or by computer; but for the sake of this exercise, the speeds quoted in the table were calculated from pitch readings taken about halfway through each side.

The most convenient method of setting speed is by means of a stroboscope, which is calculated to be read using the pulse rate of an alternating current lamp (50 Hz in UK and 60 Hz in the USA). This however does give different readings for what is nominally the same speed. For example, the nearest a 50 Hz stroboscope can get to 78 rpm is 77.92, while a 60Hz stroboscope will give the same nominal speed a reading of 78.26. Because of the aforementioned speed drift, and variations between 50 and 60 Hz electricity supplies, to keep things simple, the speeds and pitches quoted in the discography are given to the nearest one-half revolution per minute. There are several websites that offer stroboscopes or software to produce them, and the reader is recommended to enter the words "record strobo-scope" into a search engine to find what is available.

PITCH AND SPEED TABLE OF WILBUR SWEATMAN'S RECORDINGS

Matrix Number	Key(s)	Speed (RPM)
1200	F	80
2375	F	80
1201	C/B♭	80
2377	F	80
66030	F/B♭	79
66031	B♭	78
66032	C/F/B♭	79
66033	B♭/E♭	79
66037	Am/C	79
66096	B♭/F	77
77740	F	75.5
77741	F	75.5
851	F	76
852	F	76
77856	C/F/B♭	77
77857	B♭	77
77889	Gm/B♭/E♭/G	77
77924	C/F	77
78000	F/C	78
78001	F/B♭	78
78016	B♭/E♭	82
78096	B♭	77
996	B♭	76
78191	B♭/E♭	80
78192	B♭	80
1039	E♭	79
1041	B♭	79
78255	Gm/E♭	80
78256	F/B♭	80
78292	E♭	80

78294	C/F	80
1091	E♭	80
1092	G/E♭	80
78366	F	79
78367	F	79
1192	F	79
78373	F/B♭	80
78374	B♭/Gm/E♭	80
78588	E♭/E♭m	80
78692	B♭/E♭	80
79257	F/B♭	80
79277	B♭	79
9083	E♭/A♭	79
9781	E♭/A♭	81
9782	F	See Note
3847	C	79
3848	A♭/E♭	79
3296	E♭	78
3313	E♭	78
3314	E♭	78
62209	E♭	78
62210	Cm/E♭	78
62211	F	78
62212	E♭	78
17187	B♭	80
17188	E♭	80
17189	E♭	80
17190	F/B♭	80

Note: Matrix 9782 survives as a test pressing at the Edison National Historic Site and its pitch is taken from subsequent reissues.

Appendix 4

ALTHOUGH ACTUAL SALES FIGURES FOR COLUMBIA RECORDS DO NOT EXIST for records made at the time of Sweatman's tenure as a Columbia artist, it is fortunate that the Columbia files do provide details of the quantities of records shipped to Columbia dealers, which at least provides some clues as to actual sales figures. Newly released records were shipped to dealers approximately one month before their "official" catalog release date and their appearance in the monthly catalog supplements.

To give some meaningful comparison to these figures, in 1920 Bert Williams, then one of Columbia's top stars and the best-known African American performer of his age, was hitting total shipments of a million records per annum. Sweatman, as can be seen from the table below, was not far behind, with a total of 927,100 shipped records during 1919.

Title	Month released	Copies shipped
Col A2548. Regretful Blues/Everybody's Crazy 'Bout The Doggone Blues But I'm Happy...	July 1918	140,500
Col A2596. Darktown Strutters' Ball/Goodbye Alexander	October 1918	76,000
Col A2611. Indianola/Oh! You La! La!	November 1918	86,300
Col A2645. Rock-a-Bye My Baby/Those Draftin' Blues	December 1918	98,000
Col A2663. Has Anybody Seen My Corrine/Dallas Blues	January 1919	115,700
Col A2682. Ringtail Blues/Bluin' The Blues	March 1919	124,700
Col A2707. Ja-Da/Rainy Day Blues	June 1919	144,000
Col A2721. A Good Man Is Hard To Find/That's Got 'Em	July 1919	89,800
Col A2752. I'll Say She Does/Lucille	September 1919	135,200
Col A2768. Kansas City Blues/[Louisiana Five]	October 1919	180,300
Col A2775. Slide, Kelly, Slide/[Louisiana Five]	November 1919	137,400
Col A2818. Hello, Hello/I Ain't Gonna Give Nobody None O'This Jellyroll	January 1920	115,800
Col A2994. But/Think Of Me Little Daddy	December 1920	97,300

Discography

WHEN I FIRST SET OUT IN THE LATE 1980S to produce a Wilbur Sweatman bio-discography, virtually nothing of Sweatman's recorded output was available on CD or microgroove reissue. As for the Internet, downloadable music was but a pipe dream! A couple of sides had been reissued on a Neovox audio cassette in the 1980s, and one Columbia title had been released on a BBC LP devoted to music featured in their television production of F. Scott Fitzgerald's *Tender Is The Night*. Fortunately my good friends Colin Bray, John Wilby, and the late John R. T. Davies at the record label Jazz Oracle thought my idea for a CD devoted to Sweatman was a good idea, and ultimately a double CD album (Jazz Oracle BDW8036) was released, containing one take of every known track by Sweatman. Since then another CD has been produced of Sweatman's Columbia recordings, and another has been released featuring his Edison recordings. Therefore, the aspiring student of Sweatman's recorded music has numerous options available for obtaining his recordings.

What has been lacking, however, is a comprehensive discography. Brian Rust's *Jazz Records, 1897–1942*, in its various editions, has tended to gloss over Sweatman's recorded output with the minimum of detail. (Brian was never a lover of the music of Wilbur Sweatman, as has been made very clear in numerous LP liner notes he has written over the years.) What follows is my attempt to start from scratch, referring wherever possible to primary source material. Sadly, Sweatman was never closely questioned in his pitifully few interviews about the personnel of the bands he recorded with, so much of the information about the personnel of the Columbia sessions in particular is speculative. The information herein is based on contemporary sources of information as to who was working with Sweatman at the time, and also on aural identification.

ABBREVIATIONS AND USER NOTES

PERSONNEL. Much careful research has gone into ensuring the most accurate personnel possible, using contemporary documents, photographs, interviews with participating musicians, and careful listening by the author and a number of other researchers. A notable source was Wilbur Sweatman himself, who not only kept copious amounts of notes, but also had a very good, if not entirely accurate, memory. Considering the length of his recording career, from wax cylinders made in Minneapolis in 1903 to a privately recorded session in 1950 (the latter of which are not known to exist), it is not surprising that he was occasionally wrong about names and dates. Given the time span of over a hundred years from Sweatman's earliest recording session to the present day, and the lack of documentary evidence from the early days of jazz recording, much vital information as to the participants on Sweatman's records, such as cash books, checks, or recording ledgers, no longer exists in most cases. Record companies that did maintain accurate files that are still extant, such as Columbia, Edison, Victor, and Gennett, paid little heed to who actually participated on a record, paying more interest to such details as who was to be paid (in nearly all cases Sweatman himself), issue dates, pressing runs, and details of music publishers and how much they were to be paid for the use of their material. Although every effort has been taken to ensure the accuracy of personnel, there are cases where it has been impossible to supply any more than an educated guess. In these cases the musicians' names are shown in *italics*.

INSTRUMENTS are abbreviated to save space, using internationally accepted abbreviations as follows:

as—alto saxophone
bar—baritone saxophone
bb—brass bass (tuba, sousaphone etc.)
bcl—bass clarinet
bj—banjo
bsx—bass saxophone
c—cornet
cl—clarinet
Cm—C-melody saxophone
d—drums
g—guitar
ldr—leader
mb—mandolin-banjo
p—piano
sb—string bass
t—trumpet
tb—trombone
ts—tenor saxophone
v—vocal
vn—violin

RECORDING DATES. The recording dates for Columbia issues are taken from a relatively recently discovered source and are at variance with the dates quoted in published jazz discographies. The reason for this is that the dates shown on the Columbia matrix number file cards for recordings made prior to 1923 have, in the past, been assumed to be the recording dates. This is not so; the dates on the matrix number file cards are in fact the

dates when the masters were shipped from the recording studio to Columbia's processing and pressing plant at Bridgeport, Connecticut. However, another set of cards has
come to light, the Artist File cards, which list all the records made by a particular artist,
issue number, issue date, etc.; and these cards reveal the true recording date, usually a
day or so before shipping, sometimes the same date. They also show correct dates for
remake sessions, which usually occurred when a satisfactory performance could not be
chosen from the usual three takes of each tune made at a session.

MATRIX NUMBERS AND TAKES. Wherever possible, each take has been allocated an
individual entry in the discography and, in the case of the Columbia sides, the disposi-
tion as shown on the matrix information cards has been shown. Where doubt exists as
to which take was used on a particular issue (Grey Gull's numerous derivatives being
a good example), those issues are shown on a separate line where, in place of a take
number, a question mark appears. This does not imply a new or different take to those
already known to exist, merely that the issue in question has not been examined by the
author or reported to him by reliable sources. Any help in filling these gaps would be
appreciated.

LABEL DETAILS. Label details are shown exactly as they appear on the original issues,
including any typographical errors. Minor variations on multiple label issues are not
shown. Catalog numbers are shown with A or B side designations (or R and L in the
case of Edison Diamond Disc Records), where applicable, and where these are known.
A full listing of both label abbreviations and full label names, where not abbreviated,
follows. All issues are American unless otherwise noted.
BrF—Brunswick (France)
Co—Columbia
CoE—Columbia (UK)
Cr—Crescent
Dandy—Dandy
Ed—Edison
Em—Emerson
Emp—Empire
Ge—Gennett
GG—Grey Gull
Globe—Globe
LaBelle—LaBelle
LW—Little Wonder
Mad—Madison
Op—Operaphone
Pat—Pathé
PatE—Pathé (UK)
Rx—Radiex
Schu—Schubert
Spm—Supreme

VD—Van Dyke
Vi—Victor
Vo—Vocalion
World—World

KEYS OF PERFORMANCES. From the outset of this project, because of the wide variation
in recording speeds of Sweatman's recordings, it was felt that the provision of recording
speed details would be an invaluable resource, both for collectors and reissue producers.
As it was necessary to ascertain the keys in which the performances were played before
finding the correct recording speed, it was felt that the inclusion of keys would be essential, as the more musically skilled reader would have all the available information needed
to double-check for themselves the speeds shown in Appendix 3. While the keys quoted
are accurate, two points must be borne in mind. First, the speed of a record, especially
one recorded eighty-odd years ago, can vary considerably from start to finish; records
of this vintage regularly slow down toward the end, thus "speeding up" on playback.
Secondly, the stroboscope used to check the speed of the recording works on the pulses
of electric light generated by alternating current, 50 times per second in Europe and 60
times per second in the USA. Certain speeds are not wholly divisible by 50 or 60, so
variations occur between 50 Hz and 60 Hz readings. Also, if the electricity supply is not
constant, variations can occur in reading the speed on a stroboscope. The keys are the
one and only accurate constant. The speeds of all Sweatman's known recordings, shown
to the nearest one-half revolution per minute, are shown in Appendix 3.

WILBUR SWEATMAN AND HIS BAND
Instrumentation and personnel based on Sweatman's own recollections, plus contemporary sources. Charlie Minor or Jeff Smith, c; Dave Johnson, tb; Wilbur Sweatman, cl,
ldr; Laiph Mason, p; George "Pippin" Reeves, d.
Probably at the Metropolitan Music Company, 509-511 Nicollet Ave., Minneapolis, ca.
1903–4.

Maple Leaf Rag	Unnumbered Cylinder
Peaceful Henry	" "

The above cylinders were made for the Metropolitan Music Company and were issued in limited numbers. None are known to survive, although Len Kunstadt was
shown fragments of "Maple Leaf Rag" by Sweatman. It is possible that other titles by
Sweatman's band were recorded by the Metropolitan Music Company.

**CLARINET SOLO BY WILBER C. SWEATMAN [*sic*], Accompanied by Emerson
Symphony Orchestra—1
CLARINET SOLO BY WILBER C. SWEATMAN [*sic*], Accompanied by Emerson
Trio—2
CLARINET SOLO BY WILBER S. SWEATMAN [*sic*], Accompanied by Emerson
String Trio—3**

Wilbur Sweatman, cl; acc. by (1) *Arthur Bergh*, dir: t; tb; Nathan Glantz, Cm; vn; Malvin Franklin, p; bb; *James Irving Lent*, d; (2/3) Nathan Glantz, Cm; vn; Malvin Franklin, p.

3 West 35th Street, New York City, ca. December 1916.

1200-1	My Hawaiian Sunshine (L. Wolfe Gilbert)-1	Em 5166
2375-1	My Hawaiian Sunshine (L. Wolfe Gilbert)-1	Em 7120
1201-1	Down Home Rag (Wilber C. Sweatman [*sic*])-2	Em 5163
2377-1	Down Home Rag (Wilbur S. Sweatman [*sic*])-3	Em 7161

Keys: 1200-1 and 2375-1: F; 1201-1 and 2377-1: C/B♭

Matrix 2376 is by Emerson Symphony Orchestra; Sweatman is not present. The reverses of Em 7120 and 7161 are by Emerson Symphony Orchestra. Some copies of Em 7161 show Sweatman's name in both artist and composer credits as **WILBUR S. SWEATMAN**. The 5000 series Emersons are single-sided discs 5" (12.7 cm) in diameter; the 7000 series Emersons are 7" (17.6 cms) in diameter. James Lent is listed as the drummer based on aural comparison of his style on these sides with his drum solo of "The Ragtime Drummer" (Emerson 779).

MR. WILBER C. SWEATMAN [*sic*]. Clarinet solo. Unknown acc.

42 West 38th Street, New York City, Wednesday, February 28, 1917.

Boojie Rag [*sic*]   Vic test (unnumbered)

All other test recordings made at this session had piano accompaniment by Victor studio manager Eddie King. Strangely, the Sweatman entry does not credit an accompanist—possibly inferring that King was not the accompanist and that it was Sweatman's regular pianist (Dan Parrish) or even a band assembled for the occasion.

Wilbur Sweatman and His Jass Band
WILBUR SWEATMAN and His Jass Band—Pathé 20147

Wilbur Sweatman, cl, ldr; Sylvester "Vess" Williams, as; Clarence "Piccolo" Jones, Henry Minton, ts; Charlie Thorpe, bar; *Frank Withers*, bsx.

18 West 42nd Street, New York City, February-March 1917.

66030-3	Dance And Grow Thin (Meyer)	Pat 20147-A
66031-2	I Wonder Why. From "Love O' Mike" (Kern)	Pat 20145-A, Cr 10058-A, Op 4109-, World 397-, Emp 6219-, Schu 5113-
66032-2	Boogie Rag (Sweatman)	Pat 20147-B, Cr 10058-B, Op 4110-, Schu 5113-
66033-1	Joe Turner Blues (Handy)	Pat 20167-A, PatE 1046
66037-2	A Bag Of Rags (McKanlass)	Pat 20167-B, PatE 1046

Keys: 66030-3: F/B♭; 66031-2: B♭; 66032-2: C/F/B♭; 66033-1: B♭/E♭; 66037-2: Am/C

The gap in the matrix numbers may well be other titles by Sweatman; he recalled a session (he believed for Edison, but examination of 1916 and 1917 Edison Weekly Recording Reports has failed to identify a possible Sweatman session) at which he recorded "Memphis Blues," and this title may well account for one of the missing matrix numbers. See the note for the next session concerning two other titles possibly recorded at this session.

The instrumentation is confirmed by a photograph of the group in the May 1917 Pathé monthly catalog supplement, and the personnel is taken from Sweatman's own recollections of the recordings.

Crescent as **SWEATMAN'S JAZZ BAND**, Operaphone, World and Empire issues as **TEXAS JASS BAND**. Schubert as **JAZZ BAND**. The reverse of Operaphone 4110 is by Pathé Dance Orchestra as **OPERAPHONE BAND**. The reverses of Operaphone 4109 and the World and Empire issues are not known. Needle cut vertical masters (i.e., Operaphone, World, Empire, Crescent and Schubert) of 66031 and 66032 were dubbed off the master cylinders on November 23, 1917.

Wilbur Sweatman and His Jass Band

As last session
18 West 42nd Street, New York City, April 1917

66096-1	Dancing An American Rag (Ward)	Pat 20145

Keys: 66096-1: B♭/F

The correct title for this performance is "(Then You're) Dancing An American Rag." Some copies of matrix 66096 show the title as "Down Home Rag (Sweatman)" which, in view of the missing matrices from the previous session, may be a clue to the identity of one of the missing matrices. This title has usually been ascribed to the previous session, but the enormous gap in matrix numbers leads one to suspect that it is the product of another session, probably a remake from the previous session, a few weeks later.

WILBER SWEATMAN'S ORIGINAL JASS BAND [sic]

Instrumentation and personnel unknown apart from Wilbur Sweatman, cl.
104 West 38th Street, New York City, Wednesday, June 13, 1917.

61703-1	Unknown title	Co "Trial" unissued
61704-1	Unknown title	Co "Trial" unissued

WILBER SWEATMAN'S ORIGINAL JASS BAND [sic]

Probably as for June 13, 1917.
104 West 38th Street, New York City, Friday, August 17, 1917.

61704-2	Unknown title	Co "Trial" unissued

The above two sessions were trial recordings for audition purposes and were not intended for issue.

Artist credits on Sweatman's Columbia recordings vary from issue to issue, particularly on the 1918 sides; even different copies of the same record exist with differing artist credits, sometimes varying from one side to the other of individual copies! This is no doubt due to the fact that Sweatman's Columbia records sold extremely well and remained in the catalog for several years, requiring numerous label reprints over and above the original order quantity. This is borne out by some incredibly high stamper numbers on later pressings—I have seen stamper numbers on copies of Columbia A2707 (Sweatman's recording of the 1919 hit "Ja-Da") as high as 284. Over a period of time the artist credit was standardized to **WILBUR SWEATMAN'S ORIGINAL JAZZ BAND**, but issues up to and including Columbia A2611 generally misspell his forename as Wilber and include his middle initial.

The exact personnel for Sweatman's Columbia recordings are almost impossible to establish, given the lack of documentary evidence, the passage of ninety-plus years and the fact that the style of playing is purely ensemble. However, Sweatman was interviewed on several occasions by Len Kunstadt and during these interviews gave details of who he thought was present on the records. These personnel are used unchanged, apart from where (a) aural evidence points to a different musician being present in comparison to the previous session where the individual's name appeared and (b) where documentary evidence would point to another's presence.

WILBER C. SWEATMAN'S ORIGINAL JAZZ BAND [sic]

William Crickett Smith, t; Arthur Reeves or Major Jackson, tb; Wilbur Sweatman, cl, ldr; Dan Parrish, p; Ogese T. McKay or Jerome "Romy" Jones, bb; George Bowser, d. 104 West 38th Street, New York City, Thursday, March 28, 1918

77740-1	Regretful Blues (Hess)-1	Co A2548, CoE 2908
77740-2	Regretful Blues (Hess)-1	Co A2548
77740-3	Regretful Blues	Co rejected ("poor rendition")
77741-1	Ev'rybody's Crazy 'Bout The Doggone Blues But I'm Happy (Creamer and Layton)-2	Co A2548, CoE 2908
77741-2	Ev'rybody's Crazy 'Bout The Doggone Blues But I'm Happy (Creamer and Layton)-2	Co A 2548
77741-3	Ev'rybody's Crazy 'Bout The Doggone Blues But I'm Happy (Creamer and Layton)-2	Co A2548—originally "store"

Keys: 77740-1-2 F; 77741-1-2-3: F

Take combinations confirmed. Co A2548: 1/1, 1/2, 2/1, 2/2, 2/3

Matrix 77741 on all inspected copies of Co A2548 is labelled as by **WILBER C. SWEATMAN'S ORIGINAL JAZZ BAND**, but later pressings show matrix 77740 as by **WILBUR C. SWEATMAN'S ORIGINAL JAZZ BAND**. CoE 2908 as **SWEATMAN'S JAZZ BAND** with the titles in upper case. Interestingly, a pressing of A2548 has been reported that couples 77740-1 with 77740-2. Although at first glance this may be an oversight on the part of the press operator, it does highlight an important and previously unknown fact. It has been known for many years that Columbia, up until 1922 (and less frequently thereafter), regularly pressed records from multiple takes. This entry demonstrates that different takes were available at the same time in the same pressing location and may have been used on a random basis—something that has not previously been considered.

The drummer on this and several subsequent sessions has historically been listed as Henry Bowser; however, extensive searches of both American Federation of

Musicians directories and World War I draft registration cards have failed to reveal a Henry Bowser living in the New York area working as a musician. However, a George Oliver Bowser living at 218 W. 134th Street in New York was registered for the Draft on June 5, 1917. At the time he was working as a musician at Shanley's Restaurant in Yonkers, New York. The 1929 American Federation of Musicians Local 802 Directory lists among drummers George Oliver Bowser, residing at 170 W. 135th Street, New York—pretty conclusive evidence that this is the man remembered by Sweatman as Henry Bowser.

DANCE MUSIC

William Crickett Smith, t; Arthur Reeves or Major Jackson, tb; Wilbur Sweatman, cl, ldr; Dan Parrish or Palmer Jones, p; George Bowser, d.
104 West 38th Street, New York City, ca. late March–early April 1918.

| 851-2 | Ev'rybody's Crazy 'Bout The Doggone Blues | LW 851 |
| 852-2 | Regretful Blues | LW 852 |

Keys: 851-2 and 852-2: F
NB: all Little Wonder records are 5.5" (12.7 cm) in diameter and are single-sided.
The above Little Wonder records (and several subsequent issues) are shown as being recorded at separate sessions from the Columbia issues of the same titles because in general they are differently balanced and in some cases are made by groups of different instrumentation and personnel from those that made the equivalent Columbia titles.

WILBER C. SWEATMAN'S ORIGINAL JAZZ BAND [sic]

William Hicks, t; Arthur Reeves, tb; Wilbur Sweatman, cl, ldr; Dan Parrish, Palmer Jones, p; George Bowser, d.
104 West 38th Street, New York, Tuesday, May 28, 1918.

77856-1	The Darktown Strutters' Ball (Introducing (1) I'm Sorry I Made You Cry)	Co rejected ("poor start")
77856-2	The Darktown Strutters' Ball (Introducing (1) I'm Sorry I Made You Cry)	Co "store"
77856-3	The Darktown Strutters' Ball (Introducing (1) I'm Sorry I Made You Cry) (Shelton Brooks, 1-Clesi)	Co A2596
77857-1	Goodbye Alexander (Introducing (1) Oh! Frenchy)	Co rejected ("poor finish")
77857-2	Goodbye Alexander (Introducing (2) Oh! Frenchy)	Co "store"
77857-3	Goodbye Alexander (Introducing (1) Oh! Frenchy) (Creamer and Layton, 1–Conrad)	Co A2596

Keys: 77856-3: C/F/B♭; 77857-3: B♭

An interesting aside: at least two photographs of the band were taken in the Columbia studio at this session, and both were used in publicity material issued by Columbia at the time.

WILBER C. SWEATMAN'S ORIGINAL JAZZ BAND [*sic*]

William Hicks, t; Major Jackson, tb; Wilbur Sweatman, cl, ldr; Dan Parrish, p; George
Bowser, d
104 West 38th Street, New York, Friday, June 14, 1918.

77889-1	Indianola (Introducing: Those Draftin' Blues)	Co rejected ("clarinet shrill")
77889-2	Indianola (Introducing: Those Draftin' Blues)	Co rejected ("clarinet shrill")
77889-3	Indianola (Introducing: Those Draftin' Blues) (Henry and Onivas/Pinkard)	Co A2611

Keys: 77889-3: Gm/B♭/E♭/G

"Indianola" on Little Wonder 778 (as **DANCE MUSIC—BAND**) has been previously included in discographies as a Sweatman performance, but its authenticity as a
Sweatman performance is highly suspect in view of its matrix and issue number being
considerably lower than the Little Wonder issues from the March 28, 1918, session (778
would put its recording date in late 1917. NB: Prince's Band recorded a 12-inch version
of 'Indianola' for Columbia ca. December 10, 1917).

WILBER C. SWEATMAN'S ORIGINAL JAZZ BAND [*sic*]

William Hicks, t; Major Jackson, tb; Wilbur Sweatman, cl, ldr; Dan Parrish, p; unknown, d.
104 West 38th Street, New York City, Tuesday, June 25, 1918.

77924-1	Oh! You La! La! (Introducing: (1) I Want Him Back Again) (Tush, 1-Brown)	Co A2611 (originally "store")
77924-2	Oh! You La! La! (Introducing: (1) I Want Him Back Again)	Co rejected ("too jumbled")
77924-3	Oh! You La! La! (Introducing: (1) I Want Him Back Again (Tush, 1-Brown)	Co A2611

Keys: 77924-1–3: C/F

WILBUR C. SWEATMAN'S ORIGINAL JAZZ BAND

William Hicks or Russell Smith, t; Major Jackson, tb; Wilbur Sweatman, cl, ldr; Dan
Parrish, p; Jerome "Romy" Jones or Ogese T. McKay, bb; Zeno Lawrence, d.
104 West 38th Street, New York City, Friday, August 16, 1918.

78000-1	Rock-A-Bye Your Baby With A Dixie Melody from "Sinbad" (Schwartz)	Co A2645
78000-2	Rock-A-Bye Your Baby With A Dixie Melody	Co rejected ("poor rendition")
78001-1	Those Draftin' Blues (Introducing: Somebody's Done Me Wrong) (Pinkard 1-Skidmore and Friedlander)	Co A2645
78001-2	Those Draftin' Blues (Introducing: Somebody's Done Me Wrong) (Pinkard 1-Skidmore and Friedlander)	Co A2645 (originally "store")

Keys: 78000-1 F/C, 78001-1-2 F/B♭

The file card for matrix 78000 shows the comment "With Patter chorus."

WILBUR SWEATMAN'S ORIGINAL JAZZ BAND

Unknown t; Major Jackson, tb; Wilbur Sweatman, cl, ldr; Dan Parrish, p; Jerome "Romy" Jones, bb; Zeno Lawrence, d.

104 West 38th Street, New York City, Wednesday, August 21, 1918.

78016-1	Has Anybody Seen My Corrine (Introducing: (1) Down On Bull Frog's Isle; (2) Livery Stable Blues) (Graham and Johnson, 1-White, 2-Lopez and Nunez)	Co A2663 (originally "store")
78016-2	Has Anybody Seen My Corrine (Introducing: (1) Down On Bull Frog's Isle; (2) Livery Stable Blues)	Co rejected ("clarinet squeaky")
78016-3	Has Anybody Seen My Corrine (Introducing: (1) Down On Bull Frog's Isle; (2) Livery Stable Blues) (Graham and Johnson, 1-White, 2-Lopez and Nunez)	Co A2663

Keys: 78016-1: B♭/E♭

WILBUR SWEATMAN'S ORIGINAL JAZZ BAND

William Hicks or Russell Smith, t; Major Jackson, tb; Wilbur Sweatman, cl, ldr; Dan Parrish, p; Jerome "Romy" Jones, bb; Zeno Lawrence, d.

104 West 38th Street, New York City, Friday, October 4, 1918.

78096-1	Dallas Blues (Introducing: (1) At The Funny Page Ball (2) Lovin' (I Can't Live Without It) (Wand, 1-Speroy, 2-Warfield)	Co A2663
78096-2	Dallas Blues (Introducing: (1) At The Funny Page Ball (2) Lovin' (I Can't Live Without It)	Co rejected
78096-3	Dallas Blues (Introducing: (1) At The Funny Page Ball (2) Lovin' (I Can't Live Without It)	Co "store"
996-1	Dallas Blues	LW 996

Keys: 78096-1: B♭; 996-1: B♭

Little Wonder 996 as **JAZZ BAND**. Despite the labelling of this issue as "Medley Fox-trot," none of the tunes introduced into the Columbia performance are included.

WILBUR SWEATMAN'S ORIGINAL JAZZ BAND

William Crickett Smith, t; Major Jackson, tb; Wilbur Sweatman, cl, ldr; Dan Parrish, p; George Bowser, d.

104 West 38th Street, New York City, Wednesday, December 4, 1918.

78191-1	Ringtail Blues	Co rejected ("inferior to master")
78191-2	Ringtail Blues (Robinson and Williams)	Co A2682
78191-3	Ringtail Blues	Co rejected ("inferior to master")
78192-1	Bluin' The Blues (Ragas)	Co A2682
78192-2	Bluin' The Blues	Co rejected ("inferior to master")
78192-3	Bluin' The Blues	Co rejected ("inferior to master")
78192-4	Bluin' The Blues	Co rejected ("inferior to master")
1039-3	Has Anybody Seen My Corrine?	LW 1039

| 1040- | Unknown title | LW rejected |
| 1041- | Ringtail Blues | LW 1041 |

Keys: 78191-2: B♭/E♭; 78192-1: B♭; 1039-3: E♭
Little Wonder 1039 and 1041 as **JAZZ BAND**.
Little Wonder matrix 1040 is almost certainly a rejected Sweatman performance, possibly of "Bluin' The Blues," but in the absence of recording files for Little Wonder, we can only speculate. The copy of Little Wonder 1041 inspected does not show a take number.

WILBUR SWEATMAN'S ORIGINAL JAZZ BAND

Willie Lewis, Arthur Briggs, t; Frank Withers, tb; Wilbur Sweatman, cl, ldr; *unknown, possibly Mazie Mullins*, Cm; Dan Parrish, p; George Bowser, d.
104 West 38th Street, New York City, Friday, January 17, 1919.

78255-1	Rainy Day Blues	Co rejected ("poor ending")
78255-2	Rainy Day Blues (Frank Warshauer)	Co A2707
78255-3	Rainy Day Blues (Frank Warshauer)	Co A2707
78256-1	Ja-Da! (Ja-Da, Ja-Da, Jing, Jing, Jing)	Co rejected ("too confused")
78256-2	Ja-Da! (Ja-Da, Ja-Da, Jing, Jing, Jing)	Co rejected ("out of tune" or "out of time")
78256-3	Ja-Da! (Ja-Da, Ja-Da, Jing, Jing, Jing)	Co rejected ("wrong tempo")

Keys: 78255-2: Gm/E♭
A version of "Rainy Day Blues" was issued on Little Wonder 1107 (as **DANCE MUSIC—ORCHESTRA**), but it is by Yerkes' Jazarimba Orchestra.
Arthur Briggs, in an interview with Ate van Delden, stated that this was his first recording session. It is worth mentioning that the trumpet work on the next two sessions (three, if the Little Wonder session ca. March 8, 1919, was separate from the Columbia sessions) is consistent stylistically with the playing on the above sides. At this time Briggs was a member of Will Marion Cook's New York Syncopated Orchestra, so the possibility of other members of the Cook orchestra also being present on this and the following two/three dates date cannot be discounted.

WILBUR SWEATMAN'S ORIGINAL JAZZ BAND

Willie Lewis, t; *Arthur Briggs*, possible 2nd t; Frank Withers, tb; Wilbur Sweatman, cl, ldr; *George Smith*, vn; Dan Parrish, p; Jerome "Romy" Jones, bb; unknown d (and celeste on 78256).
104 West 38th Street, New York City, Wednesday, February 5, 1919.

78256-4	Ja-Da! (Ja-Da, Ja-Da, Jing, Jing, Jing) (Bob Carleton)	Co A2707
78256-5	Ja-Da! (Ja-Da, Ja-Da, Jing, Jing, Jing)	Co rejected ("poor tone")
78291-1	Lonesome Road (Introducing: Salvation Blues [A Camp Meetin' Croon])	Co rejected

78291-2	Lonesome Road (Introducing: Salvation Blues [A Camp Meetin' Croon])	Co rejected
78291-3	Lonesome Road (Introducing: Salvation Blues [A Camp Meetin' Croon])	Co rejected
78292-1	A Good Man Is Hard To Find (Introducing: Sweet Child)	Co rejected
78292-2	A Good Man Is Hard To Find (Introducing: Sweet Child) (Eddie Green/Erving and Stovall)	Co A2721, LaBelle AL 5040 (originally "store")
78292-3	A Good Man Is Hard To Find (Introducing: Sweet Child) (Eddie GreenErving and Stovall)	Co A2721

Keys: 78256-4: F/B♭; 78292-2-3: E♭

LaBelle AL 5040 as **BAND**. This issue omits both details of the introduced composition and composer credits. "Lonesome Road" was composed by Will Nash.

WILBUR SWEATMAN'S ORIGINAL JAZZ BAND

Willie Lewis, Arthur Briggs, t; Frank Withers, tb; Wilbur Sweatman, cl, ldr; *George Smith*, vn; Dan Parrish, p; unknown, d.

104 West 38th Street, New York City, Saturday, February 8, 1919.

| 78294-1 | That's Got 'Em (Sweatman) | Co A2721, LaBelle AL 5040 |
| 78294-2 | That's Got 'Em | Co rejected ("damaged when received") |

Keys: 78294-1: C/F

LaBelle AL 5040 as **BAND**. This issue omits composer credits. The LaBelle issue is a Columbia pressing with a pasted-over LaBelle label.

The note "damaged when received" refers to the receipt of the master at Columbia's processing and pressing plant at Bridgeport, Connecticut.

JAZZ BAND

Willie Lewis or Arthur Briggs, t; Frank Withers, tb; Wilbur Sweatman, cl, ldr; Dan Parrish, p; unknown, d.

104 West 38th Street, New York City, possibly February 8, 1919.

1091-1	A Good Man Is Hard To Find	LW 1091
1092-1	Lonesome Road	LW 1092 (see note)
1092-2	Lonesome Road	LW 1092

Keys: 1091-1: E♭; 1092-2: G/E♭

LW 1092-1 has been reported but is unconfirmed.

WILBUR SWEATMAN'S ORIGINAL JAZZ BAND

Willie Lewis, *Arthur Briggs*, t; Frank Withers, tb; Wilbur Sweatman, cl, ldr; *Unknown, possibly Mazie Mullins*, Cm or ts; Dan Parrish, p; unknown d (same drummer as February 5 session).

104 West 38th Street, New York City, Saturday March 22, 1919.

78366-1	Kansas City Blues	Co rejected
78366-2	Kansas City Blues (Bowman)	Co A2768
78366-3	Kansas City Blues (Bowman)	Co A2768
78367-1	Slide, Kelly, Slide	Co "store—do not use as mother"
78367-2	Slide, Kelly, Slide (Briegel)	Co A2775, LaBelle AL 5055
78367-3	Slide, Kelly, Slide	Co rejected

Keys: 78366-2-3: F; 78367-2: F

LaBelle AL 5055 as **BAND**. This issue omits composer credits. The LaBelle issue is a Columbia pressing with a pasted-over LaBelle label.

The reverses of Co A2768, A2775, and LaBelle AL 5055 are by Louisiana Five Jazz Orchestra.

JAZZ BAND

Willie Lewis, t; Frank Withers, tb; Wilbur Sweatman, cl, ldr; Dan Parrish, p; Jerome "Romy" Jones, bb; unknown d (same as March 22, 1919 session).

104 West 38th Street, New York City, *ca. mid-late March 1919.*

| 1192-2 | Kansas City Blues | LW 1192 |

Key: 1192-2: F

The above session is yet another example of a Little Wonder title recorded at a different session from the Columbia record of the same title; in this case the tenor saxophone is replaced by brass bass.

WILBUR SWEATMAN'S ORIGINAL JAZZ BAND

Willie Lewis, t; Frank Withers or John Reeves, tb; Wilbur Sweatman, cl, ldr; Dan Parrish, p; Walter Gray, bj; Arnold Joshuah Ford, Arthur Sumner Shaw, Arthur Gray, mb; unknown d (same as previous session). Someone shouts at the end of 78373.

104 West 38th Street, New York City, Saturday, March 29, 1919.

78373-1	I'll Say She Does from 'Sinbad" (Intro.: N'Everything)	Co "store, do not use"
78373-2	I'll Say She Does from "Sinbad" (Intro.: N'Everything) (De Sylva, Kahn and Jolson)	Co A2752
78373-3	I'll Say She Does from "Sinbad" (Intro.: N'Everything)	Co "store, do not use"
78374-1	Lucille	Co rejected ("poor tone")
78374-2	Lucille (Wadsworth and Arden)	Co A2752
78374-3	Lucille	Co rejected ("blasting banjos")

Keys: 78373-2: F/B♭; 78374-2: B♭/Gm/E♭

Previous discographies have shown the Little Wonder of "Lucille" (LW 1169) as being by Wilbur Sweatman. However, the artist credit for this issue is Jazzarimba Orchestra, a group under the leadership of Harry A. Yerkes, and aural examination confirms this to be correct.

WILBUR SWEATMAN'S ORIGINAL JAZZ BAND

Russell Smith, t; John Reeves, tb; Wilbur Sweatman, cl, ldr; *Bobby Lee, p; Jerome "Romy" Jones or Ogese T. McKay, bb; Herbert King, d.*
104 West 38th Street, New York City, Tuesday, July 22, 1919.

78588-1	Hello, Hello!	Co rejected ("Not up to standard")
78588-2	Hello, Hello!	Co rejected ("Not up to standard")
78588-3	Hello, Hello!	Co rejected ("Not up to standard")

WILBUR SWEATMAN'S ORIGINAL JAZZ BAND

Russell Smith, t; John Reeves, tb; Wilbur Sweatman, cl, ldr; Bobby Lee, p; Jerome "Romy" Jones, bb; Herbert King, d.
104 West 38th Street, New York City, Wednesday, September 24, 1919.

78588-4	Hello, Hello! (King)	Co A2818, LaBelle AL 5060
78588-5	Hello, Hello! (King)	Co A2818
78588-6	Hello, Hello!	Co rejected ("breaks")
78588-7	Hello, Hello! (King)	Co A2818
78692-1	I Ain't Gonna Give Nobody None O' This Jellyroll (Introducing: Just Leave It To Me)	Co rejected ("out of tune" or "out of time")
78692-2	I Ain't Gonna Give Nobody None O' This Jellyroll (Introducing: Just Leave It To Me)	Co rejected ("out of tune" or "out of time")
78692-3	I Ain't Gonna Give Nobody None O' This Jellyroll (Introducing: Just Leave It To Me)(Williams and Williams/Pinkard)	Co A2818, LaBelle AL 5060

Keys: 78588-4-5-7: E♭/E♭m; 78692-3: B♭/E♭

The labelling of LaBelle AL 5060 is somewhat unusual. Matrix 78588-4 is credited as **BAND**; matrix 78692-3 is credited as **JAZZ BAND** and gives the title as "I Ain't Gonna Give Nobody." The LaBelle issue is a normal Columbia pressing with a pasted-over LaBelle label.

Little Wonder 1234 (often mistakenly listed as 1233), previously noted as a performance of "Hello, Hello!" by Sweatman, is in fact a hitherto undocumented performance by the Louisiana Five.

WILBUR SWEATMAN'S ORIGINAL JAZZ BAND

Russell Smith or Charlie Gaines, t; Calvin Jones, tb; Wilbur Sweatman, cl, ldr; Bobby Lee, p; unknown, bj; Herbert King, d.
104 West 38th Street, New York City, Thursday, June 10, 1920.

79243-1	In Gay Havana (Tango Fox Trot)	Co rejected ("Not up to standard")
79243-2	In Gay Havana (Tango Fox Trot)	Co rejected (originally "OK")
79243-3	In Gay Havana (Tango Fox Trot)	Co rejected (originally "store")
79257-1	But (Introducing: Tiddle-Dee Winks)	Co A2994—(originally "store" -see note)
79257-2	But (Introducing: Tiddle-Dee Winks) (Berlin-Handman)	Co A2994
79257-3	But (Introducing: Tiddle-Dee Winks)	Co "store, do not use as mother"

Keys: 79257-2: F/B♭

A second take of 79257 exists, but the copy inspected is of the "sunken rim" label type, which almost invariably does not show take and mother dispositions. In view of the comments on the file card regarding 79257-3, it is reasonable to assume that 79257-1 was used.

The Columbia file cards are emphatic that all takes of 79243 were made at this session, despite the enormous gap in matrices. Whether or not the matrices were allocated for an earlier session which was canceled or whether this was an error in bookkeeping we can only surmise.

WILBUR SWEATMAN'S ORIGINAL JAZZ BAND

Russell Smith or Charlie Gaines, t; Calvin Jones, tb; Wilbur Sweatman, cl, ldr; Bobby Lee, p; Herbert King, d.
104 West 38th Street, New York City, Tuesday, June 15, 1920.

79277-1	Think Of Me Little Daddy (Introducing: I'm Going Back To My Used To Be)	Co rejected ("poor balance")
79277-2	Think Of Me Little Daddy (Introducing: I'm Going Back To My Used To Be)	Co rejected (originally "OK [suspend]")
79277-3	Think Of Me Little Daddy (Introducing: I'm Going Back To My Used To Be)	Co rejected ("poor balance")
79278-1	Sunbeams (Introducing: Rose Of Bagdad [I Love You So])	Co rejected ("poor balance")
79278-2	Sunbeams (Introducing: Rose Of Bagdad [I Love You So])	Co rejected (originally "OK")
79278-3	Sunbeams (Introducing: Rose Of Bagdad [I Love You So])	Co rejected ("poor balance")
79279-1	Su Ez A	Co rejected (originally "OK")
79279-2	Su Ez A	Co rejected ("poor balance")

WILBUR SWEATMAN'S ORIGINAL JAZZ BAND

Russell Smith or Charlie Gaines, t; Calvin Jones, tb; Wilbur Sweatman, cl, ldr; Bobby Lee, p; Herbert King, d.

104 West 38th Street, New York City, Tuesday, June 22, 1920.

79277-4	Think Of Me Little Daddy (Introducing: I'm Going Back To My Used To Be) (Whitman-Cox)	Co A2994	
79277-5	Think Of Me Little Daddy (Introducing: I'm Going Back To My Used To Be) (Whitman-Cox)	Co A2994 (originally "store")	
79297-1	Never Let No One Man Worry Your Mind (Introducing: I'm Gonna Jazz My Way Right Straight Thru' Paradise)	Co rejected ("inferior to master")	
79297-2	Never Let No One Man Worry Your Mind (Introducing: I'm Gonna Jazz My Way Right Straight Thru' Paradise)	Co "store"	
79297-3	Never Let No One Man Worry Your Mind (Introducing: I'm Gonna Jazz My Way Right Straight Thru' Paradise)	Co rejected (originally "OK")	
79298-1	Pee Gee Blues	Co rejected ("edgy")	
79298-2	Pee Gee Blues	Co rejected (originally "OK")	
79298-3	Pee Gee Blues	Co rejected ("edgy")	

Key: 79277-4–5: B♭

The reason for the change in status of 79277-5 is not known; however, copies of this take are extremely rare, so the possibility of it having been used in error cannot be discounted.

Sweatman recalled a recording session for Lyric in 1920, but the results of any such session were never issued.

WILBUR SWEATMAN AND HIS ACME SYNCOPATERS [sic]

Eugene "Bud" Aiken, Leslie Davis, t; *Calvin Jones*, tb; Wilbur Sweatman, cl, bcl, ldr; *Percy Green*, as; *Ramón Hernández*, ts; *Duke Ellington*, p; *Mike Danzi*, bj; *Jerome "Romy" Jones*, bb; *Maceo White*, d.

9-11 East 37th Street, New York City, Tuesday, August 12, 1924.

9017	Battleship Kate	Ge rejected
9017-A	Battleship Kate	Ge rejected
9018	She Loves Me	Ge rejected

WILBUR SWEATMAN AND HIS ACME SYNCOPATERS [sic]

Leslie Davis, Eugene "Bud" Aiken, t; Calvin Jones, tb; Wilbur Sweatman, cl, bcl, ldr; Percy Green, as; Ramón Hernández, ts; Edwin C. Stevens, *Walter Hall, or Claude Hopkins*, p; *Clyde Johnson or possibly Mike Danzi*, bj; Jerome "Romy" Jones, bb.

9-11 East 37th Street, New York City, Thursday, September 18, 1924.

9083	Battleship Kate	Ge rejected
9083-A	Battleship Kate (Sweatman-Rives)	Ge 5584-B
9084	She Loves Me	Ge rejected (see note)
9084-A	She Loves Me	Ge rejected

Keys: 9083-A: E♭/A♭

The reverse of Ge 5584 is by Lange-McKay Orch.

The recording engineer on both of the above sessions was Arthur J. Lyons.

Matrices 9083 and 9084 were originally scheduled for issue on Gennett 5548, but this was withdrawn before issue. The recording dates for the above Gennett sessions differ from previous discographies—however, the above dates are taken from the Gennett Recording Information cards, which are specific about date and location. The file cards show that Sweatman was paid $125 for each side at the September 18 session.

WILBUR SWEATMAN'S BROWNIES

Leslie Davis, Eugene "Bud" Aiken, t; Calvin Jones, tb; Wilbur Sweatman, cl, bcl, ldr; Percy Green, as; Ramón Hernández, ts; *Walter Hall or Claude Hopkins*, p; Harry Batcheldor, bj, v-1; Jerome "Romy" Jones, bb; Maceo White, d, v-1.

79 Fifth Avenue, New York City, Friday, October 10, 1924.

9781-A	Battleship Kate (Ada Rives & Wilbur C. Sweatman)-1	Ed 51438-L
9781-B	Battleship Kate (Ada Rives & Wilbur C. Sweatman) -1	Ed 51438-L
9781-C	Battleship Kate (Ada Rives & Wilbur C. Sweatman) -1	Ed 51438-L
9782-A	It Makes No Difference Now	Ed rejected, *Jazz Oracle BDW8046 (CD)*, *Neovox 714 (Cassette)*
9782-B	It Makes No Difference Now	Ed rejected (test exists)
9782-C	It Makes No Difference Now	Ed rejected (test exists)

Keys: 9781-A-B-C: E♭/A♭; 9782-A-B-C: F

The reverse of 51438 is by Georgia Melodians.

Tests of matrix 9782-A-B-C exist at the Edison National Historical Site at West Orange, New Jersey.

The Edison "Information for Advertising Department" sheet for Ed 51438 has the following handwritten note: "Mr. Walsh, I understand he [Sweatman] was quite a hit with Columbia at one time. Cronkhite." The release sheet also notes that matrix 9781 was played in the key of E♭. A handwritten note adds that Edison 51438 was deleted from catalog on May 19, 1926, which probably accounts for its rarity.

Previous discographies have shown John Reeves as trombonist on the above and several subsequent Sweatman sessions. That is hardly likely to be the case, as he died on April 7, 1922, having been shot five times by his wife!

The results of the following two Grey Gull sessions, as was normal practice on this and associated labels, were issued under a bewildering variety of different pseudonyms. Thus it is impossible to give an artist credit in the usual sense, as even one single issue on one label can appear under up to five pseudonyms. A full listing of known pseudonyms, and the issues they pertain to, follows the session details. The use of the question mark after the matrix number does not imply an additional unconfirmed take—merely that the issue that follows has not been visually inspected and that it is not possible to verify which take was used. It is highly likely, even probable, that alternate takes to those shown for individual issues were released, but these are all that have been examined by the author or confirmed via reliable sources.

Wilbur Sweatman, cl; acc. by Walter Hall, p; Harry Batcheldor, bj.
Probably the Emerson Recording Laboratories, 206 Fifth Avenue, New York City, ca. March 1926.

3847-A	Get It Now (Pearl)	GG 1340-B, 4193-B, 8020-B, Rx 1340-B, Globe 1340-A, 8020-B, Dandy 5156-B
3847-B	Get It Now (Pearl)	GG 1340-B, 4193-B, Rx 1340-B, 1382-B, 1402-B, 4193-B, Mad 22005-A, Spm 1340-B
3847-E?	Get It Now	Globe 1382-B
3848-A	Poor Papa (Rose-Woods)	GG 1340-A, Rx 1340-A, Globe 1340-A, Spm 1340-A
3848-B	Poor Papa (Rose-Woods)	GG 1340-A, Rx 1340-A, Dandy 5156-A

Keys: 3847-A-B: C; 3848-A-B: A♭/E♭
Take combinations confirmed: GG 1340—A/A, A/B, Rx 1340—B/B
3847-E is noted in the late Carl Kendziora's Grey Gull numerical listing, published in *Record Research* magazine, as being issued on Globe 1382 but, as no copy could be found to substantiate this, it is the author's belief that this is a misreporting of a badly stamped 3847-B. One also has to consider that Grey Gull, a company hardly renowned for their lavishness, would have taken the trouble to record at least three extra masters when they already had and were using two perfectly good ones.
Performer credits:
Grey Gull 1340: **C. Wilber, C. Wilbur, Ed Johnson, Chic Winter, The Dixie Trio, Uncredited**
Grey Gull 8020: **C. Wilber, Ed Johnson**
Radiex 1340: **The Dixie Trio, C. Wilber**
Dandy 5156: **Ed. Johnson**
Globe 1340: **C. Wilber, Ed Johnson, Chic Winter, Uncredited**
Globe 1382: **Ed Johnson, The Dixie Trio**
Radiex 1382: **The Dixie Trio**
Globe 8020: **C. Wilber, Ed Johnson, The Dixie Trio**
Supreme 1340: **C. Wilber, The Dixie Trio**
GG 4193, Rx 1402, and Madison 22005 all show the title as "Powder Puff" with the composer credit on GG4193 and Rx1402 as Sanella or Sannella, and on Madison 22005 as Thompson. All three of these issues show the performance as being a saxophone solo with piano accompaniment; the artist credit on Rx 1402 as Sanella or Sannella. Mad 22005 as Neilson, and GG/Rx 4193 is uncredited. Dandy 5156 shows the composer credit for matrix 3847-A as A. Eggers.

Reverses: Rx 1402 by Bostonian Syncopators; GG/Rx 4193 by International Orchestra; Globe/Radiex 1382 by Bostonian Syncopators (Fred Hall and his Roseland Orchestra); Grey Gull/Globe 8020 by Original Dixie Rag Pickers (Grey Gull studio band); Mad 22005 by Southern Melody Makers (Grey Gull studio band).

Wilbur Sweatman, cl; acc. by *Henry Green*, tb; *Ida Roberts*, p; *Hazel Vanverlayer*, v.
20 East 42nd Street, New York City, ca. March 1929.

3296-A	Battleship Kate (Sweatman)-v*HV*	GG 7037, 1701, Rx 1701, 7037, VD 77037-
3296-B	Battleship Kate (Sweatman)-v*HV*	Radiex 7037
3313-A	Sweat Blues (Sweatman)	Rx 1706
3313-B	Sweat Blues (Lead Pipe Blues*) (Sweatman)	Rx 1706, GG 1706, VD 901-B*, 5015-*, Mad 50015-B*, Rx 901
3314-A	Jim Town Blues (Sweatman)	Radiex 7037
3314-B	Jim Town Blues (Sweatman)	GG 7037, 1702, Rx 7037, VD 77037

Keys: 3296-A: E♭; 3313-A-B: E♭; 3314-B: E♭.

Several issues credit matrix 3313 as "with vocal chorus." Mad 50015-B and Van Dyke 901-B do not show the matrix number but instead have a control number, 152-B, both in the runoff and on the label. The composer credit on some copies of Grey Gull 1706 is (Sweatmen [sic]). The composer credit on the copy of Van Dyke 901-B is (Wilbur Sweatman).

Performer credits:
Grey Gull 1701: **Dixie Trio**
Grey Gull 1702: **Dixie Trio, Uncredited**
Grey Gull 1706: **Wabash Trio, Uncredited**
Grey Gull 7037: **Ed Johnson, Uncredited**
Radiex 901: **Joy Dispensers**
Radiex 1701, 1706, 7037: **Uncredited**
Madison 5015, 50015: **Atlanta Syncopators**
Van Dyke 901: **Wilbur Sweatman's Trio, Ed Johnson, Joy Dispensers**
Van Dyke 5015: **Atlanta Syncopators, Ed Johnson, Uncredited**
Van Dyke 77037: **Ed Johnson, Uncredited**

Reverses:
GG 1701, 1702, 1706, Radiex 1701, 1702, 1706, and 7037 are uncredited (Grey Gull studio bands). Mad 5015, 50015, and Van Dyke 5015 as Atlanta Syncopators (Grey Gull studio band). Rx 901 by Joy Dispensers (Grey Gull studio band). Van Dyke 901 as Joy Dispensers and Mike Mosiello and His Radio Stars (Grey Gull studio band). The reverse of Globe 1706 is not known.

WILBUR SWEATMAN

Wilbur Sweatman, cl, acc. by Benton Heath, p; Lester Miller, bj-1, g-2.
42 West 38th Street, New York City, Tuesday, April 29, 1930.

62209-1	Sweat Blues (Wilbur Sweatman)-1	Vi V-38597
62209-2	Sweat Blues-1	Vi rejected
62210-1	Got 'Em Blues-1,2	Vi rejected
62210-2	Got 'Em Blues (W. Sweatman)-1,2	Vi 23254
62211-1	Breakdown Blues-1,2	Vi rejected
62211-2	Breakdown Blues (Wilbur Sweatman)-1,2	Vi V-38597
62212-1	Battleship Kate (W. Sweatman)-1	Vi 23254
62212-2	Battleship Kate-1	Vi rejected

Keys: 62209-1: E♭; 62210-2: Cm/E♭; 62211-2: F: 62212-1: E♭

The personnel was recalled by Benton Heath.

According to the Victor file card, Victor 23254 sold 604 copies, though it is not known whether this is an actual sales figure or a pressing figure or, in the case of the latter, whether dealer returns had been deducted.

WILBUR SWEATMAN and his ORCHESTRA

Russell Smith, t; *Calvin Jones*, tb; Wilbur Sweatman, cl, ldr; Benton Heath, p; Eddie Gibbs, g; Ogese T. McKay, bb; Zeno Lawrence, d; Gerald "Corky" Williams, v-1.
Broadway & 57th Street, New York City, Tuesday, March 26, 1935, 10:00 a.m.–1:40 p.m.

17187-1	Whatcha Gonna Do (Williams)-1	Vo 2983-B, BrF A-86030-B
17187-2	Whatcha Gonna Do-1	Vo rejected
17188-1	The Hooking Cow Blues (Williams-Handy)-1	Vo 2983-A, BrF A-86030-A
17188-2	The Hooking Cow Blues-1	Vo rejected
17189-1	Battleship Kate (Sweatman-Rives)-1	Vo 2945-A
17189-2	Battleship Kate-1	Vo rejected
17190-1	The Florida Blues (Phillips-Jenkins-Jones)	Vo 2945-B
17190-2	The Florida Blues	Vo rejected

Keys: 17187-1: E♭; 17188-1: B♭; 17189-1: E♭; 17190-1: F/B♭

The artist credit on BrF A86030 is **Wilbur Sweatman Orchestra**. The composer credit on BrF 86030-B is Gerald-Corky-Williams. All known copies of BrF 86030 have their labels reversed.

A "rogue'" pressing has been reported that couples 17189-2 with "Sweet Violets" by the Sweet Violet Boys. Correct labels appear on both sides.

The piano on this session is generally attributed to George Rickson, but stylistically it is the same man as on the Victor session, which Benton Heath identified as being himself.

The actual recording date for this session is not as clear-cut as it ought to be, given that much relevant company data survives. The Vocalion Record Cards and the Recording Laboratories Work Order and Questionnaire sheets, on first reading, imply that two sessions were involved. Matrices 17189 and 17190 were allegedly recorded on March 26, and matrices 17187 and 17188 on March 27.

However, there are several anomalies to consider. The Work Order sheets for matrices 17187 and 17188 both show a start time of 10:00 a.m. but no finish time. The Work Order sheet for matrix 17189 shows neither a start nor finish time, and the Work Order sheet for the last recorded, matrix 17190, shows a finish time of 1:40 p.m. What are we to make of this? If we take the Record Cards and Work Order Sheets at face value, then two sessions on consecutive days were taken up recording these four sides. However, the absence of a finish time on those matrices made on March 26 and the equally absent start time for those matrices allegedly made on March 27 leads me to suspect that this is in fact a case of poor bookkeeping, and that all four sides were in fact recorded on March 26, commencing at 10:00 a.m. and finishing at 1:40 p.m. Three hours and forty minutes seems adequate time to rehearse four tunes and make a total of eight recorded masters (two of each performance).

Just to add further complications, it appears that Vocalion was not following strict numerical/date order with its matrices at this time. Matrix 17000 was recorded on March 8 and the subsequent numbers follow more or less chronologically to 17150, which was recorded on April 18. The sequence then drops back to March 20 with matrix number 17151, and then works chronologically forward again. The matrices for the Sweatman recordings are dated on the Vocalion Record Cards and Work Order cards as follows:

17184-86	26th March	17189-93	26th March (17189–90 by Sweatman)
17187-88	27th March (Sweatman)	17194-99	27th March

Aurally, the sides appear to emanate from a single session, with no discernible change in studio balance between the instruments; at any rate, doubt still remains as to whether these four sides are the product of one or two sessions.

The following is a private recording session that took place in New York in 1950.
Wilbur Sweatman, cl, bcl, ldr; Bill Hegamin, p; Eddie McLean, g; Henry Turner, sb; Herman Bradley, d; Delphine Carmichael, v.
New York City, 1950.
    Unknown titles   Private recordings

Notes

ACKNOWLEDGMENTS

1. "Early jazz" is a shorthand term frequently applied to jazz records made prior to the 1923 King Oliver Gennett recordings that featured a classic New Orleans lineup, including a youthful Louis Armstrong.

2. Len Kunstadt and Bob Colton, "In Retrospect: Wilbur Sweatman," *The Black Perspective In Music* 16 no. 2 (Fall 1988): 227.

INTRODUCTION

1. Rainer Lotz, *Black People: Entertainers of African Descent in Europe and Germany* (Bonn, Germany: Birgit Lotz-Verlag, 1997).

2. Lawrence Gushee, *Pioneers of Jazz: The Story of The Creole Band* (New York: Oxford University Press, 2005).

3. Lynn Abbott and Doug Seroff, *Out of Sight: The Rise of African American Popular Music, 1889–1895* (Jackson: University Press of Mississippi, 2002), and *Ragged But Right: Black Travelling Shows, "Coon Songs," and the Dark Pathway To Blues and Jazz* (Jackson: University Press of Mississippi, 2007).

4. Tim Brooks, *Lost Sounds: Blacks and the Birth of the Recording Industry, 1890–1919* (Urbana and Chicago: University of Illinois Press, 2004).

5. Reid Badger, *A Life in Ragtime: A Biography of James Reese Europe* (New York and Oxford: Oxford University Press, 1995).

CHAPTER 1

1. Garvin Bushell, as told to Mark Tucker, *Jazz From the Beginning* (Oxford, UK: Bayou Press, 1988), 18.

2. Perry Bradford, *Born with the Blues* (New York: Oak Publications, 1965), 114.

3. *Chicago Defender*, October 17, 1925, 6.

4. Tom Fletcher, *100 Years of the Negro in Show Business* (New York: Burdge, 1954), 152.

5. Bradford, *Born With The Blues*, 93.

6. Duke Ellington, *Music Is My Mistress* (Garden City, NY: Doubleday, 1973), 36.

7. *Record Research* (July 1961): 9.

8. *Record Research* 24 (Sept./Oct. 1959): 3.
9. Eubie Blake: Interview with Max Morath, Brooklyn, 1976.
10. Bradford, *Born With The Blues*, 114–15.

CHAPTER 2

1. *The Journals of the Lewis and Clark Expedition*, June 13, 1804.
2. Coleman Sweatman's birthplace and parental origins are somewhat confused. Although the 1880 Federal census claims that he was born in Missouri ca. 1853 and that his parents originated in Virginia, his 1900 census entry claims that he was born in Kentucky in July 1859 and gives no details of where his parents were born. To complicate matters further, his 1880 census entry omits his forename!
3. Eubie Blake: Interview with Max Morath, Brooklyn, 1976.
4. Sol Smith Russell (1848–1902) was a well-known comic actor from the 1870s to 1890s. During the Civil War he served as a drummer boy in the Union army. After touring the Midwest he went to New York in 1871 and in 1874 became a member of actor-manager John Augustin Daly's celebrated company, and toured with them throughout the United States and Europe.
5. *Record Research* 24 (Sept.-Oct. 1959): 3.
6. Rudi Blesh and Harriet Janis, *They All Played Ragtime: The True Story of an American Music* (1950) (London, Sidgwick & Jackson, 1958), 149–50.
7. *New York Tribune*, August 20, 1893, quoted in Abbott and Seroff, *Out of Sight*, 287.
8. For more details of the Dahomean Village see Abbott and Seroff, *Out of Sight*, 285–87, 289–92.

CHAPTER 3

1. Notable exceptions include the late Marshall Stearns's pioneering book on the history of dancing to jazz, *Jazz Dance*, and, more recently, German author and researcher Rainer Lotz's research into black performers in Europe and Lynn Abbott and Doug Seroff's two books on pre-jazz African American entertainment, *Out of Sight* and *Ragged But Right*).
2. "The Honey-suckle and the Bee," Gramophone Concert Record G.C.-3273; "The Rainbow Coon (My Rainbow Coon*)," Gramophone Concert Record GC-3278, Zonophone X-43029*; "The Honeysuckle and the Bee," Berliner 3244; "Just Because She Made Dem Goo-Goo Eyes," Berliner 3245.
3. A detailed essay on the career of Belle Davis, along with a CD including her performance of "The Honeysuckle and the Bee," can be found in Lotz, *Black People*, 65–87.
4. Marshall and Jean Stearns, *Jazz Dance: The Story of American Vernacular Dance* (1968; rpt. New York: Schirmer, 1979), 83.
5. "Mr. Sweatman is a native of Kansas City, MO, and began his musical career with the Original Smith Famous Pick Band." *Indianapolis Freeman*, January 29, 1910. Also reported in "At The Chicago Theaters." *Indianapolis Freeman*, October 8, 1910.
6. For an overview of Smith's career, with particular emphasis on his Chicago years,

readers are directed to "Major N. Clark Smith in Chicago" by Marian M. Ohman, *Journal of the Illinois State Historical Society* Spring 2003. findarticles.com/p/articles/mi_qa3945/is_200304/ai_n9171979.

7. Ross Russell, *Jazz Style in Kansas City and the Southwest* (Berkeley: University of California Press, 1971), 172.

8. Nathan W. Pearson, *Goin' to Kansas City* (Urbana and Chicago: University of Illinois Press, 1994), 20.

9. Laurie Wright, *Trombone Man: Preston Jackson's Story* (Chigwell, UK: Storyville Publications, 2005), 139–40.

10. *Leavenworth Herald*, November 2, 1895.

11. *Leavenworth Herald*, November 30, 1895.

12. Published by Carl Hoffman, Kansas City, 1895. The score is in the Library of Congress and a photocopy is at the Center for Black Music Research, Columbia College, Chicago.

13. For more on M. B. Curtis see article "Maurice Curtis lent Berkeley brief splendor" by Daniella Thompson at berkeleyheritage.com/eastbay_then-now/peralta_park2.html.

14. *Kansas City Star*, August 20, 1899.

15. As quoted in Abbott and Seroff, *Out of Sight*, 133.

16. Abbott and Seroff, *Ragged But Right*, 44.

17. Abbott and Seroff, *Out of Sight*, 463–64.

18. This date is confirmed by his World War I and World War II draft registration cards and his 1919 passport application. A number of other sources, including John Chilton's *Who's Who of Jazz* and several websites, incorrectly claim a birth date of August 15, 1883 in Nashville, Tennessee.

18. Lotz, *Black People*, 137–39.

19. John Chilton, *Who's Who of Jazz* (London: Bloomsbury Book Shop, 1970), 377.

20. "Brunswick Pick-Ups," *Indianapolis Freeman*, July 27, 1901.

21. Wilbur Sweatman, interview with Marshall and Jean Stearns, November 24, 1959. The quote did not appear in the published version of *Jazz Dance*.

22. Marshall and Jean Stearns, interview with Wilbur Sweatman, November 24, 1959, quoted in *Jazz Dance*, 23.

CHAPTER 4

1. "His first experience of travelling was with the P. G. Lowery Band . . . and held the position of the leader of the band, the youngest leader on the road." "At The Chicago Theaters," *Indianapolis Freeman*, October 8, 1910.

2. Fletcher, *100 Years of the Negro in Show Business*, 59.

3. For an excellent and highly detailed biography of Lowery, the reader is recommended to seek out Clifford Edward Watkins's book *Showman: The Life and Music of Perry George Lowery* (Jackson: University Press of Mississippi, 2003).

4. "A Breeze From Alabama. March and Two Step," published by John Stark & Son, St. Louis, MO, 1902. It is dedicated to ". . . P.G. Lowery. World's Challenging Colored Cornetist and Band Master."

5. Abbott and Seroff, *Ragged But Right*, 207.
6. Johnson's draft registration card is available online at www.doctorjazz.co.uk/draft cards.html#musdcwj.
7. *Indianapolis Freeman*, May 10, 1902.
8. Brooks, *Lost Sounds*, 500.
9. Abbott and Seroff, *Ragged But Right*, 160–61.
10. Fletcher, *100 Years of the Negro in Show Business*, 149.
11. *Indianapolis Freeman*, May 17, 1902.
12. *Indianapolis Freeman*, November 8, 1902.
13. Lee Collins, *Oh, Didn't He Ramble: The Life Story of Lee Collins as told to Mary Collins* (Oxford, UK: Bayou Press, 1989), 49.
14. *Indianapolis Freeman*, May 24, 31, 1902, December 6, 1902.
15. Watkins, *Showman*, 46.
16. W. C. Handy, Ed. Arna Bontemps. *Father of the Blues* (New York: Macmillan, 1941), 44.
17. *Ibid.*, 45.
18. Extensive details about Prince's show business career can be found in Larry Gushee's excellent book *Pioneers of Jazz: The Story of The Creole Band*.
19. Handy, *Father of the Blues*, 66.
20. *Indianapolis Freeman*, January 13, 1900.
21. "Wilbur Sweatman writes that he is now playing three clarinets at once . . ." *Indianapolis Freeman*, September 29, 1917.
22. Gushee, *Pioneers of Jazz*, 12.
23. *Indianapolis Freeman*, June 13, 1903.
24. Abbott and Seroff, *Out of Sight*, 49–50.
25. *Ibid.*, 332–34.
26. *Variety*, August 22, 1919 .
27. *Variety*, September 19, 1919.

CHAPTER 5

1. Andrea Stulman Dennett, *Weird & Wonderful: The Dime Museum in America* (New York: New York University Press, 1997), 134.
2. James Weldon Johnson, *Black Manhattan* (New York: Alfred Knopf, 1930), 97.
3. Fletcher, *100 Years of the Negro in Show Business*, 151.
4. *Indianapolis Freeman*, July 2, 1904.
5. Tim Brooks, *Lost Sounds*, 35.

CHAPTER 6

1. Wilbur Sweatman, interview with Marshall and Jean Stearns, November 24, 1959.
2. "At the Chicago Theaters," *Chicago Defender*, October 8, 1910.
3. William Howland Kenney, *Chicago Jazz: A Cultural History, 1904–1930* (New York: Oxford University Press, 1993), 4–5.
4. Doug Seroff, letter to author, November 7, 1994.

5. Reid Badger, *A Life in Ragtime: A Biography of James Reese Europe* (New York and Oxford: Oxford University Press, 1995), 39–40.

6. Henry T. Sampson, *Blacks in Blackface: A Source Book on Early Black Musical Shows* (Metuchen, NJ: Scarecrow Press, 1980), 427.

7. Kenney, *Chicago Jazz*, 6.

8. *Ibid.*

9. Samuel Coleridge-Taylor, dubbed "the Black Mahler," was born in London in 1875, the son of a Sierra Leonean father, Daniel Peter Hughes Taylor, and an English mother, Alice Hare Martin. He studied at the Royal College of Music under Sir Charles Villers Stanford (who conducted the first performance of Coleridge-Taylor's best-known piece, "Hiawatha's Wedding Feast") and was encouraged by Sir Edward Elgar, an early admirer and promoter of his works. He was greatly influenced by Dvorzák, especially in recognizing the importance of African American music. He made three concert tours of the United States that were met with great acclaim, especially among African American audiences. He worked with black American poet Paul Laurence Dunbar, setting some of his poems to music. Coleridge-Taylor died of overwork and influenza in 1912, aged just thirty-seven.

10. Ohman, "Major N. Clark Smith in Chicago," *Journal of the Illinois State Historical Society* (Spring 2003).findarticles.com/p/articles/mi_qa3945/is_200304/ai_n9171979.

11. Edward Berlin: *King of Ragtime: Scott Joplin and His Era* (New York and Oxford: Oxford University Press, 1994), 116.

12. Jordan's 1915 trip to Britain is extensively covered in Howard Rye, "Visiting Firemen 14: Joe Jordan," *Storyville* 134 (June 1988): 55–58.

13. A detailed essay on Jordan and his property speculations can be found in Tim Samuelson, "From Ragtime to Real Estate," *The Rag-Time Ephemeralist* 3 (2002): 201–9.

14. Charles Sengstock Jr., email to author, December 30, 2005.

15. Charles Sengstock Jr., *That Toddlin' Town: Chicago's White Dance Bands and Orchestras, 1900–1950* (Urbana and Chicago: University of Illinois Press, 2005), 76, 108.

16. Fess Williams and His Joy Boys, Dixie Stomp/Drifting and Dreaming, Vocalion 15690. Peyton made one other record, as pianist on a September 1935 recording session organized by Richard M. Jones and issued as by Jones' Chicago Cosmopolitans. The one title he appears on from the session is "Joe Louis Chant," issued on Decca 7115.

17. Dave Peyton, "The Musical Bunch," *Chicago Defender*, December 12, 1925.

18. Harrison Smith, "Wilbur C. Sweatman, Original Jazz King," *Record Research* (July 1961): 9.

19. *Indianapolis Freeman*, June 26, 1909.

20. United States Census, Jackson County, Missouri, January 3, 1920.

21. *Indianapolis Freeman*, October 9, 1909.

22. *Indianapolis Freeman*, January 29, 1910.

23. *Chicago Defender*, July 2, 1910.

24. *Indianapolis Freeman*, January 29, 1910.

25. *Ibid.*

26. *Ibid.*

27. *Indianapolis Freeman*, October 8, 1910.

28. *Chicago Defender*, July 2, 1910, and marriage certificate.

29. *Chicago Defender*, August 6, 1910.

30. *Ibid.*

31. *Indianapolis Freeman*, November 19, 1910.

32. *Chicago Defender*, May 22, 1909.

33. Blesh and Janis, *They All Played Ragtime*, 156.

34. Frank Driggs and Chuck Haddix, *Kansas City Jazz: From Ragtime to Bebop—A History* (New York and Oxford: Oxford University Press, 2005), 32.

35. His Master's Voice C-654. This version of "Down Home Rag," along with the Europe's Society Orchestra recording and one of Wilbur Sweatman's 1916 Emerson recordings of the tune, are all available on the CD *Ragtime to Jazz, Vol. 1* (Timeless CBC 1-035, [1997]).

36. Hamp later had a successful career as a vocalist, recording for OKeh in the late 1920s as "The California Blue Boy."

37. "Down Home Rag," music by Wilber C. Sweatman, lyrics by Roger Graham. Published by Will Rossiter, 1913.

38. Ben Hecht, *Gaily, Gaily* (Garden City, NY: Doubleday, 1963), 163.

39. *The Illinois Crime Survey* (Chicago: Illinois Criminal Justice Association in cooperation with the Chicago Crime Commission, 1929).

40. On a 1910 map of the Levee district, it is shown as "Colosimo Café."

41. Charles A. Sengstock Jr., *Jazz Music in Chicago's Early South-Side Theaters* (Northbrook: Canterbury Press, 2000), 39–40).

42. *Indianapolis Freeman*, January 14, 1911.

43. *Indianapolis Freeman*, January 28, 1911.

44. Abbott and Seroff, *Ragged But Right*, 290.

45. Rye, "Visiting Firemen 14," 55–58.

46. *Ibid*, 56.

47. *New York Age*, October 25, 1919.

48. *Indianapolis Freeman*, March 20, 1920.

49. "Regular Chicago Review," *Indianapolis Freeman*, July 8, 1911.

50. *Chicago Defender*, June 10, 1911.

51. *Indianapolis Freeman*, May 9, 1914.

52. Ethel Waters, *His Eye Is on the Sparrow* (New York: Doubleday 1951), 75.

53. *Indianapolis Freeman*, July 29, 1911.

CHAPTER 7

1. Fletcher, *100 Years of the Negro in Show Business*, 151.

2. *Chicago Defender*, November 1, 1913.

3. *Indianapolis Freeman*, May 9, 1914.

4. James A. Drake, *Rosa Ponselle: A Centenary Biography* (New York: Amadeus, 2003), 65.

5. *Indianapolis Freeman*, September 23, 1911.

6. *Ibid.*

7. *Indianapolis Freeman*, September 30, 1911.

8. Eubie Blake, interviews with Max Morath, Brooklyn, 1976. An edited transcript of the interviews is available online at americanheritage.com/articles/magazine/ah/1976/6/1976_6_56.shtml.

9. Gushee, *Pioneers of Jazz*, 13.

10. *Variety*, July 13, 1907.

11. "Stage Notes," *Chicago Broad Ax*, October 21, 1911.

12. *Indianapolis Freeman*, October 21, 1911.

13. *Indianapolis Freeman*, November 11, 1911.

14. H. Loring White, *Ragging It: Getting Ragtime into History (and Some History in Ragtime)* (Lincoln, NE: iUniverse, 2005), 87.

15. Sophie Tucker, *Some of These Days: The Autobiography of Sophie Tucker* (Garden City, NY: Doubleday, Doran, 1945), 148–49.

16. Robert Kimball and William Bolcom, *Reminiscing with Sissle and Blake* (New York: Viking, 1973), 81.

17. Lewis A. Erenberg, *Steppin' Out: New York Nightlife and the Transformation of American Culture 1890–1930* (Chicago: University of Chicago Press, 1981), 68.

18. *New York Age*, December 14, 1911.

19. *New York Age*, December 21, 1911.

20. *Indianapolis Freeman*, July 6, 1912.

21. *New York Age*, September 19, 1912.

22. *Variety*, December 15, 1906.

23. Thomas L. Riis, *Just Before Jazz: Black Musical Theater in New York, 1890 to 1915* (Washington: Smithsonian, 1989), 166.

24. *Ibid.*, 171.

25. Wilbur Sweatman, interview with Marshall and Jean Stearns, November 24, 1959.

26. "London News," *Variety*, March 21, 1913.

27. Advertisement, *New York Star*, March 1, 1913.

28. *Indianapolis Freeman*, May 31, 1913.

29. Eric Ledell Smith, *Bert Williams: A Biography of the Pioneer Black Comedian* (Jefferson, NC: McFarland, 1992), 168.

30. Kimball and Bolcom, *Reminiscing with Sissle and Blake*, 72.

31. For more on Europe and the Clef Club, see Badger, *A Life in Ragtime*.

32. *Indianapolis Freeman*, February 7, 1914.

33. *New York Age*, April 30, 1914.

34. *Indianapolis Freeman*, March 7, 1914.

35. *Lowell Sun*, November 7, 1914.

36. *New York Age*, December 17, 1914.

37. *Variety*, November 24, 1916.

38. Daniel L. McNamara, ed., The *ASCAP Biographical Dictionary of Composers, Authors and Publishers* (New York: Thomas Y. Crowell, 1948).

CHAPTER 8

1. Allan Sutton and Kurt Nauck, *American Record Labels and Companies: An Encyclopedia (1891–1943)* (Denver, CO: Mainspring, 2000), 278–79.

2. "Dixie Jass Band One-Step"/"Livery Stable Blues," Victor 18255. The disc was first advertised in the May 1917 Victor supplement, which was printed in mid-April.

3. Eddie Edwards, "Once Upon a Time," *Jazz Record* (May 1947), quoted in Art Hodes and Chadwick Hansen, eds., *Selections from the Gutter: Jazz Portraits from "The Jazz Record"* (Berkeley: University of California Press, 1978), 111.

4. "Johnson 'Jass' Blues," Edison 50440. This title and "Night-Time In Little Italy" are available on *Ragtime to Jazz, Vol. 1*. "Pozzo" is available on *Ragtime to Jazz, Vol. 3* (Timeless CBC 1-070). "Cute Little Wigglin' Dance" is available on *Ragtime to Jazz, Vol. 4* (Timeless CBC 1-085).

5. This is confirmed by Edvin Arnold Johnson's draft registration card, dated May 31, 1917, which states that his place of employment was "Montmarte [*sic*] Restaurant." It also shows that his employer was Marco Wolff (shown as "M. Wolfe"). As he, along with Buster Johnson, Marco Wolff, and Rudy Wiedoeft, registered for the draft in Los Angeles in the last few days of May, it is likely that they made a brief return trip to California.

6. For an in-depth examination of Pathé's activities in America, see Sutton and Nauck, *American Record Labels and Companies.*

7. Badger, *A Life in Ragtime.*

8. Handy, *Father of the Blues*, 207–8.

9. *Record Bulletins for May 1917*, Pathé Supplement.

10. "A Bag of Rags, Two-Step." Sheet music published by Daly, Boston, 1912.

11. A detailed essay on William Newmeyer Spiller and his extensive musical career is to be found in Lotz, *Black People*, 125–49.

12. Bruce Vermazen, *That Moaning Saxophone: The Six Brown Brothers and the Dawning of a Musical Craze* (New York and Oxford: Oxford University Press, 2004), 111.

13. Handy, *Father of the Blues*, 147.

14. Emerson Military Band, "Joe Turner Blues/Razzazza Mazzazza," Emerson 7147.

15. *Chicago Defender*, March 28, 1918.

16. H. O. Brunn, *The Story of the Original Dixieland Jazz Band* (Baton Rouge: Louisiana State University Press, 1960), 107.

17. Jean-Christophe Averty, "Contribution a L'Histoire de L'Original Dixieland Jass Band (II)," *Les Cahiers du Jazz* 4 (1960): 90–92.

18. *Times-Picayune*, November 4, 1917.

19. Handy, *Father of the Blues*, 170.

20. *Ibid.*, 170.

21. Albert J. McCarthy, "Darnell Howard," *Jazz Monthly* 6, no. 5 (July 1960): 7.

22. Handy, *Father of the Blues*, 174.

23. *New York Herald*, January 4, 1918.

24. Dan Parrish (1892–1965) was an important figure in the history of early jazz, one

of the pioneers who took jazz to Europe in the late teens and stayed there for many years. Born in Mound City, Illinois, on March 18, 1892, his early career is rather shadowy, but he was in Chicago by 1914 (*Chicago Defender*, March 28, 1914) and Sweatman almost certainly would have known him prior to his own move to New York. In 1919 he was one of the musicians chosen by drummer Louis Mitchell to accompany him on his return to Paris to play at Le Perroquet. Parrish was subsequently involved in a number of groups led by Crickett Smith and in 1929 recorded the only sides issued under his name, with his band accompanying the celebrated poet and writer Jean Cocteau reciting two of his poems, "Les Voleurs d'Enfants" (The Child Snatchers)/"La Toison d'Or" (The Golden Fleece), on French Columbia LFX-3. Both titles are available online at ubu.com/sound/cocteau.html. He continued to work in Paris throughout the 1930s and managed to leave France via Lisbon after the German invasion in 1940, returning to the States on the S.S. *Siboney* in April 1941.

25. R. D. Darrell, quoted in Roland Gelatt, *The Fabulous Phonograph: From Tin Foil to High Fidelity* (Philadelphia and New York: Lippincott, 1955), 233.

26. John Chilton, *The Song of the Hawk: The Life and Recordings of Coleman Hawkins* (Ann Arbor: University of Michigan Press, 1990), 72.

27. Gunther Schuller, *Early Jazz: Its Roots and Musical Development* (New York: Oxford University Press, 1968), 246–49.

28. *Chicago Defender*, October 17, 1925.

29. "When I got to New York I showed up to play, and Will knew I couldn't read notes. I could look at the page and tell where the music was going, but I never learned things note by note—I couldn't play it that way." Sidney Bechet, *Treat It Gentle* (London: Cassell, 1960), 126.

30. The activities of the Southern Syncopated Orchestra, both in the United States and Europe, have been documented in great detail, mainly by Howard Rye in *Storyville* magazine, notably issues 42: 204; 51: 95; 142: 137; 143: 165; 144: 223.

31. Columbia Records supplement, October 1918.

32. Bradford, *Born with the Blues*, 115.

33. Sutton and Nauck, *American Record Labels and Companies*, 116–18.

CHAPTER 9

1. New York City Directory, 1918–19.

2. *New York Age*, July 27, 1918.

3. *New York Age*, May 7, 1927, and *New York Times*, May 31, 1927.

4. *New York Age*, April 19, 1919, and *New York Times*, April 20, 1919.

5. A detailed history of the Jenkins Orphanage and its band is to be found in John Chilton's *A Jazz Nursery: The Story of the Jenkins' Orphanage Bands of Charleston, South Carolina* (London: Bloomsbury Bookshop, 1980).

6. Arthur Briggs, interview with Ate van Delden, Paris, May 30, 1974.

7. Letter from Warren Plath to Rainer Lotz, December 3, 1981.

8. Tour dates in Howard Rye, "Visiting Firemen 15: The Southern Syncopated Orchestra," *Storyville* 142 (June 1990): 138–39.

9. Howard Rye and Robert Pernet, Visiting Firemen 18: Louis Mitchell, *Storyville* *2000–1* e(2001): 234–35.

10. Dan Parrish interview with Jean-Christophe Averty, 1958. As quoted in "Visiting Firemen 18: Louis Mitchell," 235–36.

11. *Variety*, August 18, 1919.

12. *New York Age*, June 12, 1920.

13. Gushee, *Pioneers of Jazz*, 210–14.

14. Charlie Gaines, interview with Russ Shor, ca. 1975.

15. Russ Shor, "Charlie Gaines," *Storyville* 68 (December 1976–January 1977).

16. *Billboard*, January 17, 1920.

17. *Chicago Defender*, February 22, 1919.

18. The mandolin-banjo is a hybrid eight-stringed instrument, resembling a shortened banjo but with eight strings arranged in four rows of double strings, like a mandolin. With its resonator and vellum head, it produced far greater volume than a traditional mandolin, and was very popular with string-dominated bands in the early years of the twentieth century. One alleged reason for its popularity was that its tuning (G, D, A, E) was the same as that of a violin, and violinists thrown out of work by the demand for syncopated dance bands could easily switch instruments and find work with the hugely popular banjo bands. It is often wrongly referred to as banjolin or banjoline, which is in fact a different instrument—a mini-banjo retaining the mandolin/violin tuning but with only four strings.

19. Ted Vincent, *Keep Cool: The Black Activists Who Built the Jazz Age* (London and East Haven, CT: Pluto, 1995), 137–42.

20. "Lucille" appears to have entered the Harlem musical language; it appears again six years later, entitled "Funny Feelin' Blues," as a clarinet solo by Bob Fuller, issued on the rare Ajax label, issue number 17091.

21. *New York Clipper*, June 4, 1919.

22. *Variety*, November 10, 1919.

23. Gushee, *Pioneers of Jazz*, 257.

24. Charlie Gaines, interview with Russ Shor, ca. 1975.

25. *Chicago Defender*, March 20, 1920.

26. *New York Age*, January 24, 31, February 7, March 6, March 20, 27, April 10, 17, May 8, 1920; *Chicago Defender*, January 31, February 7, March 6, 20, April 3, 17, 1920.

27. *Chicago Defender*, July 9, 1921.

28. Garvin Bushell, *Jazz from the Beginning*, 18.

29. Bruce Vermazen, "Art Hickman's Orchestra" www.gracyk.com.

30. "Pee Gee's Blues," composed by H. Qualli Clark, published by Pace and Handy, 1919. A contemporary version was recorded ca. September 1919 by Wadsworth's Novelty Orchestra and issued on Pathé 22206.

31. *San Francisco Examiner*, October 30, 1920.

32. *New York Clipper*, June 4, 1919.

CHAPTER 10

1. Columbia had already recorded cabaret blues singer Mary Stafford in late 1920 and throughout 1921.

2. *New York Clipper*, April 19, 1922.
3. *New York Age*, July 23, 1921.
4. *New York Age*, August 12, 1922.
5. *Coshocton Tribune*, December 30, 1922; *Pittsburgh Courier*, September 8, 1928.
6. *New York Age*, March 10, 1923.
7. Stanley Dance, *The World of Duke Ellington* (New York: Scribner's, 1970), 57.
8. Sonny Greer, interviewed by Edith Exton and Brooks Kerr, New York, 1976; and Barry Ulanov, *Duke Ellington* (New York: Creative Age, 1946), 27.
9. Sonny Greer, interviewed by Stanley Crouch, January 15, 1979, quoted in Mark Tucker, *Ellington: The Early Years* (Urbana and Chicago: University of Illinois Press, 1991), 81.
10. Stuart Nicholson, *Reminiscing in Tempo: A Portrait of Duke Ellington* (Boston: Northeastern University Press, 1999), 28.
11. *Chicago Defender*, March 31, 1923.
12. Ellington, *Music Is My Mistress*, 36.
13. Letter to author from Donald Thompson, August 29, 2004.
14. Leonard Harper (1897 or 1899–1943) was one of the top nightclub and cabaret producers of the inter-war years, best known for his long association with the various Connie's Inn and Cotton Club revues in the 1920s and 1930s. In 1923 he produced *Plantation Days*, the first all-black cast revue to appear in London, which ran at the Empire Theatre from March 12 to May 12, 1923.
15. A. H. Lawrence, *Duke Ellington and His World: A Biography* (New York: Routledge, 2001), 35.
16. Bricktop and James I. Haskins, *Bricktop* (New York: Atheneum, 1983), 81–82.
17. *Pittsburgh Courier*, September 15, 1923.
18. *Baltimore Afro-American*, September 14, 1923.
19. Mark Miller, *Some Hustling This! Taking Jazz to the World, 1914–1929* (Toronto: Mercury, 2005), 47.
20. *Chicago Defender*, January 26, 1924.
21. *Baltimore Afro-American*, April 25, 1924.
22. *Billboard*, August 16, 1924.
23. Bradford, *Born with the Blues*, 130.
24. Frank Driggs, "Goodbye Fess," *Storyville* 67 (October–November 1976): 18. "One night a guy comes in from one of the big night clubs out on the highway to Schenectady and wants to hire us . . . and we go into the Colony Inn."
25. *Syracuse Herald*, July 13, 1924.
26. Bruce Bastin, *Never Sell a Copyright* (Chigwell, UK: Storyville, 1990), 21.
27. Little is known about Ada Rives; she was born in Louisiana ca. 1897 and was listed in the 1920 census as working as a theater pianist and living in Kingston City, New York, married to Coy Rives, a garage machinist. At the time of the 1930 census she and Coy Rives were rooming at a hotel in Chicago, he working as a mechanical engineer and she not working. Ada Rives appears on the cover of a number of songsheets from the mid- to late 1920s, one published in 1928 helpfully noting that she was "Solo Organist, Loew's State [Theater] New Orleans."

28. *Hot News and Rhythm Record Review* 1 (April 1935).

29. I am indebted to researcher Ken Steiner for allowing me access to his ongoing research into Ellington's early career.

30. Rainer Lotz, *Michael Danzi: American Musician in Germany, 1924–1939* (Schmitten, Germany: Norbert Ruecker, 1986), 9.

31. Rainer Lotz, "Michael 'Mike' Danzi," *Storyville* 67 (October–November 1976): 26–27.

32. Lotz, *Michael Danzi*, 9.

33. Lotz, "Michael 'Mike' Danzi," 26–27.

34. *Baltimore Afro-American*, November 22, 1924.

35. *Ibid.*

36. *Chicago Defender*, September 26, 1925.

37. *Chicago Defender*, November 21, 1925.

38. Abbott and Seroff, *Ragged But Right*, 277–78, 325–26.

39. Miller, *Some Hustling This!* 31.

40. *Variety*, August 18, 1926.

41. Eddy Determeyer, *Rhythm Is Our Business: Jimmie Lunceford and the Harlem Express* (Ann Arbor: University of Michigan Press, 2006), 26.

42. Dance, *The World of Duke Ellington*, 46.

43. *New York Age*, May 7, 1927, and *New York Times*, May 31, 1927.

44. *Kingston Daily Freeman*, January 12, 1928.

45. *Syracuse Herald*, August 26, 1928.

46. An E. Cassamore played trombone and cornet on the recordings made for the Ajax label in Montreal in 1924 by Millard Thomas and His Chicago Novelty Orchestra; presumably this is the same person.

47. George T. Simon, *Simon Says: The Sights and Sounds of the Swing Era, 1935–1955* (New Rochelle, NY: Arlington House, 1971), 447.

48. *New York Times*, January 30, 1944, 11.

49. "Sweatman had played through New Orleans with Mahara's Minstrels in 1901 [*sic*] and on the one night he had gone to town, a Sunday night, he had heard only one band and hadn't thought much of it." Samuel B. Charters and Leonard Kunstadt, *Jazz: A History of the New York Scene* (Garden City, NY: Doubleday, 1962), 236. It is interesting to note in Appendix 2 that Sweatman was in New Orleans in mid-November 1902, with P. G. Lowery's band with Forepaugh & Sells Brothers Circus, which included a Sunday night stay, and it may in fact have been on this occasion that he went into town and heard a band.

50. Bradford, *Born with the Blues*, 32.

51. *Record Research* 24 (September–October 1959): 3.

52. Berlin, *King Of Ragtime*, 246.

53. Alan Lomax, *Mister Jelly Roll* (New York: Duell, Smith and Pearce, 1950), 223–28.

54. "Afterthoughts," *Storyville* 90 (August–September 1980): 240.

55. *Chicago Defender*, August 30, 1930.

56. Peter Carr, "The Ikey Robinson Story," *Storyville* 2002–3, ed. Laurie Wright (Chigwell, UK: Storyville, 2003), 43–45.

57. *Ibid.*, 52–53.

58. *Baltimore Afro-American*, June 6, 1931.

59. *Middletown Times Herald*, August 12, 1931.

60. Carr, "The Ikey Robinson Story," 53.

61. *Chicago Defender*, June 20, 1931.

CHAPTER 11

1. *New York Times*, July 27, 1932.

2. *New York Times*, May 11, 1933.

3. *New York Age*, October 14, 1933.

4. A good example of Gibbs's style can be found on Eddie South's broadcast of "Sweet Sue," reissued on CD on AB Fable abc1-009.

5. "Battleship Kate" was also published by Alfred Music in 1946 as a piano-accordion arrangement by Anthony Galla-Rini, which leads one to suspect that Sweatman licensed the rights of these, and possibly other of his compositions, to Alfred Music for these specialist editions.

6. *New York Age*, April 25, 1943.

7. Sweatman used one of the photographs taken at the session on the cover of at least one of his songs published in the 1950s—"Down Missouri Way." It may have also been used on other sheet music covers from this period.

CHAPTER 12

1. Charters and Kunstadt, *Jazz*.

2. *Record Research* 24 (September–October 1959): 3.

3. Handy, *Father of the Blues*, 114–15.

4. *New York Times*, March 10, 1961.

5. *Ibid.*

6. *Record Research* (July 1961): 9.

7. Berlin, *King of Ragtime*, 246–47.

8. *Ibid.*, 247–48.

9. *Ibid.*, 247–48, 323.

Bibliography

CONTEMPORARY NEWSPAPERS AND PERIODICALS

The *Baltimore Afro-American*
Billboard
The *Chicago Broad Ax*
The *Chicago Defender*
The *Coshocton Tribune*
Hot News and Rhythm Record Review
The *Indianapolis Freeman*
The *Kansas City Star*
The *Kingston Daily Freeman*
The *Leavenworth Herald*
The *Lowell Sun*
The *Middletown Times Herald*
The *New York Age*
The *New York Clipper*
The *New York Herald*
The *New York Tribune*
The *New York Times*
The *Pittsburgh Courier*
The *San Francisco Examiner*
The *Syracuse Herald*
The *Times-Picayune*
Variety

BOOKS, JOURNALS, AND INTERVIEWS

Abbott, Lynn, and Doug Seroff. *Out of Sight: The Rise of African American Popular Music, 1889–1895* (Jackson: University Press of Mississippi, 2002).
———. *Ragged But Right: Black Travelling Shows, "Coon Songs," and the Dark Pathway to Blues and Jazz* (Jackson: University Press of Mississippi, 2007).
Badger, Reid. *A Life in Ragtime: A Biography of James Reese Europe* (New York and Oxford: Oxford University Press, 1995).
Bastin, Bruce. *Never Sell a Copyright* (Chigwell, UK: Storyville, 1990).
Bechet, Sidney. *Treat It Gentle* (London: Cassell, 1960).
Berlin, Edward. *King of Ragtime: Scott Joplin and His Era* (New York and Oxford: Oxford University Press, 1994).

Blesh, Rudi, and Harriet Janis. *They All Played Ragtime: The True Story of an American Music* (London: Sidgwick & Jackson, 1958).

Bradford, Perry. *Born with the Blues* (New York: Oak, 1965).

Bricktop and James I. Haskins. *Bricktop* (New York: Atheneum, 1983).

Briggs, Arthur. Interview with Ate van Delden. Paris, May 30, 1974.

Brooks, Tim. *Lost Sounds: Blacks and the Birth of the Recording Industry, 1890–1919* (Urbana and Chicago: University of Illinois Press, 2004).

Brunn, H. O. *The Story of the Original Dixieland Jazz Band* (Baton Rouge: Louisiana State University Press, 1960).

Bushell, Garvin, as told to Mark Tucker. *Jazz from the Beginning* (Oxford, UK: Bayou Press, 1988).

Charters, Samuel B., and Leonard Kunstadt. *Jazz: A History of the New York Scene* (Garden City, NY: Doubleday, 1962).

Chilton, John. *Who's Who of Jazz* (London: Bloomsbury Book Shop, 1970).

———. *A Jazz Nursery: The Story of the Jenkins' Orphanage Bands of Charleston, South Carolina* (London: Bloomsbury Bookshop, 1980).

———. *The Song of the Hawk: The Life and Recordings of Coleman Hawkins* (Ann Arbor: University of Michigan Press, 1990).

Collins, Lee. *Oh, Didn't He Ramble: The Life Story of Lee Collins as told to Mary Collins* (Oxford, UK: Bayou Press, 1989).

Dance, Stanley. *The World of Duke Ellington* (New York: Scribner's, 1970).

Dennett, Andrea Stulman. *Weird and Wonderful: The Dime Museum in America* (New York: New York University Press, 1997).

Determeyer, Eddy. *Rhythm Is Our Business: Jimmie Lunceford and the Harlem Express* (Ann Arbor: University of Michigan Press, 2006).

Drake, James A. *Rosa Ponselle: A Centenary Biography* (New York: Amadeus, 2003).

Driggs, Frank, and Chuck Haddix. *Kansas City Jazz: From Ragtime to Bebop—A History* (New York and Oxford: Oxford University Press, 2005).

Driggs, Frank. "Goodbye Fess." *Storyville* 67 (October-November 1976): 18.

Ellington, Duke. *Music Is My Mistress* (Garden City, NY: Doubleday, 1973).

Fletcher, Tom. *100 Years of the Negro in Show Business* (New York: Burdge, 1954).

Erenberg, Lewis A. *Steppin' Out: New York Nightlife and the Transformation of American Culture 1890–1930* (Chicago: University of Chicago Press, 1981).

Gushee, Lawrence. *Pioneers of Jazz: The Story of the Creole Band* (New York: Oxford University Press, 2005).

Handy, W. C. Edited by Arna Bontemps. *Father of the Blues: An Autobiography* (New York: Macmillan, 1941).

Hecht, Ben. *Gaily, Gaily* (Garden City NY: Doubleday, 1963).

Hot News and Rhythm Record Review 1 (April 1935).

Johnson, James Weldon. *Black Manhattan* (New York: Knopf, 1930).

Kenney, William Howland. *Chicago Jazz: A Cultural History, 1904–1930* (New York: Oxford University Press, 1993).

Kimball, Robert, and William Bolcom. *Reminiscing with Sissle and Blake* (New York: Viking, 1973).

Kunstadt, Len, and Bob Colton. "Daddy of the Clarinet, Wilbur Sweatman." *Record Research* 24 (September–October 1959): 3.

———. Wilbur Sweatman obituary. *Record Research* (July 1961): 9.

———. "In Retrospect: Wilbur Sweatman." *The Black Perspective in Music* vol. 16, no. 2 (Fall 1988) 227.

Lawrence, A.H. *Duke Ellington and His World: A Biography* (New York: Routledge, 2001).

Lotz, Rainer. *Black People: Entertainers of African Descent in Europe and Germany* (Bonn, Germany: Birgit Lotz-Verlag, 1997).

———. *Michael Danzi: American Musician in Germany, 1924–1939* (Schmitten, Germany: Norbert Ruecker, 1986).

———. "Michael "Mike" Danzi." *Storyville* 67 (October 1976): 24.

McCarthy, Albert J. "Darnell Howard." *Jazz Monthly* vol. 6, no. 5 (July 1960): 7.

Miller, Mark. *Some Hustling This! Taking Jazz to the World, 1914–1929* (Toronto: Mercury, 2005).

Nicholson, Stuart. *Reminiscing in Tempo: A Portrait of Duke Ellington* (Boston: Northeastern University Press, 1999).

Pearson, Nathan W. *Goin' to Kansas City* (Urbana and Chicago: University of Illinois Press, 1994).

Riis, Thomas L. *Just Before Jazz: Black Musical Theater in New York, 1890 to 1915* (Washington: Smithsonian, 1989).

Russell, Ross. *Jazz Style in Kansas City and the Southwest* (Berkeley: University of California Press, 1971).

Rust, Brian. *Jazz Records, 1897–1942. 5th Revised and Enlarged Edition* (Chigwell, UK: Storyville, 1982).

Rye, Howard. "Visiting Firemen 14: Joe Jordan." *Storyville* 134 (June 1988): 55.

———. "Visiting Firemen 15: The Southern Syncopated Orchestra." *Storyville* 142 (June 1990): 137.

Rye, Howard, and Robert Pernet. "Visiting Firemen 18: Louis Mitchell." *Storyville 2000–1* (Chigwell, UK: Storyville, 2001), 221.

Sampson, Henry T. *Blacks in Blackface: A Source Book on Early Black Musical Shows* (Metuchen, NJ: Scarecrow, 1980).

Samuelson, Tim. "From Ragtime to Real Estate" *Rag-Time Ephemeralist* 3 (2002): 201.

Schuller, Gunther. *Early Jazz: Its Roots and Musical Development* (New York: Oxford University Press, 1968).

Sengstock Charles A., Jr. *Jazz Music in Chicago's Early South-Side Theaters* (Northbrook, [IL?]: Canterbury, 2000).

———. *That Toddlin' Town: Chicago's White Dance Bands and Orchestras, 1900–1950* (Urbana and Chicago: University of Illinois Press, 2005).

Shor, Russ. "Charlie Gaines." *Storyville* 68 (December 1976–January 1977): 45.

Simon, George T. *Simon Says: The Sights and Sounds of the Swing Era, 1935–1955* (New Rochelle, NY: Arlington House, 1971).

Smith, Eric Ledell. *Bert Williams: A Biography of the Pioneer Black Comedian* (Jefferson, NC: McFarland, 1992).

Stearns, Marshall, and Jean Stearns. *Jazz Dance: The Story of American Vernacular Dance* (1968; rpt. New York: Schirmer, 1979).

Sutton, Allen, and Kurt Nauck. *American Record Labels and Companies: An Encyclopedia (1891–1943)* (Denver, CO: Mainspring, 2000).

Sweatman, Wilbur. Unpublished interview with Marshall and Jean Stearns. November 24, 1959.

Tucker, Mark. *Ellington: The Early Years* (Urbana and Chicago: University of Illinois Press, 1991).

Tucker, Sophie. *Some of These Days: The Autobiography of Sophie Tucker* (Garden City, NY: Doubleday, Doran, 1945).

Ulanov, Barry. *Duke Ellington* (New York: Creative Age, 1946).

Vermazen, Bruce. *That Moaning Saxophone: The Six Brown Brothers and the Dawning of a Musical Craze* (New York and Oxford: Oxford University Press, 2004).

Vincent, Ted. *Keep Cool: The Black Activists Who Built the Jazz Age* (London and East Haven, CT: Pluto, 1995).

Waters, Ethel. *His Eye Is on the Sparrow* (New York: Doubleday, 1951).

Watkins, Clifford Edward. *Showman: The Life and Music of Perry George Lowery* (Jackson: University of Mississippi Press, 2003).

White, H. Loring. *Ragging It: Getting Ragtime into History (and Some History in Ragtime)* (Lincoln, NE: iUniverse, 2005).

Wright, Laurie. *Trombone Man: Preston Jackson's Story* (Chigwell, UK: Storyville, 2005).

Index